EVOLUTION

NATURE AND SCRIPTURE IN CONFLICT?

EVOLUTION

NATURE AND SCRIPTURE IN CONFLICT?

Pattle P. T. Pun

Academie Books
Grand Rapids, Michigan
Zondervan Publishing House

ACADEMIE BOOKS are published by Zondervan Publishing House,
1415 Lake Drive, S.E., Grand Rapids, Michigan 49506

EVOLUTION: NATURE AND SCRIPTURE IN CONFLICT?
Copyright © 1982 by The Zondervan Corporation
Grand Rapids, Michigan

Library of Congress Cataloging in Publication Data

Pun, Pattle P. T.
    Evolution: nature and Scripture in conflict?

    Includes index.
    1. Bible and evolution. I. Title.
BS659.P86   231.7'65   81-19776
ISBN 0-310-42561-1   AACR2

Edited by Dr. Russell R. Camp and Norma C. Camp
Designed by Martha Bentley

Printed in the United States of America

84 85 86 87 88 89 90 / 10 9 8 7 6 5 4 3 2

To the serious doubters

Contents

Part I

Scientific Bases of the Theory of Evolution

Part II

A Christian View of the Origin of Life

Part III

Brief Survey of the Interrelationship of Naturalism and Darwinism

Part IV

A Christian Attitude on Evolution

Figures

Tables

Foreword

To understand the theory of evolution and the doctrine of creation one needs a background in anthropology, botany, biochemistry, geology, paleontology, zoology, and physics. Pattle P. T. Pun is well versed in these fields and has an ongoing communication with scholars in the various disciplines. He is also aware of current thinking in the evolution-creation issues. In addition, Dr. Pun is a graduate of San Diego State University and the State University of New York at Buffalo with research in biochemistry and microbiology; therefore, he is well qualified to interpret the findings of investigators seeking the origins of life and species.

Dr. Pun's book deals with both the factual data and the probable mechanisms involved in bringing living organisms onto the planet. The intricacies of cell biology and gross anatomy are presented in concise statements that show the significance of such knowledge. The evidence leads the author to conclude that there has been some descent with modification following the creation of the original species. However, Dr. Pun does not accept the total theory of evolution even in its so-called theistic form. This volume is especially commendable for stating alternative viewpoints and evaluating each. However, the reader is given the information needed to make the decisions.

Material not readily found in popular textbooks is presented, and even advanced students of origins will find material not usually dealt with in many courses dealing with creation and evolution. For example, the volume contains a fascinating account of Genesis contrasted with Babylonian stories of creation; judgments on methods of dating the age of the earth and Christian views correlating Genesis with conclusions of the geochronologists; history of the growth of ideas in both theological and scientific areas; and conclusions based on "empirical adequacy" and "rational coherency," which are two of the author's criteria.

Few individuals are scholars in all areas and equipped to fully comprehend all phases of this book. However, each of us can profit according to his training from the comprehensive treatment that Dr. Pun has produced. I predict that this volume will have an impact in the apologetic field, and I commend it to you for your thoughtful reading.

RUSSELL L. MIXTER
Professor of Biology

Wheaton College, Wheaton, Illinois

Preface

Ever since the publication of *Origin of Species* by Charles Darwin in 1859, a storm of controversy has been raging among theologians and scientists. Some proponents of Darwin's theory have elevated it as a new paradigm to be used to reinterpret the human experience. Others have identified the theory of evolution as the work of the devil with no scientific merit and have committed themselves to a fight against the theory, as if the fight were against the devil himself. Most people stand somewhere in between these two opinions. Richard Bube summarized the controversy in this way: "If the evolutionists usually put too much emphasis on these empirical data, the antievolutionists usually put too little."*

How much emphasis *should* one put on the scientific data related to the theory of evolution? This treatise attempts to analyze these data, delineate the strengths and weaknesses of the theory of evolution, and point out that the discussion of evolution revolves not so much around empirical scientific evidence but, rather, around philosophical presuppositions.

This book is an expanded version of a paper published in the June 1977 issue of the *Journal of the American Scientific Affiliation* written during the Faith and Learning Seminar held at Wheaton College, Wheaton, Illinois, in 1976. The project was supported by a grant from the Wheaton College Alumni Association.

I would like to express deepest appreciation to Dr. Raymond Brand and Dr. Albert Smith of the Biology Department of Wheaton College for their insightful and substantive reviews on Part I of this book. The contribution in the final revision of Part II and Part IV of Dr. Alan Johnson of the Bible Department is greatly appreciated.

I want also to thank other Wheaton faculty members for reviewing Part III: Dr. Arthur Holmes, Philosophy Department; Dr. Zondra Lindblade, Sociology Department; and Dr. James Rogers, Psychology Department. I am indebted to Dr. James O. Buswell, III for his generosity in making available his collection of books pertaining to the evolution controversy to aid in this writing project. The helpful comments on the sections in geology and physical anthropology by Dr. David DeVries of the Geology Department and by Dr. Dean Arnold of the Anthropology Department respectively are also appreciated. Last but not least, the courteous cooperation of Mrs. Kathy Driscoll who helped type the manuscript for this book is gratefully acknowledged.

---

*Bube, R. The human quest. Waco, TX: Word; 1971: 207.

PART I

SCIENTIFIC BASES
OF THE THEORY OF EVOLUTION

CHAPTER 1

Historical Development of the Theory of Evolution

1.1 Antiquity of Evolutionary Thought

The evolution controversy began many centuries ago. It has had a stormy history no matter what the nomenclature or who was involved. The development of the theory has produced a fascinating struggle that needs to be understood by Christians with an interest in science so that they can better comprehend current world views.

The development of the theory reaches far back into history. Even in ancient Greece two opposing views on cosmological change (evolution) were popular. Parmenides (515 B.C.-?) advocated a concept of eternal absolute being. This view adopted the concept of the changeless quality of true being. Apparent changes in the world of phenomena were explained away on the basis of the rearrangement, separation, and union of small unalterable particles. Heraclitus (540–475 B.C.), on the other hand, conceived of the cosmos as being in a continual, universal process of flux, involving cycles of generation and decay. Individual things were perceived as maintaining themselves permanently against the universal process of destruction and renovation (1).

Aristotle (382–322 B.C.), who believed in a purposive force directing all natural phenomena, first approached the nature of change in the living world by classifying plants and animals. He stated that all the different "forms" of living organisms were abruptly created from a primordial mass of "living" matter, a theory later recognized as *spontaneous generation* (2). The influential philosophy of Aristotle and the later adoption of his thoughts by the medieval church and states stifled further attempts to explain change in the living world for more than a millennium. However, from ancient times, the existence of diverse races of men and breeds of domestic animals gave evidence of continual minor changes within species. Variations in the living world caused the curious to search for an intellectual explanation, and the belief that organisms have not changed since their creation was challenged by the opposing view that parental life experiences can lead to the acquisition of new traits in the offspring.

After the Copernican revolution and the Enlightenment, the intellectual atmosphere was more conducive to the pursuit of new ideas regarding change within living organisms. Maupertuis (1698–1759) may have been the first to propose a general theory of evolution (2). He based his theory on a study of the history of four generations of a human family in which polydactyly (a congenital defect involving the appearance of a web of muscle and skin between fingers and the production of additional fingers) was inherited. This was later recognized as a dominant gene. He noted that this trait could be transmitted by either parent who was affected and suggested that certain particles from the parents, which might be changed by climatic and nutritional influences or by irregularities of their distribution, were responsible for the inherited change in the offspring. Thus, he recognized the phenomenon of descent with possible modification. However, Maupertuis made little impression on the biologists of his time.

George de Buffon (1707–88) maintained that species were separately created, but he supported a limited evolution within species due to climatic and nutritional effects on inheritance. He also speculated about possible evolution above the species level by adopting less rigid criteria for defining a species (see I. 1.2).

Darwin's grandfather Erasmus Darwin (1731–1802) first alluded to the term *evolution* to designate the process that involved "the power of acquiring new parts, attended with new propensities, directed by irritations, sensations, volitions and associations and thus possessing the faculty of continuing to improve by its own inherent activity and of delivering these improvements by generation down to its posterity world without end" (3). However, his thesis was highly speculative and had little effect on biological thought.

Chevalier de Lamarck (1744–1829) developed a theory using an echelon of progress from inert matter to a simple form of life that finally culminated in the existence of man. He recognized branching in his echelon of progress that he attributed to the inheritance of acquired characteristics as a result of the organism's adaptation to the changing environment. His theory also allowed for occasional organismal degeneration instead of progress. Lamarck's ideas produced a dynamic impact on his contemporaries and were little refuted until early in the twentieth century. However, Geoffrey Saint-Hilaire (1772–1844) suggested that the occasional deviant form of an organism may be the raw material for the evolution of new types, provided the abnormal form survived. Saint-Hilaire's theory helped lay the groundwork for the understanding that mutations provide a source of genetic diversity needed for evolution to occur through *natural selection*.

The concept of natural selection was separately conceived by two social scientists, namely, Thomas Malthus (1776–1834) and Herbert Spencer (1820–1903). Malthus in his *Essay on Population* argued that every population outgrows its food supply, and eventually starvation, disease, and war set in to prune the population because an arithmetically increasing food supply cannot catch up with a geometrically increasing population. Later, Herbert Spencer showed how the Malthusian theory can be used to explain the force behind the progress of human society. He recognized that there was a societal tendency to place a premium upon skill, intelligence, self-control, and the power to adapt through technological innovation; thus, there was a selection of the best of each generation for survival. Spencer coined the term *survival of the fittest*. This term and the term *struggle for existence*, previously set forth by Malthus, were later used by Charles Darwin (1809–82) as slogans for his concept of natural selection.

Darwin's contribution to the development of evolutionary thought was to provide a mechanism, natural selection, to account for the observed changes in domesticated livestocks and natural populations. While on a sailing expedition to South America in 1831, he was impressed by the seemingly isolated occurrence of large groups of mammals not found in the Old World and particularly the multiple species of plants and animals peculiar only to the Galapagos Islands off the coast of Ecuador. This led him to speculate that immigration of species from old to new isolated habitats resulted in the origin of new varieties and species.

In the same period Alfred R. Wallace (1823–1913) proposed the identical theory as a result of his studies on the distribution of animals in the Malay region. Darwin and Wallace successfully attracted the attention of the scientific community by presenting their theory in London to the Linnaean Society in 1858. Upon the publication of *The Origin of Species by Means of Natural Selection* in 1859, the public became exposed to Darwin's idea of evolution. Since Darwin's theory revolves around the concept of *species*, it is essential to establish a working definition of the term.

References 1.1

1. Nordenskiold, E. The history of biology. New York: Tudor; 1928. Eyre, L. B., translator.
2. Glass, B. Maupertuis, pioneer of genetics and evolution. Glass, B.; Temkin, O.; Strauss, Jr., W. L. 1745–1859 eds. Forerunners of Darwin. Baltimore: John Hopkins; 1959: 51–83.
3. Darwin, E. Zoonamia. Vol. 1. Boston: Thomas and Andrews; 1803 (Preface).

1.2 Definitions of Species

John Ray (1628–1705) made the first systematic attempt to classify living organisms. He used the criterion of the similarity in the form and structure (morphology) of the seeds of organisms to classify the individuals belonging to a species. He argued that one species could never spring from the seed of another (1).

Carolus Linnaeus (1707–78) elaborated Ray's ideas and developed a system of generic and specific names for all known plants and animals. He adopted Ray's criteria of the morphological form and the possibility of producing a fertile offspring to arrange members into the smallest units of taxonomy and called the units species. Linnaeus adhered to the concept of the *fixity of species*. It states that there existed at that time just as many species as God had created in the beginning.

Linnaeus's species concept stimulated the cataloging of different varieties of organisms by a multitude of collectors and taxonomists. Soon the number of species became enormous, producing a refinement in the Linnaean classification scheme. Linnaeus in his later work found so much difficulty in defining species that he questioned whether it might not be the genera (e.g., oak tree) rather than the species (e.g., white oak) that were separately created. His ideas were challenged by Buffon and Lamarck, who set the stage for Darwin's *Origin of Species*. Today, although the taxonomic system of Linnaeus is still being used, his scheme of classification has been repeatedly revised.

According to Mayr (2) there are three species concepts currently being used:

1. *The Typological Species Concept.* According to this concept, if two organisms are morphologically different, they are considered two distinct species. Using this criterion, even two organisms in the same reproductive community that show only slight morphological differences from one another would be two distinct species.

2. *The Nondimensional Species Concept.* This concept fixes the individuals of a species as those found at a single locality (sympatric) and

occurring at the same time (synchronous). The separation of a species from another by space and time is emphasized. However, sometimes the territories of species are not obvious, and ambiguity is introduced in defining local population.

3. *The Interbreeding-population Concept.* The criterion of interbreeding between two populations is used to determine a species. It considers species as a group of individuals that actually or potentially interbreed with each other. This concept has the advantage of being multidimensional in that populations occupying different geographical regions or living in different time periods are classified on the ability to interbreed. The difficulty, however, of the practical application of "potentially" interbreeding is apparent; nevertheless, this concept provides an operational definition of species.

The most widely accepted current definition of species among scientists represents a synthesis of elements from all three of the above concepts, namely (3):

1. *Species are defined by distinctness rather than by difference.*

2. *Species consist of populations rather than of unconnected individuals.*

3. *The decisive criterion of the classification of species is the reproductive isolation of populations rather than the fertility of individuals within the population.*

Some difficult problems still exist for taxonomists in the currently used concept of a species. A commonly encountered problem is the attempt to categorize dimorphism (two forms distinct in structure and color in the same species), age differences, genetic polymorphism (plant or animal in several forms or color varieties), and nongenetic behavioral differences.

Differences between two populations may be very subtle, making it difficult to determine whether both are distinct or the same species. For example, if two members of the genus *Drosophila* were brought together and they failed to produce fertile offspring, they would normally be classified as two separate species. However, the reproductive isolating barriers both premating and postmating have to be considered.

Premating barriers prevent the mating of two individuals. These barriers may be in the forms of (1) habitat isolation, the different preference of habitat of two populations; (2) seasonal isolation, the difference in breeding seasons; (3) ethological barriers, the incompatibilies in mating behavior; and (4) mechanical isolation, the structural differences in genital armatures that prevent mating. In contrast, postmating barriers prevent gene exchange in the offspring of the two individuals after mating has occurred. They include (1) gametic mortality, the insemination reaction that kills the sperms; (2) zygotic mortality, the irregularities of the development of the zygote that leads to its abortion; (3) hybrid inferiority and sterility, the genetic incompatibilities of the hybrid that either impose a selective disadvantage on the hybrid in mating or cause it to be sterile (4).

The criterion of interbreeding cannot be applied to organisms that reproduce asexually only. Attempts to categorize microorganisms by morphological standards alone have not been adequate. Many other criteria had to be employed in the taxonomical studies of asexual haploid organisms, and no consensus has been reached as to the best solution for these difficulties.

The application of the biological species concept to paleontological collections is also a difficult task. Since fossil specimens cannot interbreed, other criteria are used by the paleontologist to assess the taxonomic status of natural populations that became fossilized. A certain degree of subjectivity has to be invoked in the classification of fossils. Paleontologists have to rely on not only morphological, but ecological, stratigraphical, and distributional evidence to arrive at a probable species identification of fossil organisms.

Notwithstanding all these difficulties, the advantages of having a nonarbitrary definition of a biological species far outweighs its shortcomings, and the biological concept of species is widely accepted as a working definition in classifying the living world.

References 1.2

1. Bedall, B. G. Historical notes on avian classification. Systematic Zool. 6:129–36; 1957.
2. Mayr, E. Animal species and evolution. Cambridge, MA: Harvard Univ. Press; 1963: 16–30.
3. Mayr, E. Animal species and evolution. 20.
4. Mayr, E. Animal species and evolution. 92–106.

1.3 Mechanisms of Evolutionary Changes: Lamarckism vs. Mendelism

In order for a population to survive under natural selection it has to adapt to changing environmental conditions and also pass on to its offspring its capacity to survive, so-called *directional selection (see I. 1.4.5)*. In Darwin's time little was publicly known about the science of genetics even though Mendel's work was published in 1865, a mere six years after Darwin's *Origin of Species*. The dominant view of inheritance at that time was a *blending* type. The hereditary information from the two parents was believed to be blended in the offspring, just as a container of white paint mixed with a container of red paint blends into a pink liquid. This theory would predict that half of the variations carried by the parents were lost in each generation. Eventually the source of diversities would be eliminated, and natural selection would run out of raw material for operation.

Chevalier de Lamarck was the first person to propose a comprehensive theory known as "the inheritance of acquired characteristics" to explain evolutionary change. Lamarck believed that the evolutionary process that started out with the simplest organism became progressively more complex in succeeding generations. The process was triggered by the environmental effect on an organism's *vital fluid*. This fluid was a source of energy that differentiated an organism from the nonliving world. Organizational gains in an organism were conserved and passed on to the offspring.

Lamarck argued that temperature around the world affected the life processes of plants differently, and variations of plants were distributed according to the temperature zones of the world. He maintained that animals also could adapt to new environments through the use of organs and features best suited to a new surrounding. The vital fluid associated with these organs and features would be stimulated, assuring their further development, but if some parts did not suit the new environment, they would deteriorate, and only the well-adapted parts of the organism would be inherited by the offspring. In this way, the diverse forms of life evolved.

Darwin did not publicly agree with Lamarck but was more or less influenced by his theory in his formulation of a hypothesis to account for the transmission of parental variation. He believed that different parts of the body sent *particles* into the blood as messengers to the gonads, the sexual reproductive structures. As the body organs change under environmental influences, so would the messenger particles. Therefore, the new variations transmitted by these particles would be constantly replenished. However, Darwin's hypothesis was not really satisfactory because it could not account for the patterns of inheritance of parental characteristics.

Francis Galton (1822–1911) tested Darwin's hypothesis by attempting to produce hybrid rabbits with intermediate color by injecting blood from male rabbits of one color into the female rabbits of another. Darwin's theory would predict that the offspring would have coat colors intermediate between those of the parents and the blood donors because they had received a mixture of messenger particles carried by the blood of the donors and the parents. However, the coat colors of the offspring were consistently the same as those of the parents with no sign of being influenced by the blood donors (1).

Gregor Mendel (1822–84) proposed another theory. He described the hereditary units as particulate *traits* or *genes* instead of vital fluid. Mendel tried to test the validity of the dominant blending view of heredity by mating different parental stocks and analyzing the characteristics of the offspring to see if there were any specific patterns of inheritance. Mendel was successful in discovering two basic laws of inheritance while most of his colleagues who were involved in more or less the same kind of experimentation failed to come up with any significant conclusions. This was no accident, for he had set up his experiments carefully.

Mendel chose the garden pea *Pisum sativum* for experimentation. The pea had several advantages that allowed Mendel to have direct answers to his questions. First, the fertilization process could easily be controlled since the plant normally undergoes self-fertilization. This permitted Mendel to develop a technique to allow easy cross fertilization of different pea plants by removing the stamens (pollen organs) from one plant before self-fertilization and transferring them to another unfertilized de-stamenized plant. Second, because the generation time of the pea plant was brief, Mendel could trace the distribution of parental characteristics in many generations in a relatively short time. Third, peas had many sharply defined characteristics each represented in two alternative forms that Mendel called traits.

Mendel did two sets of experiments with the garden peas. In the first set of experiments he mated pure breeding plants showing alternative traits for a specified characteristics. He then observed the distribution of a given pair of traits in the offspring. From the results of these experiments, he formulated the *law of segregation*. In the second set of experiments Mendel traced the patterns of inheritance of two pairs of traits. These experiments led him to formulate the *law of independent assortment*. The parental generation was designated as P, and the first generation and second generation offspring were designated as F_1 (first filial generation) and F_2 (second filial generation), respectively.

The first set of experiments Mendel performed were monohybrid crosses involving one pair of traits. The second set of experiments were dihybrid crosses in which the distribution of two pairs of traits was followed. Mendel observed that all the traits of pure breeding parents did not always appear in the F_1 generation. Apparently one form of each paired trait took precedence over the other. He termed those traits that appear in the F_1 generation *dominant characters* and the traits that are not seen (latent) in the F_1 generation *recessive characters*.

Figure 1.1 summarizes the traits that Mendel examined, and Table 1.1 lists all the combinations of the monohybrid crosses. The uniformity in

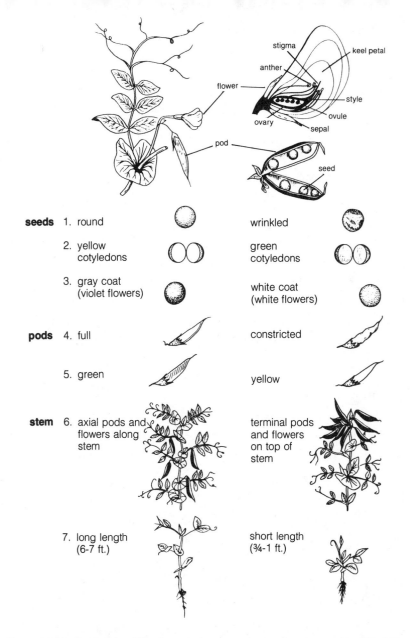

Figure 1.1. Seven characteristics in peas that were observed and scored by Mendel in his published experiments. As in other legumes such as various species of beans *(Phaseolus),* each flower produces a seed pod, containing up to 10 seeds (7 ovules). Reprinted, with permission, from Strickberger, M. W. Genetics. New York: Macmillan Publishing Co.; 1976. © 1976.

Table 1.1. Mendel's results from crosses involving single character differences. See Figure 1.1 for further description of these characters.

Parental phenotypes (pure breeding)		F_1 phenotypes	F_2 phenotypes*	F_2 ratio
seeds	round x wrinkled	all round	5/474 round 1/850 wrinkled	2.96 1
	yellow x green	all yellow	6/022 yellow 2/001 green	3.01 1
	gray x white	all gray	705 gray 224 white	3.15 1
pods	full x constricted	all full	882 full 299 constricted	2.95 1
	green x yellow	all green	428 green 152 yellow	2.82 1
stem	axial x terminal	all axial	652 axial 207 terminal	3.14 1
	long x short	all long	787 long 277 short	2.84 1

*The F_2 generation results from self-fertilization of F organisms.

the F_1 generation expressing the dominant characters and the apparent 3:1 distribution of the dominant versus the recessive characters in the F_2 generation could best be explained by assuming that the appearance (phenotype) of the dominant character is controlled by an A gene, and the phenotype of the recessive trait is controlled by an a gene. The parental genetic compositions (genotype) would be AA (homozygous dominant) and aa (homozygous recessive).

During the process of sexual reproduction, the genes of each parent *segregate* into gametes. In this case only one type of gamete will be obtained from each of the parents as a result of segregation, namely, A and a. When these gametes are brought together again in the fertilization process, then the genotype of the hybrid will be Aa (heterozygous). Since A gene is dominant over a gene, the only phenotype that is expressed in the F_1 generation will be the dominant character. This accounts for the observation of the uniformity in the appearance of the dominant traits in Mendel's F_1 offspring. During the subsequent mating among the F_1 generation, segregation occurs again, but now two different gametes can be obtained from each parent. Thus the possible combinations of genotype will be $AA:Aa:aa$ with a 1:2:1 ratio. Since A is the dominant gene, AA and Aa will both have the phenotype of the dominant characters. This gives rise to the 3:1 phenotypic ratio in the F_2 generation.

In Mendel's dihybrid crosses where he mated pure breeding plants characterized by round yellow seeds with pure breeding plants characterized by wrinkled green seeds, he got the following results:

F_1 generation: All plants had round yellow seeds

F_2 generation: 315 had round yellow seeds

101 had round green seeds

108 had wrinkled yellow seeds

32 had wrinkled green seeds with the four phenotypes occurring in a ratio of roughly 9:3:3:1

Again the concepts of segregation explains the data. If the genotypes of the plants in the parental generation with round yellow seeds and those with wrinkled green seeds are represented by $RRYY$ (homozygous dominant) and $rryy$ (homozygous recessive), respectively, during the F_1 generation, only one genotype is possible, namely, $RrYy$ since each parent can produce only one type of gamete by segregation, i.e., RY and ry, respectively. However, in the crosses among the F_1 offspring, segregation can give rise to several possible combinations of gametes. Since each gamete must contain one type of inherited factor from each gene pair, a condition that Mendel had established from the monohybrid crosses, the gametes produced by a heterozygous F_1 generation $(RrYy)$ will have the composition of RY, Ry, rY, or ry. If each of these compositions are produced at equal frequency, i.e., the segregation of the two pairs of traits is independent of each other, then sixteen combinations with nine genotypes are possible, namely, $RRYY$, $RRYy$, $RRyy$, $RrYY$, $RrYy$, $Rryy$, $rrYY$, $rrYy$, and $rryy$ with a ratio of 1:2:1:2:4:2:1:2:1, respectively. These genotypes will give a phenotypic ratio of 9:3:3:1. This interpretation is shown in Figure 1.2.

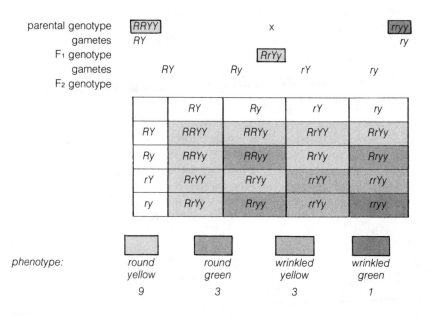

Figure 1.2. Schematic drawing showing the outcome of Mendel's second law of segregation. See text for explanation.

Although Mendel's work was first published in 1865, it went unnoticed until 1900, when Correns, de Vries, and Tschermak rediscovered and confirmed his findings. Furthermore, Hugo de Vries (1848–1935) proposed a new concept of mutation (2) that he used to describe changes in *Oenothera*, a plant commonly known as evening primrose. *Oenothera* brought about new types apparently at a single step. Mutations have since been shown to involve changes in single genes. Although de Vries coined the term *mutation* to describe sudden and abrupt changes, it has been found subsequently that a single mutation usually results in only a slight or barely perceptible modification of a phenotypic characteristic. This concept will be discussed further in the next section. With the reintroduction of Mendelian principles and de Vries's concept of mutation, the mechanism of evolutionary change was redefined with a more precise genetic framework.

The source of variation Darwin failed to explain by natural selection is essentially the mutations that occur in genes and that can be rearranged by genetic recombination. However, through the process of natural selection new varieties can evolve by the adaptation of the preexisting mutants to the new environment.

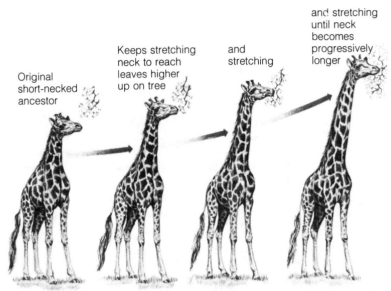

Original short-necked ancestor

Keeps stretching neck to reach leaves higher up on tree

and stretching

and stretching until neck becomes progressively longer

Lamackian view: Inheritance of acquired characteristics driven by inner need.

Mendelian view: Inheritance of intrinsic characteristics controlled by particulate genes that undergo mutation and recombination.

Original group exhibits variation in neck length

Natural selection favors longer necks: better chance to get

higher leaves Favored character passed on to next generation

After many, many generations the group is still variable, but shows a general increase in neck length

Figure 1.3. Comparison of the ideas of Lamarckian and Mendelian theories of evolutionary change. Adapted, with permission, from Savage, J. M. Evolution. 2nd ed. New York: Holt, Rinehart, and Winston; 1969. © 1969.

Therefore, the Lamarckian theory and the Mendelian theory of inheritance differ basically in the explanation of the source of diversification. Lamarckism interpreted it as a result of the inheritance of environmentally induced characteristics driven by the inner need of the vital fluid that stimulates development. Mendelism perceived it as the intrinsic characteristics of individuals controlled by particulate genes that can undergo mutation independently of environmental changes. The two interpretations of evolutionary change can best be illustrated by the hypothetical evolutionary scheme of the giraffes depicted in Figure 1.3 (3).

After additional research by August Weismann (1834–1914), Lamarckism fell into disfavor. Weismann believed that alterations of body characteristics by adaptation to the environment cannot be transmitted through the gametes. The failure to demonstrate the inheritance of acquired characteristics in experimental animals was consistent with his thesis. Characteristics in human populations also seem to conform to Weismann's interpretation. For ages Chinese women have had their feet tightly bundled shortly after birth, yet today's Chinese women have feet of regular size.

Lamarckian followers argue that since germ cells and body cells can be differentiated only in sexually reproducing organisms, Weismann's theory cannot be applied to asexual organisms, such as bacteria. Therefore, the Lamarckian view continued to be popular among bacteriologists in the early part of this century.

The Nobel laureate Joshua Lederberg (b. 1925) and his associates devised an ingenious experiment shown in Figure 1.4 to refute the Lamarckian view and establish the Mendelian view (4). The idea was to test the source of streptomycin-resistant mutant in a bacterial culture that was sensitive to the killing effects of streptomycin, a drug that inhibits the protein synthesis process in the bacteria. If the streptomycin-resistance trait can be shown to be inherent in the bacterial culture and not the result of the exposure to streptomycin, the Lamarckian theory that predicts the drug-resistant characteristic is produced only by the adaptation of the bacteria to the drug is refuted.

Lederberg developed a simple technique he called *replica plate* for his experiment. A wooden block was covered with a piece of sterile velveteen. The block was slightly smaller than the petri dish containing the solid agar medium that would support the growth of the bacteria. A few bacteria taken from a culture that was sensitive to streptomycin were spread on the surface of the agar plate containing no streptomycin. After an appropriate incubation time, each bacterium gave rise to a colony (an area of bacterial growth on an agar plate) containing millions of bacterial cells with the same genetic make-up. This is represented by the dark dots on the agar plate in Figure 1.4. The cover of the plate was removed, and the velveteen was used as a stamp on which an imprint of each colony was made by gently tapping the plate onto the velveteen. The imprint was correlated with the actual position of the master plate, i.e., the plate containing the original colonies. The imprint on the velveteen was trans-ferred to an agar plate that was supplemented with streptomycin by the same procedure as the original stamp making. The principle behind the procedure was that the velveteen's sticky hairlike texture picked up bac-teria from each colony on the master plate and introduced them to the streptomycin plate at the same location.

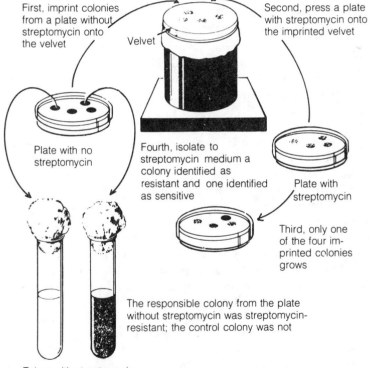

Figure 1.4. Diagrams illustrate the replica plating technique used by Lederberg to demonstrate that streptomycin resistance results from mutations that can occur quite independently of exposure of the culture to the drug. Explanation in the text. Adapted, with permission, © 1961, from Sager, R.; Ryan, F. Cell heredity. New York: John Wiley & Sons; 1961.

After incubation, the colony that survived on the streptomycin plate was scored, and by comparing it with the position of the imprint, the corresponding colony of the master plate was identified as the streptomycin-resistant clone. This was demonstrated by taking a few bacteria from the clone and transferring them to a liquid medium containing streptomycin. They multiplied and made the liquid medium in the tube cloudy, whereas the control colony as identified by the replica plating technique did not grow in the tube with the same medium. Thus, bacterial cells that had never been exposed to the drug streptomycin were shown to be resistant to the drug. The inheritance of acquired characteristics was ruled out by this experiment.

References 1.3

1. Lerner, I.M.; Libby, W. J. Heredity, evolution and society. 2nd ed. San Francisco: Freeman; 1976: 5.
2. de Vries, H. Die mutations theorie. Leipzig: Veit; 1901.
3. Savage, J. M. Evolution. 2nd ed. New York: Holt, Rinehart, and Winston; 1969.
4. Lederberg, J.; Lederberg, E. M. J. Bacteriol. 63:399; 1952.

1.4 Classical Mutation Theory vs. Neo-Darwinian Evolution

1.4.1 *Mutation*. When Hugo de Vries postulated the term *mutation*, he believed that mutation alone can bring about the abrupt changes of genetic constitution. He divorced evolution from natural selection by maintaining that natural selection merely has the negative effect of "pruning" the genetic varieties that are unfit to survive and thus plays no role in the diversification of genic variation that is the essence of evolution. This has been known as the classical mutation or *saltation* theory.

De Vries's contemporary W. Johannsen (1857–1927) added impetus to the classical mutation theory by demonstrating that variation in the size of garden beans did not respond to the effect of natural selection (1). From a seed lot of a single variety he selected out the largest beans and the smallest ones. He found that only in the first generation did the cross between plants grown from the larger beans produce slightly larger beans than a cross between plants grown from smaller beans. In the subsequent generations, the selection of the size of the bean during mating had no effect on the offspring. He concluded that natural selection had no effect on the fluctuating variations Darwin observed in the natural populations. Other geneticists who supported the mutation theory thereby stressing the importance of the sudden origin of discontinuous variations as a source of evolutionary change were William Bateson (1861–1920) (2) and

S. I. Korzhinsky (1861–1900) (3). Their criticisms dampened the enthusiasm of the Darwinists, who believed that natural selection was the major driving force for evolution.

The concept of mutation was later elaborated by the Nobel laureate Thomas Hunt Morgan (1866–1945) and his associates, who refined de Vries's conclusion by their experiments with the mutability of the fruit fly *Drosophila melanogaster* (4, 5, 6). They showed that the effects of the mutations that occurred in the flies were of varying degrees of severity. The effects ranged from ones so drastic that the mutants were lethal to moderate effects to those barely detectable. Mutants with drastic changes were easily recognized by an untrained eye, and they were most useful in genetic analysis. They reexamined de Vries's data and found that the mutants he obtained were actually an assemblage of diverse mutations that appeared to be drastically different from its parental plant. These findings led de Vries to conclude that sudden mutation gives rise to new species that he understood to mean a new line of pure-breeding genetically identical individuals.

Morgan's work was later elaborated by his student, Nobel laureate H. J. Muller (1890–1967) who related the frequency of mutation to the effects of radiation (7, 8, 9). He measured the frequencies of certain classes of mutations and showed that they can be increased experimentally, i.e., by the effect of x-irradiation. His work also stimulated the search for other mutagenic radiations and chemicals. The work of Morgan, Muller, and their colleagues paved the way for the Neo-Darwinian view that mutation provides the raw material for evolution.

1.4.2 *Recombination.* A further source of diversity, namely, recombination, was also discovered and later contributed directly to the Neo-Darwinian view of the origin of variation in the living world. William Bateson, Reginald Punnet (1875–1967), and their associates first observed the departure from the Mendelian ratio expected from independent assortment in crosses between different varieties of sweet peas (10). They found that parental plants of different flower color and pollen shape gave rise to F_1 and F_2 offspring in which the genes for flower color and pollen shape did not assort independently. These genes seemed to be tied together (later termed linkage) so that the F_2 offspring showed ratios of too many of the original parental genotypes and too few of the newly combined genotypes. The correlation of the Mendelian paired factors (alleles) with homologous chromosomes that paired up during meiosis by W. S. Sutton (1877–1926) (11) and T. Boveri (1862–1915) (12) clarified the mechanism of this unexpected genetic phenomenon. Furthermore, Morgan helped clarify the picture by his study of sex-linked characteristics in

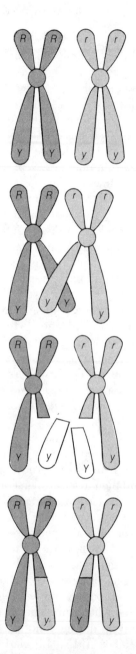

*Two homologous chromosomes pair up during meiosis

*Crossing over of chromatid arms

*Random breakages occur at region of chromatid overlap

*Reunion of "wrong partner" causes exchange of y and Y genes.

Figure 1.5. Schematic model of crossing over. c: centromere that connects chromatids on the chromosome R, r, Y, y genes; same designations as those of Figure 1.2.

Drosophila melanogaster (13). The characteristics that did not assort in-dependently during meiosis were located on the same chromosome. Therefore, during the segregation process, they stayed together. As a result, the genotypes of the F2 comprised a majority of the parental types while the rare newly combined genotypes arose by the process of crossing over or recombination. These events are illustrated in Figure 1.5.

With these added features of the genetic explanation of variation, the classical theory was slightly modified. For the classicist, variation arising from mutation and recombination is removed by the purifying force of natural selection that rejects all but the fittest type. This is the so-called *stabilizing selection* (*see* I. 1.4.4). Therefore, natural selection was seen as antithetical to variation, and a genetic basis for evolution was unsubstan-tiated.

The theory of evolution via natural selection was held at low esteem between 1900 and 1925. The position of many evolutionists during this period can best be represented by the following excerpts from William Bateson's speech given at the 1921 convention of the American Associa-tion for the Advancement of Science (14):

> I may seem behind the times in asking you to devote an hour to the old topic of evolution. Discussions of evolution came to an end primarily because it was obvious that no progress was being made. . . . When students of other sciences ask us what is now currently believed about the origin of species, we have no clear answer to give. Faith has given place to agnosticism . . . we have absolute *certainty* that new forms of life, new orders and new species have arisen on earth. That is *proven* by the paleontological record . . . our faith in evolution stands unshaken. (Italics mine)

1.4.3 *Agnostic Period.* Although the mechanism of evolution by natural selection fell into disrepute, evolutionists clung onto their faith by relying on the circumstantial evidence of the fossil record. Edward O. Dodson and Peter Dodson named this period "The Agnostic Period" of development of modern evolutionary thought (15). Although the classical mutationist position was gradually replaced by the modern dominant view of Neo-Darwinism, it was recently revived by the advent of the field of molecular evolution (a study of evolution by the modern techniques of molecular biology) in the form of *neutral mutation theory* that R. C. Lewontin called *neo-classicist* (16). We shall return to the discussion of the neutralist-selectionist debate in a subsequent section (see I.3.3.2.a.1).

The restoration of Darwinian natural selection as the principle guiding factor in evolution began when J. B. S. Haldane (1892–1964), R. A. Fisher (1890–1962), S. Wright (b. 1889), and S. S. Chetverikov (b. 1880) inde-pendently worked out the theoretical models to study the variations in population. However, the modern synthetic version of the Neo-Darwinian theory was not formulated systematically until the publication of Dobzhansky's *Genetics and the Origin of Species* in 1937 (17). Theodosius Dobzhansky (1900–75) correlated mathematical models in population genetics with the refined chromosomal theory of heredity by the Morgan school. Dobzhansky's work was supplemented by writings of J. S. Huxley (b. 1887), E. Mayr (b. 1904), G. G. Simpson (b. 1902), and G. L. Stebbins (b. 1906), all of whom attempted to present a strong case for the synthetic theory of evolution.

For the Neo-Darwinist, evolutionary changes take place when the genic variation by mutation and recombination is subject to the process of natural selection. These changes are determined at the population level by the way in which the environment is changing relative to the adaptation of the organisms in the population. Based on the different organism-environmental interactions, natural selection seems to be operating in three different ways, namely, *stabilizing selection, directional selection,* and *disruptive selection.* These are depicted in Figure 1.6.

1.4.4 *Stabilizing Selection.* Stabilizing selection (normalizing selection) eliminates any marked deviations from an already well-adapted population. It is essentially the type of selection referred to by the classicists. But contrary to the classicist's view that this was the only role of natural selection in evolution, Neo-Darwinism maintains that stabilizing selection is only one of several ways natural selection can work in evolution.

An example of stabilizing selection can be seen in the predator-prey relationship of owls and field mice. Mice with normal color are protected from owls because the field is the color of the mice. However, mice with deviant color are quickly eliminated from the population because they are more visible to owls. Thus, selection tends to maintain the color of the mice within a narrow range that is determined by the color of the field.

1.4.5 *Directional Selection.* Directional selection is the force that drives the population to undergo evolutionary changes in one direction with respect to certain adaptive characteristics. Here deviants are not always eliminated as in the case of stabilizing selection. Deviants from the norm in one direction tend to survive more often and leave more offspring than deviants in the opposite direction.

Directional selection can most easily be observed when a population is subjected to a progressive change in environment. The most famous example of directional selection is *industrial melanism* as seen in the peppered moth and is discussed in detail in I.3.2.1.b.

1.4.6 *Disruptive Selection.* Disruptive selection has a somewhat opposite effect from stabilizing selection. The latter favors homogeneity of a population by eliminating extreme variants, whereas disruptive selection tends to eliminate the majority of a population and establish the extreme variants.

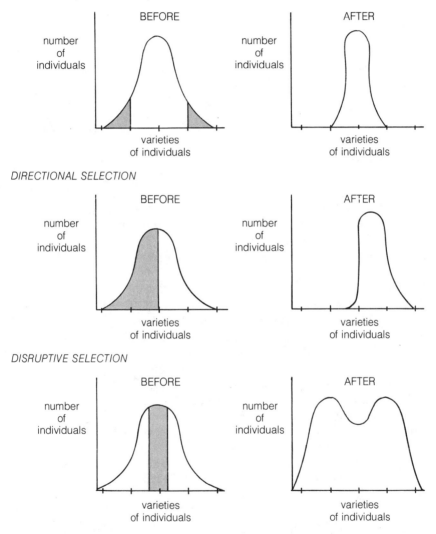

Figure 1.6. Diagrams illustrating the effects of stabilizing (normalizing), directional, and disruptive selection. Varieties of individuals can be represented by phenotypic variations such as height, skin color, etc., that are controlled genetically. Shaded and open areas on the *Before* selection curves represent adverse and favorable selections respectively.

An example of disruptive selection is seen in the development of the seed size of some plants when certain beetles specialize in feeding only on intermediate-size seeds. The result is the elimination of seeds of intermediate size and the plants producing the intermediate seeds. The outcome is two distinct populations of plants. One population has small seeds and the other large seeds.

References 1.4

1. Johannsen, W. Elemente der exakten Erblichkeitslehre. Jena: Gustav Fischer; 1909. Reprint; 1926.
2. Bateson, W. Materials for the study of variation. London: Macmillan; 1894.
3. Korzhinsky, S. I. Heterogenesis and evolution. St. Petersberg: Academy of Science; 1899. Russian.
4. Morgan, T. H. Science. 33:534–37; 1911.
5. Morgan T. H. The physical basis of heredity. Philadelphia: Lippincott; 1919.
6. Morgan, T. H.; Sturtevant, A. H.; Muller, J. J.; Bridges, C. B. The mechanism of Mendelian heredity. New York: Holt; 1915.
7. Muller, H. J. Science. 66:84–87; 1927.
8. Muller, H. J. Zeitschrift Fuer Induktive Abstammungs-Und Vererbungslehre. Suppl. Vol. 1, 1928: 234–60.
9. Muller, H. J.; Genet, J. 13:279–357; 1928.
10. Bateson, W.; Saunders, E. R.; Punnett, R. C. Experimental studies in the physiology of heredity. Reports to the Evolution Committee Royal Society II. London: Harrison and Sons; 1905.
11. Sutton, W. S. Biol. Bull. 4:213–51; 1903.
12. Boveri, T. Ergebnisse uber die Konstitution der chromatischen Substanz des Zellkerns. Jena: G. Fischer; 1904.
13. Morgan, T. H. Science. 34:384; 1911.
14. Bateson, W. Science. 55:55; 1922.
15. Dodson, E. O.; Dodson, P. Evolution: process and product. 2nd ed. New York: Van Nostrand; 1976: 97.
16. Lewontin, R. C. The genetic basis of evolutionary change. New York and London: Columbia Univ. Press; 1974: 197.
17. Dobzhansky, T. Genetics and the origin of species. 1st, 2nd, 3rd ed. New York: Columbia Univ. Press; 1937, 1941, 1951.

1.5 Microevolution, Macroevolution, and the Synthetic Theory

The first systematic attempt to categorize different levels of evolution was made by Richard B. Goldschmidt (1878–1958) (1). He took the original allusion of Dobzhansky (2) to microevolution as the evolutionary process observable within man's lifetime and gave it an experimental meaning. Goldschmidt believed geneticists could use microevolution to analyze the variants of natural populations as well as observe evolutionary changes in controlled breeding studies in the laboratory. Macroevolution (megaevolution), a term coined by Simpson (3), was perceived as the territory of the paleontologist, the comparative anatomist, and the embryologist. Therefore, Goldschmidt interpreted microevolution as the observable changes that give rise to variations in experimental and natural populations within a species and macroevolution as the historical evolution of the "good" species that have been placed in the higher taxonomic categories. Furthermore, these macroevolutionary changes have been correlated with the geological time scale.

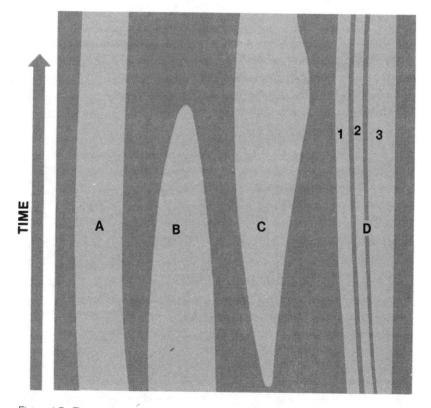

Figure 1.7. The adaptive grid. Adaptive zones are indicated by letters and subzones by arabic numbers, ecologically unstable zones are shaded. Reproduced, by permission © 1969, Savage, J. M. Evolution. 2nd ed. New York: Holt, Rinehart, and Winston; 1969.

Neo-Darwinists claimed that the accumulation of gene mutations and the isolation and selection of new variants that continue to undergo the same process accounted for all evolutionary diversification. Goldschmidt argued that these processes cannot be an all-encompassing mechanism and thus did not suffice for an understanding of macroevolution. He challenged the Neo-Darwinists to explain the evolution of 18 features by accumulation and selection of small mutations. The features included hair in mammals, feathers in birds, segmentation of arthropods and vertebrates, visceral arches, muscles, nerves, teeth, shells of mollusks, ectoskeletons, compound eyes, blood circulation, and alternation of generations. He proposed a novel concept of *systemic mutation* to account for macroevolution. This concept will be discussed in detail in I.3.3.2.a.3. Neo-Darwinists, while unable to meet the challenges posed by

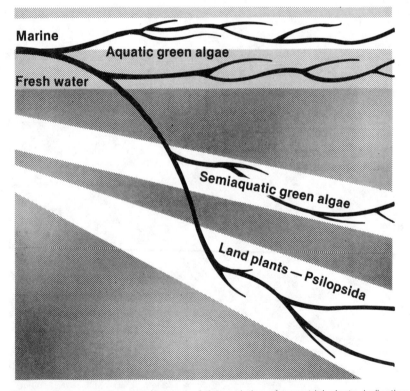

Figure 1.8. An adaptive grid diagram of the evolution of terrestrial plants, indicating major breakthroughs and invasions of new adaptive zones. Reprinted, by permission, copyright 1969. Savage, J.M. Evolution. 2nd ed. New York, Holt, Rinehart, and Winston; 1969.

Goldschmidt, found his alternative explanation untenable and adhered to their assertion that microevolution and macroevolution are not qualitatively distinct. They believed the accumulation of point-mutations by natural selection not only will lead to the development of new varieties within a species, but it can also account for the major features of macroevolution (3).

According to present-day Neo-Darwinists, the interaction of organisms and their environment produced a series of adaptive zones or fields (4). Each adaptive zone may also consist of subzones (Figure 1.7). For example, all aquatic green algae occur in the aquatic adaptive zone, but the fresh water and the marine green algae are confined by their respective adaptive subzones. Microevolution involves the crossing of evolutionary lines within subdivisions of the subzones. However, macroevolution involves the crossing of evolutionary lines between one major zone or subzone into another. Evolution among green algae in the marine and fresh water subzones would be called microevolution, whereas macroevolution would involve major breakthroughs into new adaptive zones. A hypothetical macroevolutionary scheme constructed on the basis of geographical distribution of algae and land plants is represented in Figure 1.8.

1.5.1 *Speciation.* Neo-Darwinists account for the origin of species by the process of speciation. It is an extrapolation of variations seen in populations subjected to artificial selection. The major criterion that establishes a new species is the formation of reproductive isolation. Several of the mechanisms of reproductive isolation have been described earlier in this section. While Goldschmidt maintained that speciation occurs apart from the point mutation-selection scheme by a process of macrogenesis or saltation in which a "hopeful" monster arises by a rearrangement of the intrachromosomal pattern, this is rejected by the Neo-Darwinists. The mode of speciation advocated by Goldschmidt and others involves the establishment of reproductive isolation followed by development of geographical barriers. This view has been called sympatric speciation. It is a much refined form of the classical mutationist position that states that speciation takes place when reproductive isolation of a new population occurs in the presence of the parent species by disruptive selection, seasonal isolation, and polyploidy. In contrast, most Neo-Darwinists maintain that geographic speciation followed by reproductive isolation is the dominant evolutionary mode (5).

Neo-Darwinists have developed several patterns of evolution to account for trends in the evolutionary scheme constructed from the fossil record and the morphological differences observed in natural populations.

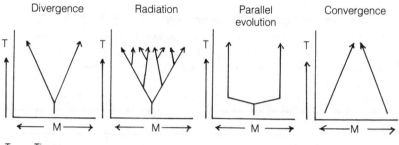

T = Time
M = Morphological changes

Figure 1.9. Some common evolutionary patterns as indicated by morphological changes among different lineages.

Rensch (6) first used the term *kladogenesis* (or cladogenesis) to describe phylogenetic branching and *anagenesis* to describe the development toward higher phylogenetical levels. Certain laws of evolution were laid down that characterize the fossil record and natural populations. The *law of the unspecialized* states that unspecialized organisms will survive, but the overspecialized will be eliminated by changing environments (7). Furthermore, *Dollo's law* indicates that major evolutionary steps, once taken, are never reversed, i.e., a reptile cannot become a fish again (8). Although there are exceptions to these laws, they can be used to describe the major features of evolution.

Several patterns of morphological change are also apparent during macroevolution. *Divergence* is the splitting of a lineage into two adaptive pathways. Chimpanzee and man are presumed to be the descendants of a common ancestor that subsequently diverged into two adaptive pathways. *Radiation* is a multiple divergence in which a number of lineages split from a primitive form and diverge to occupy a number of distinctive niches and regions in the biosphere. The various species of finches in the Galapagos Islands first described by Darwin were probably the result of adaptive radiation from an ancestral form that migrated from the mainland of South America (*see* I.2.4, Figure 2.29 for details). *Parallel evolution* results when two distinct lineages undergo the same morphological changes due to adaptation to similar environments. The eye of a squid is remarkably similar to that of man although the two lineages evolved independently. This is the result of parallel evolution. And finally, *convergence* occurs when separate lineages become morphologically similar. The flippers of whales resemble the fins of fish. However, fish and whales are little related in the evolutionary tree. Therefore, the resemblance is due to convergence. Figure 1.9 illustrates these patterns (9).

1.5.2 *Synthetic Theory*. The modern synthetic theory of organic evolution involves three categories: (1) the origin of life (abiogenesis), (2) microevolution, (3) macroevolution. Attempts have been made to correlate the origin of life with the physical and chemical reactions that are occurring in the inorganic world. Since the spontaneous generation of life is no longer thought to be possible under present earth conditions, evolutionists resort to the assumption that life may have occurred by the random collision of inorganic molecules on the surface of the primitive earth. These collisions were thought to be aided by physical and chemical catalysts resulting in the production of increasingly complex organic molecules by a mechanism analogous to natural selection (10). Several experiments have been set up that have simulated presumed primitive earth conditions in order to test the above hypothesis (*see* I.3.3, Figure 3.10; 3.11).

Much circumstantial evidence is available to support most of the contentions of the synthetic theory; however, the backbone of this huge structure is still in the process of construction. G. A. Kerkut, in the conclusion of his book *The Implication of Evolution* (11) summarized the current status of the synthetic theory of evolution, which he calls the "General Theory of Evolution" (macroevolution), as compared to the "Special Theory of Evolution" (microevolution) as follows:

> There is a theory which states that many living animals can be observed over the course of time to undergo changes so that new species are formed. This can be called "The Special Theory of Evolution" and can be demonstrated in certain cases by experiments. On the other hand there is the theory that all the living forms in the world have arisen from a single source which itself came from an inorganic form. This theory can be called the "General Theory of Evolution" and the evidence that supports it is not sufficiently strong to allow us to consider it as anything but a working hypothesis. It is not clear whether the changes that bring about speciation are the same nature as those that brought about the development of new phyla. The answer will be found by future experimental work and not by dogmatic assertions that the General Theory of Evolution must be correct because there is nothing else that will satisfactorily take its place.

Since Kerkut's statement, not much progress has been made toward the resolution of the status of the "General Theory of Evolution." Recent hypotheses attempting to account for possible genetic variabilities have placed a great deal of strain on the Neo-Darwinists who advocate the universal sufficiency of natural selection in evolution. The following section examines the evidence for the theories of evolution and attempts to evaluate the strengths and weaknesses of the theories.

References 1.5

1. Goldschmidt, R. D. The material basis of evolution. New Haven, CT: Yale Univ. Press; 1940.
2. Dobzhansky, T. Genetics and the origin of species. 1st, 2nd, 3rd ed. New York: Columbia Univ. Press; 1937, 1941, 1951.
3. Simpson, G. G. The major features of evolution. New York: Columbia Univ. Press; 1953 (chapter 11).
4. Savage, J. Evolution. 2nd ed. New York: Holt; 1969 (chapter 10).
5. Mayr, E. Animal species and evolution. Cambridge, MA: Harvard Univ. Press; 1963: 481.
6. Rensch, B. Evolution above the species level. New York: Columbia Univ. Press; 1960 (chapter 6).
7. Rensch, B. Evolution above the species level. 237.
8. Dodson, E. O.; Dodson, P. Evolution: process and product. 2nd ed. New York: Van Nostrand; 1976: 256.
9. Dobzhansky, T.; Ayala, F. J.; Stebbins, G. L.; Valentine, J. W. Evolution. San Francisco: Freeman; 1977: 326–27.
10. Oparin, A. I. Genesis and evolutionary development of life. New York: Academic; 1968.
11. Kerkut, G. A. Implications of evolution. New York: Pergamon; 1960: 157.

CHAPTER 2

Evidence
for
Evolution

2.1 Antiquity of the Earth

2.1.1 *Principle of Uniformitarianism.* Since evolutionary processes require long periods of time, the establishment of the antiquity of the earth through geology is a prerequisite for the credibility of the evolutionary theories. Geologists concerned with estimating the earth's age use fossils as one source of data.

In medieval times fossils were thought of as a product of some plastic force in the earth, or unusual concretion, or curiously figured stones. Leonardo da Vinci (1452–1519) was the first person to make some sense out of the curiosity of fossils. He believed fossils he found in northern Italy had been formed on the sea floor by burial of living animals in silt and mud. In 1517 Fracastoro's thinking was similar, and he concluded that the fossils at Verona, Italy, were produced by natural burial of shells. He also dismissed the Noachin Deluge as a possible cause of these fossils. Fracastoro believed a temporary inundation such as the Flood would have scattered the shells rather than bury and preserve them (1).

René Descartes agreed in principle with Fracastoro in his *Philosophiae Principia* published in 1644. He argued that the "laws of nature" should be used to trace the origin and progress of the earth (2). Also in agreement with Fracastoro was Robert Hooke. In his work published posthumously in 1705, he maintained that the Noachin Flood was not adequate to explain the voluminous sediment and the fossils it contains (3). He suggested that natural phenomena should be used to explain the changes in the earth. Hooke was also the first to recognize the possibility of establishing a chronology of the earth's history from the fossil record, although he did not elaborate on the details.

After studying the earth's surface, George de Buffon pointed out the power of rivers and currents in the erosion of lands over a long period. He also suggested on the basis of fossil findings that the earth has not always been as it is at present and that the positions of the land and seas have changed. In 1778, Buffon attempted to arrange earth history into six long indeterminate intervals of time in his book *Epoques de la Nature*. The careful documentation of his novel ideas won acceptance among his contemporaries.

a) *Modern Geology*. Modern geology, however, was not brought into being until the *principle of uniformitarianism* had been systematically worked out by James Hutton (1726–97) in his *Theory of the Earth* published in 1795. He assumed that the past history of the earth can be explained only by what is observed or recorded to be happening at present or during the immediate past. Therefore, according to Hutton, the present must be the key to the past (4). Charles Lyell (1794–1875), the father of modern geology, built on Hutton's foundation and expounded the view of uniformitarianism in his epoch-making thesis *Principles of Geology* as follows (5):

> All past ages on the globe had been brought about by the slow agency of existing causes. The imagination was at first fatigued and overpowered by endeavoring to conceive the immensity of time required for the annihilation of whole continents by so insensible a process; and when the thoughts had wandered through those interminable periods, no resting place was assigned in the remotest distance. . . . Such views of the immensity of past time, like those unfolded by The Newtonian philosophy in regard to space, were too vast to awaken ideas of sublimity unmixed with a sense of our incapacity to conceive a plane of such infinite extent.

b) *Historic Geology*. One theory after another was developed to explain the appearance of the earth's surface. The opposing view of historic geology was first presented by Baron George Cuvier (1769–1832). He believed catastrophes and restorative creations were the explanation of the fossils in the geological timetable (6). Twentieth-century catastrophists are found among the followers of Velikovsky (7), who proposed that the irregularities in the solar system's orbit indicated that the earth was involved twice in global upheavals. His ability to assemble great masses of ancient records suggestive of past catastrophes drew much attention despite his untenable theories (8, 9).

Flood geologists (10) also believe that the sedimentary deposits of the earth were caused by a catastrophe, namely, the universal Deluge. They express this belief as follows: "A tremendous cataclysm of water pouring down from the skies and up from the subterranean deeps, produced a year long debacle of erosion and deposition of sediments that could have accounted for at least most of the sedimentary deposits in the earth's crust" (11).

c) *Contemporary View of Uniformitarianism.* Uniformitarianism is favored among most contemporary geologists for essentially two reasons: (1) It has the merit of simplicity. Since rocks can be interpreted using the physical and chemical processes observable in the present, physical geologists can develop hypotheses and subject them to verification by observation. (2) Uniformitarianism also takes into consideration the occasional catastrophes experienced by the earth. It is evident that geologic processes have acted in the same way throughout earth's history but not always with the same intensities. Some catastrophic events in the earth's history can be analyzed by their present-day counterparts, such as earthquakes and volcanic eruptions. Others, such as the Noachin Flood, can be examined only by comparing the modern processes of sedimentation with the geological record. (This comparison has led most geologists to seriously doubt the validity of the Flood geologists' claim that most, if not all, of the earth's sediments were deposited during the temporary inundation of the Flood [12]).

There are still many questions for which advocates of uniformitarianism have not found satisfactory answers. For example, the origin of the magma (the molden material underneath the earth's surface), the formation of plutonic rocks (rocks formed within the earth's crust presumably by the crystallized magma), and the forces of mountain building are not understood. Unfortunately, these phenomena are concealed from observation and cannot be analyzed (13). Nevertheless, uniformitarianism has been the foundation of modern historical geology and is a helpful guide in deciphering physical geology, but it is a concept that requires some comprehension of geologic time.

2.1.2 *Dating of the Geological Column.* There are two methods of dating the geological column, namely, *relative dating* which gives only the order of events, and *absolute dating* (finite dating), which measures the duration of time from a fixed reference point (14).

a) *Relative Dating.* The main method of relative dating makes use of fossils. One of the first attempts to classify geologic time in terms of the presence or absence of fossils was made by J. G. Lehmann (1719–67) in 1967. He called the oldest layer of rocks that did not contain any fossils the Primitive Class. The fossiliferous rocks formed by secondary processes from the Primitive Class were named Secondary Class. The third and most recent layer of rocks was the Third Class and contained abundant organic life.

The systematic application of fossils to date rocks was not widely used until George Cuvier (1769–1832, an antievolutionist), Alexandre Brongniart (1770–1847), and William Smith (1769–1839) independently came up with comparable geological ages, using fossils in France and England. They have shown that layers of comparable age in different places have similar fossils, with different fossils in layers above and below. Cuvier and Brongniart recognized ancient (extinct) and modern (living) fossils and used them to subdivide into groups the rocks where they occurred. These approaches were later clarified by Lyell (15). He classified European fossiliferous rocks into periods and groups in a form similar to the modern geological column.

In dating the geological record by fossils, two fundamental laws were used. The first is the *law of superposition* and states that undisturbed strata are in the order of their deposition of formation. The justification for the law is obvious, for the deeper layers must be formed earlier than the more superficial layers by all observable processes of rock formation. The second law is the *law of faunal and floral succession* and stipulates that plants and animals have progressively changed through time and that each period of geological time is characterized by distinctive fossil groups. This is verified by the observation that each geological period has a unique array of fossils and comparable ones can be located in a similar geological period throughout the continents. The nonrecurrence of these species has been a major advantage for the paleontological "clock."

Certain fossils called *index* or *guide* fossils are found to be very useful in correlating geologic time. These fossils must have the following characteristics: wide geographical distribution, ecological tolerance, abundance, and rapidly changing morphological features (16). Most paleontologists, however, prefer to work with a collection of fossils because even if index fossils are missing, the chances of correlating the last and first appearance of certain fossils is increased. However, some scholars believe the use of fossils to establish the geological time scale or vice versa is circular reasoning. The charge of using circular reasoning in the relative dating method (17, 18) is not justified in light of the above generalizations and also when the more quantitative techniques of *absolute dating* are considered. Attempts are made also to correlate relative dating with absolute radiometric age (19).

b) *Absolute Dating.* There are several methods for the estimation of absolute or finite age of rocks on the earth. The older techniques were quantitative and used physical and chemical parameters applicable to geological formations.

One method used to estimate the earth's age deals with the salinity of the oceans. It is assumed that the oceans were originally fresh water and that the salt content was derived from the progressive erosion of rock salt carried into the ocean by way of rivers and streams. Fresh water from the ocean was constantly distilled by the heat of the sun and returned to the environment in the form of clouds, rain, and snow. During this circulation, it is assumed, the salinity of the ocean is directly proportional to the amount of salt carried from the rivers and streams. If the rate of transport of salt and the absolute salt content in the ocean were known, the age of the ocean, which would presumably correspond to the age of the earth, could be calculated. The figure of 100 million years was obtained by this calculation. However, since no reliable methods are available to estimate whether the amount of water that was lost by evaporation from the oceans equaled the influx from the rivers and streams, this estimate is deemed unreliable (20).

The rate of accumulation of sedimentary rocks is also used to estimate the age of sedimentary deposits of the earth. The thickness of the deposit divided into the rate of accumulation would give the time for the whole deposit to have occurred. The limitation of this scheme is the difficulty involved in determining the total thickness of continuous deposition. Also, the rate of deposition seems to vary from place to place and from time to time, being faster during episodes of mountain building and slower in flooded lowlands. Therefore, the figure estimated by this method of 95 million years since the Cambrian period was not accurate (20). This system has proved useful only in special situations when thin layers of deposit mark a given length of time that can be confirmed by radiometric dating.

The assumption that the earth has gone through a period of cooling off from its original molten state without gaining heat from sources other than the sun led Lord Kelvin (1824–1907) to calculate the age of the earth as between 25 to 100 million years. However, he qualified his estimate by assuming that it was valid only if no other internal source of heat was present in the earth's history. The estimate became meaningless when heat was found to be produced during radioactive decay in minerals found in the earth's mantle and crust.

The discovery of radioactivity provided geochronological studies (chronology of the earth based on geological data) with a powerful tool. There are five conditions that have to be met before radioactivity can be applied to geochronology (21, 22).

(1) The parent atom A by a random process becomes radioactive.
(2) The parent atom A, by radioactive disintegration is transformed (decays) to a daughter atom B.

(3) The rate that A is decaying into B is a constant with an accurately known parameter.

(4) The system of the parent and daughter atoms must remain closed since the formation of the system, e.g., time of crystallization of volcanic rock. There must be no exchange of parent and daughter atoms with the surroundings during this period.

(5) The sample analyzed is representative of the geological formation analyzed.

Since radioactive dating is the most quantitative method of geochronological studies and has been severely criticized by some (23, 24), an extensive elaboration of principles is in order.

(1) *Nature of Radioactivity.* An atom consists of several types of particles. The best understood are the electrons, protons, and neutrons. Electrons revolve around the nucleus in electron shells and are negatively charged. Protons are positively charged, and neutrons are neutral, but both are bound by nuclear forces in the nucleus of the atom. The mass of the electrons is negligible as compared to that of the protons and the neutrons that have similar mass. Therefore, the *mass number* of an atom is the number of protons plus the number of neutrons. The *atomic number* of an atom in an un-ionized state is the number of protons or the number of electrons that are equal to each other.

The chemical properties of an atom are determined by its atomic number. Therefore, the number of neutrons in an atom can vary without changing its chemical properties. Oxygen, for example, has 8 protons, but different oxygen atoms can have either 8, 9, or 10 neutrons with corresponding mass numbers of 16, 17, and 18. These different nuclides of oxygen are its *isotopes.* Atoms can be split or caused to split artificially by bombardment with neutrons. However, some isotopic forms of certain elements undergo spontaneous disintegration because the nuclear forces cannot bind the excess numbers of neutrons with the protons that are constantly vibrating inside the nucleus. The net result will be the breakdown of the nuclei into different particles. This is *radioactivity.* Some isotopes do not undergo spontaneous disintegration. They are called stable isotopes, and they are of little use in geochronology.

The nuclei of radioactive atoms can break down in several ways. The first is by losing a fragment containing two neutrons and two protons. This corresponds to the nucleus of a helium atom having a mass number of four. The process is called the emission of an *alpha particle.* The loss of an alpha particle reduces the number of neutrons and protons in the parent atom each by two thus changing it to a new element with a different set of chemical properties. The emission of alpha particles also brings the parent nucleus to an *excited state* that is not stable. The nucleus will soon return to its stable *ground state* by losing the energy it has in the excited state in the emission of gamma rays.

A second way of radioactive disintegration is by the ejection of an electron or a *beta particle*. It is derived from the neutron in the nucleus. The loss of the electron causes the neutron to acquire a positive charge, and it turns into a proton. Therefore, after a beta emission the atomic number of the atom increases by one while the loss of the negligible mass of the beta particle does not change the mass number. A small particle called *neutrino* is also given off accompanying a beta emission while the parent atom is changed to a new element.

The third type of radioactive decay is called *electron capture*. In this type the nucleus of an atom captures an electron from its innermost orbital shell accompanied by the emission of a neutrino and a gamma ray. This results in the loss of one proton whose positive charge has been neutralized by the negative charge of the electron while maintaining the same mass number. The atomic number is decreased by one and a new element is formed. Figure 2.1 summarizes the three types of radioactive decay.

Some radioactive isotopes may decay in two or more ways, and the choice of which alternative paths to take is purely random.

1. Emission of alpha particle ($^4_2$He)

   $^{230}_{190}$ Th $\longrightarrow$ $^{226}_{188}$ Ra $+$ $^4_2$ He $+$ gamma ray
   (Thorium)   (Radium) (Helium)

2. Emission of beta particle ($^0_{-1}$e)

   $^{35}_{16}$ S $\longrightarrow$ $^{35}_{17}$ Cl $+$ $^0_{-1}$e $+$ neutrino
   (Sulphur)   (Chlorine)

3. Electron capture

   $^{11}_{16}$ C $+$ $^0_{-1}$e $\longrightarrow$ $^{11}_{15}$ B
   (Carbon)   (Boron)

Figure 2.1. Three types of radioactive decay. Superscripts are mass numbers. Subscripts are atomic numbers.

(2) *Quantitation of Radioactive Decay and Age Determination.* Radioactivity can be treated as the probability that a given nuclide will spontaneously disintegrate into another nuclide. If the probability is very small, the nuclide is a stable isotope. If it is large, then the nuclide is highly radioactive. If an individual radioactive nuclide is considered, it is impossible to predict exactly when it will decay. One can only estimate the probability that certain atoms will disintegrate within a given span of time. However, by taking large numbers of radioactive atoms into account and measuring the average rate of decay, a prediction of the proportion

that will have disintegrated within a certain time can be obtained.

The more radioactive nuclides present in the beginning, the higher the probability that radioactive disintegration will occur within a given span of time. Therefore, the number of atoms that actually undergo decay will be directly proportional to the number of parent atoms present originally. Since disintegration is a continuous process, the number of parent atoms will continually decrease while the number of daughter atoms will continually increase, provided that the daughter atoms are stable nuclides. A *decay constant* can be used to express the proportionality between the number of atoms decaying per unit time to the number of parent atoms. Each radioactive nuclide is characterized by a specific decay constant that is not affected by known physical or chemical processes. It is reasonable to assume, then, that the decay constants of radioactive nuclides in rocks used in geochronology also were unchanged during the geological time.

Since the quantitation of radioactivity is a statistical treatment, it is best to use a large sample and a long time span so that the detection of radioactivity will result in less fluctuation and a more accurate average decay rate. Because the atoms of a given radioactive nuclide decay at a certain average rate, it will require a definite amount of time for half of the initial atoms to undergo disintegration. This time is said to be the *half-life* of the radioactive nuclide. In other words at the end of a period equal to one half-life, only half of the original radioactive atoms are left, and at the end of two half-lives, one quarter, and so on. The relationship between the decay constant, the original number of atoms present, and the elapsed time can be shown in the following equation:

$$- \frac{dn}{dt} = \lambda N \qquad (1)$$

Where t $\quad$ = elapsed time
λ $\quad$ = decay constant
N $\quad$ = number of atoms present
dn $\quad$ = change in # of radioactive atoms

The negative sign indicates that the number of radioactive atoms decreases with time. By rearranging and integrating equation (1), the following equation is obtained.

$$N = N_0 e^{-\lambda t} \qquad (2)$$

Where N_0 $\quad$ = number of atoms present at time = 0
e $\quad$ = base of natural logarithms
N $\quad$ = number of atoms present now.

Equation (2), illustrated in Figure 2.2, gives the proportion of the number of atoms remaining at present to the number of atoms present at the beginning (N/N_0) and is plotted against the time in numbers of half-lives.

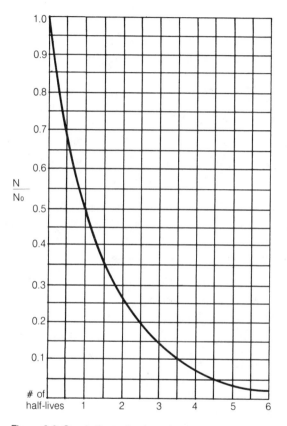

Figure 2.2. Graph illustrating law of radioactivity with proportion of radioactive parent remaining (N/N_0) drawn on line or scale.

If we assume that the parent radioactive nuclides directly disintegrate into a single stable isotope or into a series of intermediate radioactive daughter atoms that eventually decay into a single stable isotope at a rate much faster than the rate of the decay of the parent atoms, we may adopt equation (2) to express relationship between the number of parent atoms existing at the beginning and at present. This equation then can be written:

$$P_i = P_p \cdot e \; \lambda t \qquad\qquad (3)$$

Where P_i = the number of atoms of parent initially existing

P_p = the number of atoms of parent existing at present

t = elapsed time separating P_i and P_p

e = base of natural logarithms

λ = decay constant

Since we have assumed the parent decays to daughter directly or indirectly but through a brief transient stage, the difference between the number of daughter atoms existing initially and the number of daughter atoms existing at present must be equal to the difference of P_p and P_i. This relationship can be expressed as:

$$D_p - D_i = P_i - P_p \qquad\qquad (4)$$

Where D_i = number of atoms of daughter existing initially

D_p = number of atoms of daughter existing at present

In other words, the number of daughter atoms is constantly growing larger at the expense of the parent atoms whose number is constantly growing smaller.

By substituting equation (3) into equation (4) we get:

$$D_p - D_i = P_p \cdot e \; \lambda t - P_p \qquad\qquad (5)$$

that can be rewritten as:

$$D_p - D_i = P_p \cdot (e \; \lambda t - 1) \qquad\qquad (6)$$

Rearranging equation (6) to solve for t, we get the following equation:

$$\frac{D_p - D_i}{P_p} = e\lambda t - 1 \qquad\qquad (7)$$

$$e\lambda t = \frac{D_p - D_i}{P_p} + 1 \qquad\qquad (8)$$

$$\lambda t = \log_e \frac{D_p - D_i}{P_p} + 1 \qquad\qquad (9)$$

$$t = \frac{1}{\lambda} \log_e \frac{D_p - D_i}{P_p} + 1 \qquad\qquad (10)$$

Equation (5) represents an adaptation of the fundamental equation (2) for calculating age. Since one can determine the amount of daughter (D_p) and parent (P_p) existing at present by analysis and since the decay constant (λ) is known, we may calculate the age (t) of a rock if the amount of daughter (D_i) existing initially is known. (D_i is usually assumed to be equal to zero.)

(3) *Conventional Techniques of Radiometric Dating.* There are seven radiometric techniques used to date rocks. The carbon-14 (C-14) method is used to date specimens that are 40 000 years old or younger. Methods used to date rocks one million years of age and older include: uranium-238/lead-206, uranium-235/lead-207, thorium-232/lead-208, lead-207/lead-206, potassium-40/argon-40, and rubidium-87/strontium-87. Tables 2.1, 2.2, and 2.3 represent the sequences of events and half-lives of the uranium-238/lead-206, uranium-235/lead-207, and thorium-232/lead-208 series with respective half-lives of 4.51×10^9, 7.1×10^8, and 1.39

Table 2.1. The ^{238}U (Uranium) series. Decay constant of ^{238}U is 1.54×10^{-10} per year.*

Nuclide	Manner of decay	Half-life
^{238}U	α	4.51×10^9 years
^{234}Th	β^-	24.10 days
^{234m}Pa	β^-	1.175 min
^{234}Pa	β^-	6.66 h
^{234}U	α	2.48×10^5 years
^{230}Th	α	8.0×10^4 years
^{226}Ra	α	1622 years
^{222}Rn	α	3.8229 days
^{218}Po	α, β^-	3.05 min
^{214}Pb	β^-	26.8 min
^{218}At	α, β^-	1.5-2 sec
^{214}Bi	β^-, α	19.7 min
^{218}Rn	α	0.019 sec
^{214}Po	α	1.64×10^{-4} sec
^{210}Tl	β^-	1.32 min
^{210}Pb	β^-	19.4 years
^{210}Bi	β^-, α	5.013 days
^{206}Tl	β^-	4.19 min
^{210}Po	α	138.401 days
^{206}Pb	stable	—

*NOTE: Adapted, with permission, from Hamilton, E. I. Applied geochronology. London: Academic Press Inc.; 1965. © 1965 E. I. Hamilton.

Table 2.2. The ^{235}U (actinium) series. Decay constant of ^{235}U is 9.71 x 10^{-10} per year.*

Nuclide	Manner of decay	Half-life
^{235}U	α	7·1 x 10^8 years
^{231}Th	$\beta-$	25·64 h
^{231}Pa	α	3·43 x 10^4 years
^{227}Ac	$\beta-$, α	21·6 years
^{223}Fr	$\beta-$, α	22 min
^{227}Th	α	18·17 days
^{219}At	α, $\beta-$	0·9 min
^{223}Ra	α	11·68 days
^{215}Bi	$\beta-$	8 min
^{219}Rn	α	3·92 sec
^{215}Po	α, $\beta-$	1·83 x 10^{-3} sec
^{211}Pb	$\beta-$	36·1 min
^{215}At	α	~10^{-4} sec
^{211}Bi	α, $\beta-$	2·16 min
^{207}Tl	$\beta-$	4·79 min
^{211}Po	α	0·52 sec
^{207}Pb	stable	—

*NOTE: Adapted, with permission, from Hamilton, E. I. Applied geochronology. London: Academic Press Inc.; 1965. © 1965 E. I. Hamilton.

Table 2.3. The ^{232}Th (thorium) series. Decay constant of ^{232}Th is 4.99 x 10^{-10} per year.*

Nuclide	Manner of decay	Half-life
^{232}Th	α	1·39 x 10^{10} years
^{228}Ra	$\beta-$	6·7 years
^{228}Ac	$\beta-$	6·13 h
^{228}Th	α	1·910 years
^{224}Ra	α	3·64 years
^{221}Rn	α	51·5 sec
^{216}Po	α	0·158 sec
^{212}Pb	$\beta-$	10·64 h
^{212}Bi	$\beta-$, α	60·5 min
^{208}Tl	$\beta-$	3·10 min
^{212}Po	α	3·04 x 10^{-7} sec
^{208}Pb	stable	—

*NOTE: Adapted, with permission, from Hamilton, E. I. Applied geochronology. London: Academic Press Inc.; 1965. © 1965 E. I. Hamilton.

x 10^{10} years. Figure 2.3 depicts the decay curves of each of these three series.

(a) *Uranium-lead, Thorium-lead, Lead-lead Methods.* The uranium-lead and thorium-lead methods are based on the decay of uranium-238, uranium-235, and thorium-232 into lead-206, lead-207, and lead-208 respectively, all of which are stable isotopes. The decay of intermediate radioactive atoms in all three series is much faster than the decay of the parent atoms. Therefore, all the intermediate atoms are disregarded in the age calculation. A fourth naturally occurring isotope of lead, lead-204 (common lead) is not produced by radioactive decay, and it is extremely stable. Uranium-238, uranium-235, and thorium-232 frequently occur together, allowing at least three independent age determinations from the same rock.

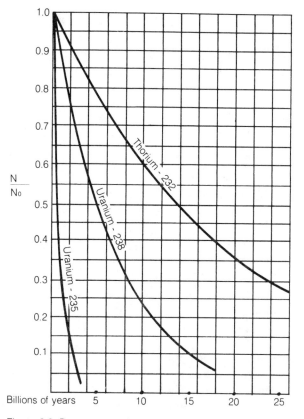

Figure 2.3. Decay curves for uranium - 235, uranium - 238, thorium - 232.

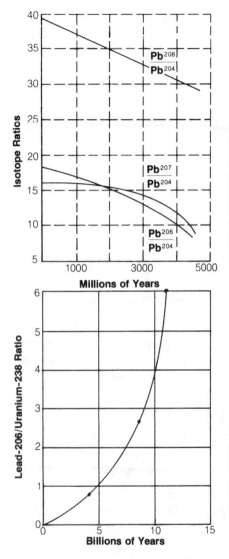

Figure 2.4. Graphs showing changes in isotope ratios in common lead in the earth during the past 4.5 billion years. Curves are based on mass spectrometric analysis of many samples. Individual data points are not shown. Reproduced, by permission, from Harbaugh, J. W. Stratigraphy and the geologic time scale. 2nd ed. Dubuque, IA: Wm. C. Brown Co. Publishers; 1974: 168. © Wm. C. Brown Co.

Figure 2.5. Graph showing ratio of lead-206/uranium-238 with respect to time. Reproduced by permission, from Harbaugh, J. W. Stratigraphy and the geologic time scale. 2nd ed. Dubuque, IA: Wm. C. Brown Co. Publishers; 1974: 168. © 1974 Wm. C. Brown Co.

The lead present with each of the above radioactive parents may not have been derived from the radioactive parents. The lead (common lead), assumed to have been present when the mineral was formed (D_i in equation [10]), must be taken into consideration when age determination is to be carried out. This can be done by correcting for the amount of common lead in the sample. Geochronologists assume that when the earth was first formed, the proportion of the three lead isotopes (Pb 206, 207, 208) was fixed with respect to common lead-204 (25).

In making age determinations it is necessary to subtract the common lead from the radiogenic lead. Two things have to be kept in mind in doing this: the approximate age of the mineral and the proportion of lead-204. By referring to Figure 2.4, one can deduce the amount of lead 206, 207, or 208 that is due to common lead. Then by subtracting these quantities from the age equation (10), a more precise age can be determined. Figure 2.5 represents the age determination by uranium-238/lead-206 after corrections have been made.

In addition to the uranium-thorium-lead ratios, the ration of lead-207 to lead-206 is useful in age determination. Since the half-life of uranium-235 (0.7 billion years) is much less than that of uranium-238 (4.5 billion years), the amount of lead-207 produced by decay of uranium-235 increases much more rapidly than that of lead-206 produced from uranium-238. Consequently, the ratio of lead-207/lead-206 is a good indication of the age of rock and is useful for dating specimens half a billion years old or older. Moreover, the lead-207/lead-206 ratio is less likely to be affected by partial loss of lead due to erosion, for both lead-207 and lead-206 have essentially the same chemical properties; therefore, any loss of lead will probably be the same. A graph of lead-207/lead-206 ratio versus time is shown in Figure 2.6

(b) *Potassium-argon Method.* The potassium-argon method of age dating has certain advantages over the uranium-thorium-lead methods because potassium is more widely found among rocks in different areas. The element potassium consists of three isotopes, namely, potassium-39, potassium-40, and potassium-41, and only potassium-40 is radioactive. Potassium-40 decays via two alternate routes, but 88% of the time it decays into calcium-40 by emitting a beta particle while 12% of the time it decays by electron capture yielding argon-40. The half-life of either of these decay routes is 1.3×10^9 years. Therefore, age determination can be carried out either by potassium-40/calcium-40 ratio or by potassium-40/argon-40 ratio. But since nonradiogenic calcium-40 is ubiquitous, it tends to complicate the dating procedure. Therefore, the potassium-40/argon-40 is used exclusively for dating purposes.

Argon-40 is a gas and is assumed to be absent from rocks during their formation because of high heat. Extreme care is taken by geochronologists to insure the preservation of this gas in the rock. In order to insure against loss of argon gas, a new technique involving the conversion of potassium-39 to argon-39 is used. Neutron activation is followed by heating the sample in stages to release argon-39 together with the argon-40. In

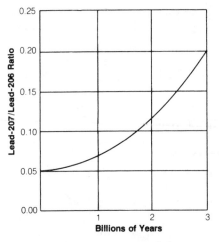

Figure 2.6. Graph of radiogenic lead-207/lead-206 ratio versus time. Reproduced, by permission, from Harbaugh, J. W. Stratigraphy and the geologic time scale. 2nd ed. Dubuque, IA: Wm. C. Brown Co. Publishers; 1974: 168. © Wm. C. Brown Co.

a sample that has preserved the argon gas generated both radiogenically and artificially, the two isotopes are expected to reside in fixed proportion in equivalent crystal sites since they have both been produced from potassium. Therefore, the ratio of argon-39/argon-40 can be related to potassium-40/argon-40 in a simple way (26, 27). Care is also taken to detect the contamination of argon-40 by the argon in the air. The argon-36 isotope present in the air is used for the detection and subtraction of the amount of argon-40 absorbed by the sample from the air. However, since the leakage of argon-40 sometimes poses a problem in rocks that are known not to behave as a closed system, potassium-40/argon-40 dating is usually taken as the minimum age limit.

(c) *Rubidium-strontium.* The rubidium-strontium method is based on the decay of rubidium-87 to strontium-87 by the emission of a beta particle with a half-life of 4.7×10^{10} years. Rubidium-87 is much more abundant than potassium and tends to occur in minerals that are rich in potassium. Therefore, two independent dating methods can be applied to the same sample containing potassium and rubidium.

(d) *Carbon-14.* The carbon-14 decay clock is widely used for more recent samples (less than 40 000 years old). It is produced when a nitrogen-14 atom absorbs a neutron in the nucleus and in turn emits a proton. Carbon-14 decays by emitting a beta particle with a half-life of 5730 years, reverting back to nitrogen-14. Carbon-14 is produced in the atmosphere above 3000 feet where nitrogen-14 is subjected to bombardment by neutrons produced by cosmic rays, consisting of a large number of high-speed protons that collide with the atmospheric gases. Newly created carbon-14 atoms continually enter the world, and some of them change into radioactive carbon dioxide. Much of the radioactive carbon dioxide is taken up by photosynthetic plants and enters the food chain of the living world. Thus, carbon-14 is present in all living materials and forms a major internal radiating source inside the bodies of the organisms.

The carbon-14 dating method is based on removal of the material containing carbon-14 from the world exchange reservoir of carbon. As soon as an organism dies and becomes fossilized, it will stop participating in the food chain of the living world. Therefore, the amount of carbon-14 trapped in the dead organism is limited and will diminish with time. The major assumption made in carbon-14 dating is that the carbon-14 in the world is at a steady state, i.e., the rate of formation of carbon-14 in the atmosphere by cosmic rays is equal to the rate of the decay of carbon-14 that already exists. This assumption was used to calculate the number of disintegrations per minute (17.2 dpm) for the carbon-14 exchange reservoir in the earth, and it agrees closely with the observed rate of 16.1 ± 0.5 dpm (28). Therefore, the assumption is a reasonable one. It is further assumed that the time required for exchange of carbon-14 in the organism with the environment is relatively short compared with the subsequent time that is to be measured after the organism has died. Thus, if a tree grew 200 years and yielded wood specimens that are 10 000 years old at present, the 200 years that the carbon-14 in the tree was exchanged with the environment is relatively short compared with the present age and will not enter into the calculation of age.

(4) *Reliability of Age Determination and the Geological Column of the Earth.* The reliability of the age determination by radioactive dating has been challenged (17, 23, 24). Arguments used to refute the validity of the radioactive dating methods include: the lack of assurance of the absence of environmental interchange in the uranium/lead and thorium/lead dated rocks; the inaccurate estimate of the contamination of the potassium-40/argon-40 clock by the argon-40 in the atmosphere; the unwarranted assumption of the time index in the common lead; and discrepancy in the carbon-14 exchange equilibrium hypothesis. While many of these criticisms may be justified, the close agreement of the results of the various radioactive methods when used to date rocks from different parts of the world impress many because of their reproducibility.

Table 2.4 lists a comparison of the ages of the rocks taken from different parts of the world as determined by five different radioactive dating methods. The agreement, except in the first case, was well within $\pm 10\%$, a degree of error commonly encountered in many scientific experiments. These ages are termed *concordant ages* because of their close agreement. There are well-documented cases of *discordant ages*, ages showing large

Table 2.4. Degree of concordance between age estimates determined by different methods.*

Region	Mineral	Calculated Ages in Millions of Years				
		$\dfrac{\text{Lead-206}}{\text{Uranium-238}}$	$\dfrac{\text{Lead-207}}{\text{Uranium-235}}$	$\dfrac{\text{Lead-208}}{\text{Thorium-232}}$	$\dfrac{\text{Lead-207}}{\text{Lead-206}}$	$\dfrac{\text{Pctassium-40}}{\text{Argon-40}}$
(1) Union of South Africa	Zircon	330	354	237	525	
(2) Quebec	Thorianite Biotite	995	975	940	990	925
(3) South Dakota	Uraninite	1580	1600	1440	1630	
(4) Quebec	Uraninite Biotite	2000	1945	2120	1925	2015
(5) Southern Rhodesia	Monazite	2260	2470	2650		
(6) Southern Rhodesia	Monazite Mica	2675	2680	2645	2680	2310

*NOTE: Reprinted, by permission, from Harbaugh, J. W. Stratigraphy and the geologic time scale. 2nd ed. Dubuque, IA: Wm. C. Brown Company Publishers; 1974: 168. © 1974 Wm. C. Brown Co.

discrepancy as determined by different methods, but they are usually within a three- or fourfold difference (Table 2.5). Moreover the discordant ages seem to follow a regular pattern, and in some cases they can be explained by the contamination or loss of the parent intermediate, final products in the sample, or by the continuous diffusion of lead from the rock into the environment.

The quantitative analytical techniques utilized by geochronologists have produced reliable information. The decay constants of most of the radioactive elements used in the dating methods can be known to within at least 5%, and in the case of uranium-238, uranium-235, and rubidium-87, the error is probably less than 3%. The ratio or isotopes can also be accurately measured to within 1–3% standard errors. For example, five laboratories in the United States analyzed a sample from the Department of Geophysics of Massachusetts Institute of Technology. The reported values of argon-40 in the sample were all within 1% of the mean. In a critical sample, several duplicate analyses are routinely made, and intercalibrations on at least one sample were made by all laboratories involved in the dating process to avoid systematic errors (40). Therefore, gross experimental errors are eliminated.

Recently six different methods of radioactive dating on the moon rocks,

Table 2.5. Concordant and discordant ages based on four dating methods.*

Mineral	Locality	Lead isotope ages (million years)				Reference
		$^{238}U{-}^{206}Pb$	$^{235}U{-}^{207}Pb$	$^{207}Pb{-}^{206}Pb$	$^{232}Th{-}^{208}Pb$	
Concordant ages						
Zircon	Wichita Mts. Oklahoma, U.S.A.	520±12	527±10	550±30	506±12	(29)
Zircon	Ceylon	540±12	544±16	555±30	538±25	(29)
Pitchblende	Katanga, Belgian Congo	575±5	595±5	630±40	—	(30)
Uraninite	Wilberforce, Canada	1000	1015	1030	1010	(31)
Uraninite	Romteland, Norway	890	892	920	900	(32)
Samarskite	Spruce Pine, N. Carolina, U.S.A.	314	316	342	302	(33)
Thucolite	Witwatersrand, S. Africa	2110	2080	2070	—	(34)
Pitchblende	Katanga, Belgian Congo	610	615	650		
Discordant ages						
Zircon	Capetown, S. Africa	330±10	356±15	530±50	238±20	(29)
Zircon	Beartooth Mts. Montana, U.S.A.	770±25	1400±40	2580±50	—	(35)
Zircon	Montana, U.S.A.	1660±50	2380±70	3080±50	870	(35)
Zircon	Quartz Creek, Colorado	930	1130	1540	515	(36)
Pitchblende	Sunshine Mine, Colorado	805±10	860±20	1035±35	—	(30)
Monazite	Huron Claim, Manitoba, Canada	3220	2840	2590	1830	(37)
Xenotime	Uncompahgre, Colorado	3180	2065	1640	1100	(38)
Euxenite	Wakefield, Quebec	620	710	1000	550	(39)

*NOTE: Adapted, with permission, from Hamilton, E. I. Applied geochronology. London: Academic Press Inc.; 1965. © 1965 E. I. Hamilton.

namely, uranium-238/lead-206; uranium-235/lead-207; thorium-232/lead-208; rubidium-87/strontium-87; argon-39/argon-40; and lead-207/lead-206, yielded dates of 4.70; 4.67; 4.60; 3.4–4.5; 3.7; and 4.75 billion years, respectively (41, 42, 43). These are in close agreement with each other and with the age of the earth that is estimated to be 4.5 billion years using the same methods.

It has been charged that since some of the noble gases found on the lunar surface have been derived from solar wind (a constant stream of particles from the sun), the potassium-argon dating of moon rock is unreliable (44). However, the potassium-argon dating was done with the interior portions of the crystalline rocks thus avoiding the outer portion of the rocks that may have been contaminated by solar wind. Moreover, analysis of the ratios of the noble gases in the lunar surface showed that their concentrations were inversely proportional to the particle size. However, these ratios were significantly different from solar values. The ratios of the isotopes, on the other hand, were found to be similar to those in meteorites. Corrections using the solar values measured in the outer portions of crystalline rocks were routinely done in the potassium-argon dating method, and these solar corrections were found to be negligible in almost all cases (45, 46, 47).

The moon was believed to have been heated up "recently" to temperatures between 1000°C and 1300°C. At such heat all the elements used in radiometric dating would have been melted, thus rendering the dating methods useless (44). This view apparently was not held in high regard by the moon-rock scientists, for none of the articles in the "Moon" issue of *Science* (30 January 1970) referred to it. It was estimated, however, that

Table 2.6. Comparison of ages obtained by radiocarbon dating with material of known ages. L (50, 51; B (52); C (53).*

No.	Sample	Lab.	Expected age	^{14}C age
1	Inca sample	L	444±25	450±150
2	Roman ship	B	1190±3	2030±200
3	Ptolemy	C	2149±150	2300±450
4	Etruscan tomb	B	2600±100	2730±240
5	Tayinot	C	2624±50	2600±150
6	Sesostris	C	3700±400	3792±50
7	Nippur	C	4125±200	4802±210
8	Zoser	C	4650±75	4979±350
9	Hemalca	C	4900±200	4883±200

*NOTE: Reprinted, with permission, from Hamilton, E. I. Applied geochronology. London: Academic Press Inc.; 1965. © 1965 E. I. Hamilton.

the moon was crystallized at a temperature range of 1140°C to 1170°C and that it had been reduced to a greater extent during crystallization than had the earth (48). The assumptions in the radiometric dating were apparently that the radiogenic elements were derived from components that surfaced during the process of crystallization. Since the surface of the moon is atmosphere-free (49), the erosion and diffusion processes that are usually associated with the contamination and loss of radioactive atoms in a sample rock are minimized. The remarkable agreement of the age of moon rock with that of earth rock increased the credence of the radioactive dating methods.

A comparison of the carbon-14 dated samples with known ages also indicated that the method is reliable within the limits of experimental errors (Table 2.6). Recently a new carbon-14 dating method was introduced that utilizes a cyclotron that increases the maximum determinable age to 100 000 years while reducing the sample size required. Scientists hope that this will increase the efficiency of the carbon-14 method (54).

A new method of dating human fossils too old for C-14 that depends on the constant rate of the racemization of amino acids has also been developed. This process changes an optically active compound that can rotate plane polarized light into an optically inactive or *racemic* mixture. Since only L-amino acids are found in living organisms, the D-amino acids detected on human fossils can be attributed to the process of racemization. Of particular interest in dating because of its long-time constant and ease of measurement is the reaction involving L-isoleucine and D-allo-isoleucine. L-isoleucine and D-allo-isoleucine are separable on the buffered columns of the automatic amino acid analyzer.

Constant temperature is the critical requirement in dating by racemization of amino acids. Using this method, fossils found in caves with relatively constant environments can be dated with only ±5 to 10% uncertainty. Samples within the C-14 range dated by this method have yielded concordant ages with those using C-14 dating. The maximum age that can be obtained by this method for caves with temperatures of 10°C and 20°C would be approximately 1.3×10^6 and 1.9×10^5 years respectively. This method has become quite useful for dating human fossils between 40 000 and 1 million years of age (55).

Each geological stratum in the earth's crust (geological column) has been correlated with quantitative measurements of radiometric data, resulting in the construction of a geologic time scale. Dated materials are used as *tiepoints* between geologic strata in constructing the time scale. The best candidates for tiepoints are layered volcanics, which consist of lava flows and deposits of volcanic ash. They have the advantage of having

Table 2.7. Radiometric dates that have been applied to geologic time scale.*

Epoch or Period	Stratigraphic Position	Locality	Rock Type	Mineral Analyzed	Radiometric Dating Method	Age in Millions of Yrs.
Pleistocene	Pleistocene-Pliocene boundary	Sierra Nevada California	Tuff	Biotite	Potassium-argon	1.0 ± 0.5
Pliocene	Latest Pliocene	Sutter Buttes California	Rhyolite	Biotite	Potassium-argon	1.7 ± 0.4
	Pliocene-Miocene boundary	Nevada	Rhyolite Tuff	Biotite	Potassium-argon	12 ± 0.5
Miocene	Middle Miocene	Colorado Washington	Granite Granite	Monazite Biotite	Uranium-lead Potassium-argon	16 ± 17 ± 0.5
	Lower Miocene	Austria	Sandstone	Glauconite	Potassium-argon	25 ± 1
Oligocene		Oregon Texas	Tuff Tuff	Biotite Biotite	Potassium-argon Potassium-argon	25.7 ± 0.8 33.1 ± 1.0
Eocene	Upper Eocene	USSR	Granite	Biotite	Potassium-argon	38 ± 4
	Mid-lower Eocene	Texas	Sandstone	Glauconite	Potassium-argon	52 ± 2
	Lowermost Eocene	New Jersey	Sandstone	Glauconite	Potassium-argon	62 ± 2
Paleocene		Colorado	Ore	Pitchblende	Uranium-lead	59 ± 2
Cretaceous	Uppermost Cretaceous	Alberta	Coal Seam	Biotite	Potassium-argon	63 ± 2
	Mid-upper Cretaceous	Germany	Sandstone	Glauconite	Potassium-argon	81 ± 2
	Uppermost Lower Cretaceous	USSR	Sandstone	Glauconite	Potassium-argon	117 ± 12
Jurassic	Upper Jurassic	California	Granite	Biotite	Potassium-argon	127 ± 4
	Middle Jurassic	Georgia	Granite	Biotite	Potassium-argon	165 ± 3
Triassic	Upper Triassic	New Jersey	Diabase	Biotite	Potassium-argon	195 ± 5
	Middle Triassic	Arizona	Diabase	Pitchblende	Uranium-lead	218
Permian	Middle Permian	USSR	Evaporite sequence	Sylvite	Potassium-calcium	241 ± 8
	Lower Permian	Norway	Nordmarkite	Zircon	Uranium-lead	260 ± 5

Pennsylvanian	Upper Pennsylvanian	Australia	Toscanite	Biotite	Potassium-argon	287	± 9
Mississippian	Lower Mississippian	USSR	Granite	Biotite	Potassium-argon	340	± 10
Devonian	Upper Devonian	Australia	Lava	Biotite	Potassium-argon	350	
	Lower Devonian	England	Granite	Biotite	Potassium-argon & Rubidium-strontium	395	± 5
Silurian	Lower Silurian	Ohio	Sandstone	Glauconite	Potassium-argon	410	± 15
Ordovician	Upper Middle	Alabama	Bentonite	Zircon	Uranium-lead	445	
	Ordovician	Sweden	Bentonite	Sandstone	Potassium-argon	452	± 10
				Biotite	Rubidium-strontium	447	
Cambrian	Upper Cambrian	Sweden	Shale	Whole rock	Uranium-lead	500	
	Middle Cambrian	USSR	Rhyolite	Glauconite	Potassium-argon	533	± 50
	Lower Cambrian	USSR	Rhyolite	Glauconite	Potassium-argon	577	± 58
	Lower Cambrian	USSR	Rhyolite		Potassium-argon	610	± 61
Precambrian		Finland	samples from same deposit	Galena	Lead-207/lead-206	775	± 20
		Quebec		Thorianite	Uranium-lead	965	± 55
		Quebec	samples from same deposit	Biotite	Potassium-argon	965	± 65
				Phlogopite	Potassium-argon	1060	± 25
		Australia		Uraninite	Uranium-lead	1070	
		Arizona	Granite	Monazite	Uranium-lead	1190	
		Scotland	Gneiss	Biotite	Rubidium-strontium	1300	
		Arizona	Pegmatite	Biotite	Rubidium-strontium	1470	± 55
		Finland		Muscovite	Rubidium-strontium	1530	
		Ukraine		Galena	Lead-207/lead-206	1800	
		Ontario		Monazite	Uranium-lead	2000	± 100
		Quebec	Rhyolite	Biotite	Rubidium-strontium	2215	
		Finland	Granodiorite	Galena	Potassium-argon	2400	
		Ukraine	Gneiss	Orthite	Lead-207/lead-206	2530	
					Uranium-lead	2700	± 100

*NOTE: Reprinted, by permission, from Harbaugh, J. W. Stratigraphy and the geologic time scale. 2nd ed. Dubuque, IA: Wm. C. Brown Co. Publishers; 1974. © 1974 Wm. C. Brown Co.

been deposited quickly, and often they occur interstratified within a sequence of fossiliferous sedimentary rocks, permitting an establishment of their position in relation to the layers of rock.

Furthermore, layered volcanics frequently contain minerals used in several radioactive dating techniques. Many volcanic rocks have yielded concordant ages, lending credence to the geological time scale. Other rocks, such as bracket intrusives and glauconites, are used occasionally as tiepoints. However, they are problematic either because they span too many stratigraphic layers, or they are continually being formed after the sedimentation of the layer has been completed. Despite these shortcomings, the geological time scale has as much validity as is allowed by the current stratus of geochronological science. Table 2.7 summarizes the geological column as correlated by representative samples to the absolute radiometric age.

References 2.1

1. Geikie, A. The founders of geology. London: Macmillan; 1905: 50–51.
2. Geikie, A. The founders of geology. 79.
3. Lyell, C. Principles of geology. 9th ed. New York: D. Appleton; 1853: 29.
4. Geikie, A. The founders of geology. 299.
5. Lyell, C. Principles of geology. 52.
6. Moore, J. R. J. Am. Sci. Affil. 22:18–23; 1970.
7. Velikovsky, I. Worlds in collision. New York: Delta; 1950.
8. Steinhauser, L. J. Am. Sci. Affil. 25:129–33; 1973.
9. Yamauchi, E. M. J. Am. Sci. Affil. 25:134–39; 1973.
10. Whitcomb, J. C.; Morris, H. M. The genesis flood. Philadelphia: Presbyterian and Reformed; 1961.
11. Morris, H. In: Why not creation? Lammert, W. ed. Grand Rapids, MI: Baker; 1970: 118.
12. Morris, H.; Roberts, F. Debate: Cataclysm and uniformitarianism. Wheaton College, Wheaton, IL: 1974 Nov. 19.
13. Mears, B. The changing earth: an introductory geology. New York: Van Nostrand; 1970: 216.
14. Mears, B. The changing earth. 217–42.
15. Lyell, C. Elements of geology. London: John Murray; 1841.
16. Raup, D. M.; Stanley, S. M. Principles of paleontology. San Francisco: Freeman; 1971: 333.
17. Moore, J. N.; Slusher, H. S., editors. Biology, a search for order in complexity. Grand Rapids, MI: Zondervan; 1970: 414.

18. Morris, H. M. Impact series. No. 48. San Diego, CA: Institute for Creation Research; 1977.
19. Wonderly, D. J. Am. Sci. Affil. 27:145; 1975.
20. Livingstone, D. A. Geochim, cosmochim Acta. 27(10):1055; 1963.
21. Hamilton, E. I. Applied geochronology. London and New York: Academic; 1965. (The section on radioactive decay was essentially extracted from this source.)
22. Harbaugh, J. W. Stratigraphy and geologic time. Dubuque, IA: Wm. C. Brown; 1968 (chapter 6).
23. Lammerts, W., editor. Why not creation? Grand Rapids, MI: Baker; 1970 (chapter 4).
24. Lammerts, W., editor. Scientific studies in special creation. Grand Rapids, MI: Baker; 1971 (chapters 8, 9).
25. Russell, R. D.; Farquhar, R. M. Lead isotopes and geology. New York: Inter Science; 1960.
26. Turner, G. Science. 167:466–68; 1970.
27. Turner, G. Meteorite research. Dordrecht, Holland: Reidell; 1969.
28. Hamilton, E. I. Applied geochronology. 41.
29. Tilton, G. R.; Davis; G. L.; Wetherill; G. W.; Aldrich, L. T. Trans. Am. Geophy. Un. 38:360; 1957.
30. Eckelmann, W. R.; Kulp, J. L. Bull. Geol. Soc. Am. 67:35; 1956.
31. Nier, A. O. J. Appl. Phys. 12:342; 1941.
32. Kulp, J. L.; Eckelmann, W. R. Am. Min. 42:154; 1957.
33. Eckelmann, W. R.; Kulp, J. L. Bull. Geol. Soc. Am. 68:1117; 1957.
34. Louw, J. D. Nature. 175:349; 1955.
35. Catanzaro, E. J.; Kulp, J. L. Geochim. Cosmachim. Acta. 28:87; 1964.
36. Carnegie Report. 1954–55.
37. Nier, A. O. Physiol. Rev. 55:150; 1939.
38. Tilton, G. E. Trans. Am. Geophys. Un. 32 (2):224; 1956.
39. Robinson, S. L.; Loveridge, W. D.; Rimsaite, J.; van Petegehm, J. Canad. Min. 17 (3):533; 1963.
40. Kulp, J. L. Science. 113:1105; 1961.
41. Tatsumoto, M.; Rosnolt, J. N. Science. 167:461–63; 1970.
42. Turner, G. Science. 167:466–68; 1970.
43. Gopalan, K. et al. Science. 167:471–73; 1970.
44. Coppedge, J. F. Evolution: possible or impossible? Grand Rapids, MI: Zondervan; 1973: 250.
45. Heymann, D. et al. Science. 167:555–58; 1970.
46. Eberhardt, P. et al. Science. 167:558–60; 1970.
47. Funkhouser, J. G. et al. Science. 167:561–63; 1970.

48. Anderson, A. T. et al. Science. 167:587–89; 1970.
49. Lunar sample analysis planning team. Summary of Apollo 11 lunar science conference. Science. 167:450–51; 1970.
50. Kulp, J. L.; Feely, W. H.; Tryon, L. E. Science. 114:565; 1951.
51. Kulp, J. L.; Volchok, H. L.; Holland, H. D. Trans. Am. Geophy. Un. 33:101; 1952.
52. Ballaria, C. Science. 121:409; 1955.
53. Arnold, J. R.; Libby, W. F. Science. 110:678; 1949.
54. Muller, R. A. Science. 196:489; 1977.
55. Bishop, W. W.; Miller, J. A., editors. Recent advances in isotope and other dating methods applicable to the origin of man. Edinburgh: Scottish Academic Press; 177–85; 1972.

2.2 Paleontological Evidence

Many evolutionists have claimed that the fossil record is conclusive evidence that evolution has occurred. However, if the paleontological evidence is closely scrutinized, the proof for evolution can be questioned.

2.2.1 *Problems Encountered by Paleontologists*

a) *Incompleteness of the Fossil Record.* As soon as an organism dies, its remains are subjected to three kinds of destructive forces: *biological degradation, mechanical destruction,* and *chemical erosion.*

Biological agents of degradation are ubiquitous, and there are hardly any natural habitats that are devoid of these agents. Scavengers devour all the edible parts of dead organisms. Smaller degradative agents, such as saprophytic bacteria and fungi, digest the remains. Even sturdy structures of dead organisms are subject to decay. For example, the structure of an oyster shell is made up largely of calcium carbonate. However, the structural matrix is held together by a network of organic degradable material. Therefore, as soon as the oyster dies, its shell is subject also to deterioration by biodegradation in combination with chemical erosion. This may account for the relative scarcity of empty shells in sea bottoms heavily populated by living shelled organisms other than the well-preserved shells of the delicate protozoa, foraminiferans, and radiolarians. The burial of the organism immediately after death by sedimentation does not completely insulate the remains from biodegradation. Bacteria are found to be heavily concentrated in unconsolidated sediments in an aquatic environment.

Mechanical destruction may be an important abrasive factor if the early post-mortem history of an organism takes place in high-energy environments, i.e., areas where the action of wind, waves, and currents are strongly felt. It was found in simulated experimental conditions that skeletons of bryozoans and calceraous algae were more sensitive to mechanical abrasion—such as tumbling with other pointed, unpolished pebbles—than were gastropods. Results such as this shed some light on the possible explanation of the relative fossil abundance of some organisms.

After the remains have been biodegraded and mechanically abraded, whatever is left, usually the skeleton, still has to withstand erosion and solution by chemical means. Chemical solution can take place at any time after the organism dies—even after the remains of the organism have become fossilized. The chances of a fossil being eroded by chemical solution depend on its chemical composition as well as that of its environment. Sometimes hollow cavities in rocks are all that remain after chemical erosion of some fossils, but these cavities are still recognizable and can be useful for paleontological classification.

Due to the operation of biological, mechanical, and chemical destructive forces, the parts of an organism that are most likely to be preserved are the hard, sturdy structures having high content of mineral instead of organic matter. Thus skeletons are preserved, whereas soft tissues are easily degraded or eroded. Therefore, the fossil record contains a *biased selection* of parts and types of organisms, according to their potential for preservation. Some knowledge derived from extinct mammals is based on fossils of teeth alone, due to their extraordinary durability. Because of the poor preservability of pigments, only very rarely do paleontologists have any fossil evidence that allows them to deduce the color of extinct organisms. The skeletons of various groups were also preserved to different degrees of completeness according to their chemical composition. For example, trilobite skeletons contain more pure calcium carbonate than those of crabs and are therefore more abundant.

An environment where burial by sedimentation or other physical forces is rapid is more likely to produce an abundance of fossils. However, areas being eroded by physical and chemical forces are less conducive to fossilization. Therefore, parts of the earth that are above sea level will be less apt to preserve fossils than areas below sea level because sea bottoms are constantly receiving sediments carried by rivers and streams. This may account for the overwhelming abundance of marine as compared with terrestrial fossils.

A biologically inactive environment is conducive to excellent fossil preservation. The spectacular preservations of vertebrates in tar pits and insects in amber represent the effect of completely biologically inert environments. Since these environments are not the normal habitats of the preserved organisms, catastrophic events must have occurred during the process of fossilization.

Habitat influences the preservability of all organisms. Some organisms may be fossilized in an environment far away from their normal habitat by post-mortem transport, meaning an organism dies one place and is carried to another. Pollens and spores of terrestrial plants are prone to be transported by wind. Remains of terrestrial plants or animals were carried by rivers into the ocean before they sank to the sea bottom and become fossilized. The effects of post-mortem transport on the distribution of fossils are hard to evaluate. However, paleontologists are extremely careful in trying to reconstruct the local environmental conditions according to the fossil record.

In summary, the fossil record is incomplete (1) and biased as to the parts and types of organisms preserved. Although large numbers of organisms lived during the earth's history, providing many fossils, the interpretation of the fossil record must be done with extreme care. Catastrophes may contribute to the fossil record although to an unknown degree. If catastrophes are shown eventually to be causing widespread fossilization, the principle of uniformitarianism (see I.2.1.1) has to be reevaluated. Paleontologists have to rely on large numbers of preserved samples to construct classification schemes. However, few fossils have been found of some organisms, and no conclusive information can be derived from scanty evidence.

b) *The Somewhat Arbitrary Fossil Classification Scheme.* As alluded to earlier (see I.1.2), the most objective basis for classifying the living world is the species concept proposed by Mayr as follows: "A species is an array of populations which are actually or potentially interbreeding and which are reproductively isolated from other such arrays under natural conditions." This concept cannot be applied to the classification of fossils because they simply cannot interbreed. Therefore, most paleontological classifications are based on observable characteristics of appearance, habitat, behavior, or geographic or stratigraphic occurrence. However, the relationship between different kinds of fossils cannot be established by morphological differences alone since phenotypic polymorphism (i.e., inherited variations in a population) is well known in the living world. Therefore, a presupposed phylogenetic relationship (the development or evolution of a kind or type of animal or plant) is the basic assumption of the modern paleontological classification scheme. To quote from a recent paleontology text:

> If classification is to serve primarily for communication and identification, utility is the principal criterion for choosing one system over another. With the

rise of interest in evolution there has inevitably been a move toward using classification to express evolutionary relations also (2).

Although the earliest taxonomists (e.g., Linnaeus and Buffon) recognized the possibility that limited changes may occur within a group of organisms after its creation, and there was speculation as to what taxa correspond to the "kinds" of creation recorded in Genesis 1 (3), modern taxonomists largely reject these interpretations. They adhere to an evolutionary presupposition and classify organisms according to their presumed phylogenetic relationships. The prominent taxonomist and paleontologist, George G. Simpson states the position of evolutionary taxonomist this way (4):

> The principles of modern taxonomy are evolutionary and the approach to classification here taken is correspondly evolutionary or in a somewhat special sense phylogenetic. Many evolutionary processes can be observed in action, both in the field and laboratory, and so can extremely short segments of phylogeny. Those brief segments have great value for exemplification and for developing valid principles, but they have little practical application to classification beyond the lowest taxonomic levels, at best. Even the long series provided in many instances by paleontology are phylogenetic only by inference: the actual processes of reproduction and descent are not observed. . . . It is therefore time that evolutionary classification uses, for the most part, concepts and definitions for which the data are not directly observable. This is not a feature peculiar to taxonomy. It is shared in greater or lesser degree by most of the inductive sciences. They are not, on that account, less scientific, nor are their conclusions necessarily any less, or more, certain than if direct observation were possible. In an analogous way, although for quite different reasons, atomic physics deals with things that have never been directly observed, but no one would question the validity or utility of its interpretations in terms of particles and processes that are known only by inference.

The claim made by Simpson that the inferential nature of taxonomic concepts is similar to that of atomic physics is not legitimate. While elementary particles are not directly observable, their existence and interactions can be empirically vindicated or falsified. For example, the *law of parity*, a theory dealing with weak interactions of atomic particles constructed by inference, was disproved by experimental findings (5). The existence of the J particle was discovered by empirical studies of interactions between light and lightlike particles (6). These empirical findings led to the establishment of new concepts in atomic physics, and the scientists involved were awarded the Nobel prize. However, although the hypothesis of the mechanisms of evolutionary change can be empirically vindicated or falsified (*see* I.1.3) and the processes of microevolution

Table 2.8. Geologic time scale.*

Era	Period	Epoch	Duration in Millions of Years	Time from Beginning of Period to Present (Millions of Years)	Geologic Conditions	Plant Life	Animal Life
Cenozoic (Age of Mammals)	Quaternary	Recent	0.011	0.011	End of last ice age; climate warmer	Decline of woody plants; rise of herbaceous ones	Age of humans
		Pleistocene	1.9	1.9	Repeated glaciation: 4 ice ages	Great extinction of species	Extinction of great mammals; first human social life
	Tertiary	Pliocene	4	6	Continued rise of mountains of western North America; volcanic activity	Decline of forests; spread of grasslands; flowering plants; monocotyledons developed	Man evolved from humanlike apes; elephants, horses, camels almost like modern species
		Miocene	19	25	Sierra and Cascade mountains formed; volcanic activity in northwest U.S.; climate cooler		Mammals at height of evolution; first humanlike apes
		Oligocene	13	38	Lands lower; climate warmer	Maximum spread of forests; rise of monocotyledons, flowering plants	Archaic mammals extinct; rise of anthropoids; forerunners of most living genera of mammals
		Eocene	16	54	Mountains eroded; no continental seas; climate warmer		Placental mammals diversified and specialized; hoofed mammals and carnivores established
		Paleocene	11	65			Spread of archaic mammals
	Rocky Mountain Revolution (Little Destruction of Fossils)						
Mesozoic (Age of Reptiles)	Cretaceous		70	135	Andes, Alps, Himalayas, Rockies formed late; earlier inland seas and swamps; chalk, shale deposited	First monocotyledons; first oak and maple forests; gymnosperms declined	Dinosaurs reached peak, became extinct; toothed birds became extinct; first modern birds; archaic mammals common
	Jurassic		46	181	Continents fairly high; shallow seas over some of Europe and western U.S.	Increase of dicotyledons; cycads and conifers common	First toothed birds; dinosaurs larger and specialized; insectivorous marsupials

Era	Period			Physical conditions	Plant life	Animal life
Paleozoic (Age of Ancient Life)	Triassic	49	230	Continents exposed; widespread desert conditions; many land deposits	Gymnosperms dominant, declining toward end; extinction of seed ferns	First dinosaurs, pterosaurs and egg-laying mammals; extinction of primitive amphibians
	Appalachian Revolution (Some Loss of Fossils)					
	Permian	50	280	Continents rose. Appalachians formed; increasing glaciation and aridity	Decline of lycopods and horsetails	Many ancient animals died out; mammal-like reptiles, modern insects arose
	Pennsylvanian (Carboniferous)	40	320	Lands at first low; great coal swamps	Great forests of seed ferns and gymnosperms	First reptiles; insects common; spread of ancient amphibians
	Mississippian (Carboniferous)	25	345	Climate warm and humid at first, cooler later as land rose	Lycopods and horsetails dominant; gymnosperms increasingly widespread	Sea lilies at height; spread of ancient sharks
	Devonian	60	405	Smaller inland seas; land higher, more arid; glaciation	First forests; land plants well established; first gymnosperms	First amphibians; lungfishes, sharks abundant
	Silurian	20	425	Extensive continental seas; lowlands increasingly arid as land rose	First definite evidence of land plants; algae dominant	Marine arachnids dominant; first (wingless) insects; rise of fishes
	Ordovician	75	500	Great submergence of land; warm climates even in Arctic	Land plants probably first appeared; marine algae abundant	First fishes, probably fresh water; corals, trilobites abundant; diversified mollusks
	Cambrian	100	600	Lands low, climate mild; earliest rocks with abundant fossils	Marine algae	Trilobites, brachiopods dominant; most modern phyla established
	Second Great Revolution (Considerable Loss of Fossils)					
Proterozoic		1000	1600	Great sedimentation; volcanic activity later; extensive erosion; repeated glaciations	Primitive aquatic algae and fungi	Various marine protozoa, towards end; mollusks, worms, other marine invertebrates
	First Great Revolution (Considerable Loss of Fossils)					
Archeozoic		2000	3600	Great volcanic activity; some sedimentary deposition; extensive erosion	No recognizable fossils; indirect evidence of living things from deposits of organic material in rock	

*NOTE: Adapted, by permission, from Villee, C. A. Biology. 7th ed. Philadelphia: W. B. Saunders Co.; 1977. © 1977 W. B. Saunders.

can be observed in the laboratory and nature, the inference that macroevolution "has occurred" in the past and that the phylogenetic tree can thus be derived can neither be empirically verified nor falsified. In a subsequent section (*see* I.3.3.2.a) it will also be seen that the mechanisms established empirically to account for microevolution are insufficient to account for macroevolution. Therefore, the extrapolation of the theory of microevolution, which Simpson indicated above as being documented empirically, into the still poorly explained areas of macroevolution is not well founded. The morphological data supporting the phylogenetic classification scheme at most can be taken as circumstantial evidence, and this evidence is not necessarily subject to an exclusively evolutionary interpretation.

2.2.2 *General Distribution of Fossils in the Geological Column.* The most widely accepted scheme of distribution of biological taxa in the earth's history that has been constructed from the fossil record is shown in Table 2.8. It should be stressed that this table does not show the time of origin of different classes of organisms but instead only the time of *dominance* or first appearance in the fossil record. The origin of each major group of organisms can only be *extrapolated* from the fossil record.

Transitional forms possessing morphological characteristics of more than one major group are sought to bridge the gaps in the presumed phylogenetic tree. The scarcity or total absence, in many cases, of these transitional fossils has long been a mystery to paleontologists. However, there are cases of transitional fossils that may represent a gradual transformation between species, genera, subfamilies, and occasionally families. This evidence supports microevolution if one bears in mind that the classification of fossils is based essentially on morphological features defining the lowest taxa. However, in the higher categories where morphological features are clearly distinct there are systematic interruptions, as Simpson frankly admitted (7):

> In spite of these examples (of transitional forms) it remains true, as every paleontologist knows, that most new species, genera, and families and that nearly all new categories above the level of families appear in the (fossil) record suddenly and are not led up to be known, gradual, completely continuous transitional sequences . . . Almost all paleontologists recognize that the discovery of a complete transition is in any case unlikely. Most of them find it logical, if not scientifically required, to assume that the sudden appearance of a new systematic group is not evidence for special creation or for saltation, but simply means that a full transitional sequence more or less like those that are known did occur and simply has not been found in this instance. Nevertheless, there are still a few paleontologists, and good ones, who are so impressed by

how much has been found that they conclude that most, at any rate, of what has not been found never existed, and there are some neontologists, also some good ones, who accept this interpretation.

Kerkut (8) has pointed out that missing links exist *between* members of each of the following five major groups of organisms: (1) viruses, bacteria, and *Protozoa;* (2) *Protozoa* and *Metazoa;* (3) various invertebrate phyla; (4) invertebrate and vertebrate; (5) major groups of vertebrates. The transitional fossils that document evolutionary relationships *within* these groups are scarce or lacking.

The interpretation of the few *transitional* forms between major groups are not without dispute. Fossil onychophorans, which resemble annelids (segmented worms) except for their locomotive appendages, have been claimed to be an annelid-arthropod interphylum intermediate (9) (*see* Figure 2.7). However, while arthropods (e.g., trilobites) had reached a high development by lower Cambrian time, onychophorans were just developing appendages for locomotion. Moreover, extant onychophorans and arthropods show marked differences anatomically. This leads to speculation of the polyphyletic (developed from more than one ancestral type) origin of *Arthropoda* and the *Onychophora.* Alternatively, the *Onychophora* and *Arthropoda* may have diverged from a remote ancestral annelid stock (10).

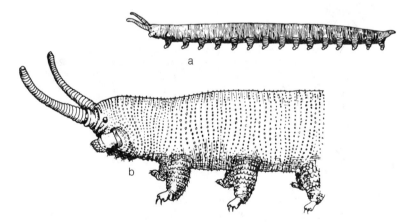

Figure 2.7. Living onchyophoran (superphylum *Protarthropoda*), *Peripatus novae-zealandiae;* (a) complete individual; (b) lateral view of anterior part of body; note antennae, oral papilla, legs, eye. Reproduced by permission of the Smithsonian Institution Press from *Smithsonian Miscellaneous Collections.* Vol. 97, No. 6. "Evolution of Annelida, Onychophora, and Arthropoda." Snodgrass, R. E. pp. 51, fig. 21. Smithsonian Institution, Washington, D. C. 1938.

In another example, fossil monoplacophorans were believed to be the transitional form between phylum *Mollusca* and phylum *Annelida* (11). A recent monoplacophoran living fossil *Neopilina* has possible internal segmentation similar to that of the annelid worms and arthropods. However, it has the typical features of *Mollusca* that sharply discriminate it from annelid worms and arthropods: restriction of an ectodermal cuticular skeleton to the dorsal side, the muscular feet, and the pallial (mantle) groove with gills (*see* Figure 2.8). Therefore, its transitional status is inconclusive and more a matter of hypothesis and opinion.

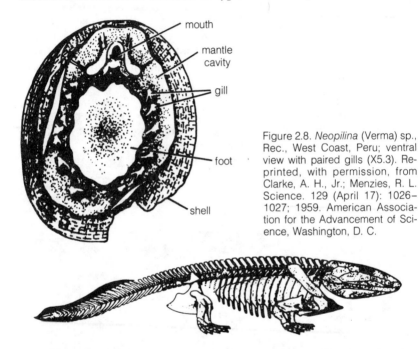

Figure 2.8. *Neopilina* (Verma) sp., Rec., West Coast, Peru; ventral view with paired gills (X5.3). Reprinted, with permission, from Clarke, A. H., Jr.; Menzies, R. L. Science. 129 (April 17): 1026–1027; 1959. American Association for the Advancement of Science, Washington, D. C.

Figure 2.9. The oldest known Amphibian skeleton, *Ichthyostega* of late Devonian, about 3 feet long. Reprinted, with permission, from Romer, A. S. Vertebrate paleontology. 3rd ed. Chicago: The University of Chicago Press; 1966.

The fish-amphibian transition *Ichthyostega* (12) has many features shared by the advanced bony fish crossopterygian and the primitive amphibian labyrinthodont (see Figure 2.9). However, three aberrant features of *Ichthyostega* have puzzled evolutionists. (1) The intertemporal bone in the skull is absent in *Ichthyostega*. This is presumably primitive in the amphibian, being retained by later labyrinthodonts but absent in more advanced amphibians. (2) The cheek region, which is still rather flexibly articulated with the skull roof in some Carboniferous forms, is already firmly consolidated in *Ichthyostega*. The movability of this basal articulation is considered a primitive amphibian feature and is not present in more advanced forms. (3) *Ichthyostega*, crossopterygians, labyrinthodonts, and all of the modern higher vertebrate classes have the *arch* vertebra or its modified form, while many of the early Palaeozoic amphibians and all the modern amphibians have the *husk* vertebra. (The arch type of vertebra is characterized by two sets of ossified arch structures formed in the central region of the vertebra—the anterior ones termed the *intercentra* [hypocentrum] and the posterior, the *pleurocentra* [Figure 2.10c, d]. The husk vertebra [Figure 2.33], on the other hand, is characterized by a single structure often spool shaped and pierced lengthwise by a hole for the notochord [Figure 2.10, a, b].) The noted absence of transitional forms linking the fin of the crossopterygian and the

(a) Lateral view of vertebrae of *Lysorophus* (husk).

(b) Anterior view of vertebrae of *Lysorophus* (husk).

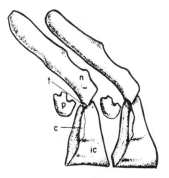

(c) Lateral view of vertebrae of the crossopterygian *Eusthenopteron* (arch).

(d) Lateral view of vertebrae of the late Devonian *Ichthyostega* (arch).

Figure 2.10. The vertebrae of Paleozoic lepospondyls, *(a, b);* and the vertebrae of labyrinthodonts, *(c, d)*. *c,* articulation for capitulum of rib; *ic,* intercentrum; *n* or *na,* neural arch; *p,* pleurocentrum; *t,* attachment for tuberculum of rib. Reprinted, with permission, from Romer, A. S. Vertebrate paleontology. 3rd ed. Chicago: The University of Chicago Press; 1966.

foot of *Ichthyostega* is also perplexing in the attempt to determine the relationship between the two groups. It is thus difficult to see the links between crossopterygian, *Ichthyostega*, and modern amphibians. Therefore, the conclusions drawn from this fossil *are very tentative*.

The interpretation of another fish-amphibian transitional fossil *Elpistostege* is uncertain also. The only available evidence, a skull-roof fossil from the early upper Devonian period, shows no trace of the transverse break behind the parietal bones that in crossopterygians is associated with the bipartite braincase. However, there is an absence of any postcranial skeleton that may bear fins or legs (13).

The amphibian-reptile intermediates *Seymouria* and *Diadectes* exemplify the lack of definitive skeletal distinctions among the fossil amphibians and reptiles (14) (Figure 2.11). Modern reptiles can be distinguished from living amphibians by their bony structure, e.g., reptiles have only one condyle in the skull, modern amphibians, two; reptiles, typically have five toes in the manus, whereas modern amphibians have four or fewer; the sacrum in reptiles includes at least two vertebrae, modern amphibians only one. However, the fossil evidence of amphibians and reptiles is not clear-cut, for primitive Paleozoic reptiles share so many of the skeletal characteristics of the earliest amphibians that it is almost impossible to tell where the boundary lines are between the two classes.

The major definite character of reptiles is the amniote egg that they lay

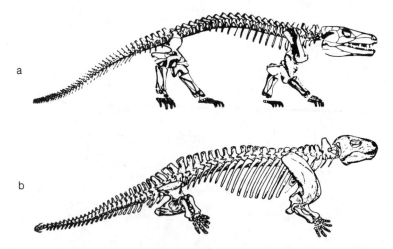

Figure 2.11. The seymouriamorph. *(a) Seymouria,* an early Permian seymouriamorph; *(b) Diadectes,* a highly specialized seymouriamorph of the early Permian. Maximum length about 10 feet. Reprinted, with permission, from Romer, A. S. Vertebrate paleontology. 3rd ed. Chicago: The University of Chicago Press; 1966.

on land. This type of egg, similar to a bird's egg, contains a large supply of nourishing yolk. The reptilian amniotic egg containing an amniotic cavity filled with fluid provides an aqueous environment equivalent to the aquatic environment of free-living larva (tadpoles) of amphibians. Thus, the amniotic egg helps explain the absence of the tadpole stage that is present in amphibians. However, it has not been possible to determine whether or not fossil reptiles were amniotic. It is also of interest to note that both *Seymouria* and *Diadectes* appeared in the early Permian era (approximately 280 million years ago); however, the oldest known reptile, *Hylonomus* was found in early Pennsylvania rock (approximately 320 million years ago). It appears that the transitional forms may have arrived 40 million years too late to beget the first known reptile!

Archaeopteryx has been cited frequently as the transitional type between reptiles and birds (14). It has a birdlike skull and wings with feathers (Figure 2.12). The reptilelike features are represented by clawlike appendages, the possession of teeth, and the long vertebral column that extends into the tail. The flying power of this organism was presumably slight, for the wingspread is much less than that of the poor fliers among modern birds.

Since most skeletal features of birds can be matched by some archosaurian reptiles, feathers have been considered the only distinctive feature of birds. Feathers are essential to birds for insulation against loss of body heat, and this contrasts greatly with reptiles since they are cold-blooded. Therefore, *Archaeopteryx* was definitely a bird. However, the presumed small sternum, the primitive reptilian structure of wing bones, and especially the long tail set *Archaeopteryx* apart from most modern birds, requiring a separate subclass to represent it. However, some of the reptilian structures of this fossil are shared by some modern-day birds. For example, the juvenile stages of *Opisthocomus hoatzin* of South America (13) and *Touraco cory thaix* of Africa (15) possess claws, and both are fliers.

Diarthrognathus (Figure 2.13), a late *Triassic* fossil, has been claimed to be a transitional form between reptiles and mammals. This form possesses a quadrate-articular joint that is a feature characteristic of tritylodonts, the last survivors of the most advanced group of the mammallike reptiles *Therapsida*. Interestingly, a minor part of the same joint is a squamosal-dentary contact, a more mammalianlike feature. However, *Diarthrognathus* lacks the dental specialization of the tritylodonts; thus, its transitional status can be questioned.

The skeletal remains of many "transitional" forms, such as *Diarthrognathus*, are fragmentary. Furthermore, the demarcation between the rep-

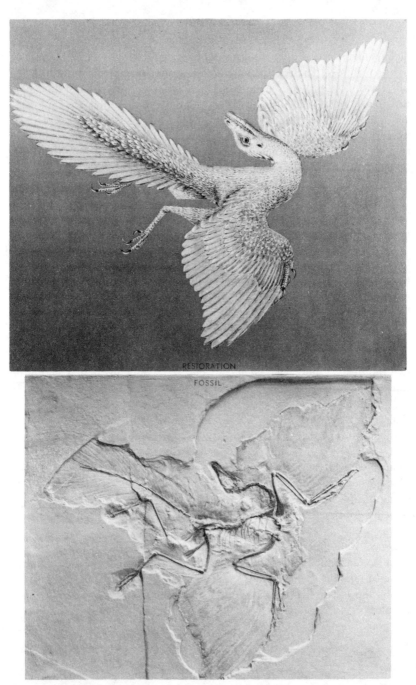

Figure 2.12. Fossil (below) of the primitive bird *Archaeopteryx,* and a restoration (above) or model depicting the appearance of this primitive animal. Courtesy of The American Museum of Natural History, New York.

tilian and mammalian structures is becoming blurred as knowledge about each group increases. The diagnostic characteristics of the class *Mammalia* essentially reside in the soft anatomy and physiology that cannot be determined from skeletal remains. Therefore, the classification of mammalian fossil according to skeletal features is tentative. In addition, the almost simultaneous appearance of *Diarthrognathus* (late Triassic era) and the first known mammal fossil (Triassic-Jurassic boundary) leaves little time for the evolution of mammals from this presumed transitional form.

In summary, the transitional forms cited above are subject to various interpretations. It seems premature to base phylogenetic trees of organisms on these forms for which we have only fragmentary morphological evidence. More specifically, L. de Nouy, an evolutionist, commenting on the status of *Archaeopteryx*, has made a very succinct statement concerning the establishment of "true links" between major groups. While recognizing the morphological similarities of *Archaeopteryx* to reptiles and birds, he nevertheless concluded:

> By link, we mean a necessary stage of transition between classes such as Reptiles and Birds, or between smaller groups. An animal displaying characters belonging to two different groups cannot be treated as a true link as long as the intermediary stages have not been found, and as long as the mechanisms of transition remain unknown (16).

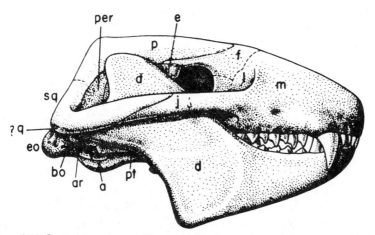

Figure 2.13. Skull of the advanced therapsid *Diarthrognathus;* original about 1.5 inches long. Abbreviations for this skull: *a,* angular; *ar,* articular; *bo,* basioccipital; *d,* dentary; *e,* epipterygoid; *eo,* exoccipital; *f,* frontal; *j,* jugal; *m,* maxilla; *p,* parietal; *per,* periotic; *pt;* pterygoid; *q,* quadrate; *sq;* squamosal. Reprinted, with permission, from Romer, A. S. Vertebrate paleontology. 3rd ed. Chicago: The University of Chicago Press; 1966.

It is sufficient to conclude that even if the "missing links" can eventually be found (a proposition on which no one can have assurance), the paleontological data can be used only as circumstantial evidence that has to be examined by *inference* instead of by experimental observations.

References 2.2

1. Raup, D. M.; Stanley, S. M. Principles of paleontology. San Francisco: Freeman; 1971 (chapter 1).
2. Raup, D. M.; Stanley, S. M. Principles of paleontology. 122.
3. Marsh, F. L. Evolution, creation and science. Washington, D.C.: Review and Herald Publishing Assoc.; 1944.
4. Simpson, G. G. Principles of animal taxonomy. New York: Columbia Univ. Press; 1967: 68.
5. Yang, C. N.; Lee, T. D. Physiol. Rev. 105:1671; 1957.
6. Ting, S. C. C. Science. 196:1167; 1977.
7. Simpson, G. G. The major features of evolution. New York: Columbia Univ. Press; 1953: 360.
8. Kerkut, G. A. Implication of evolution. New York: Pergamon; 1960.
9. Olson, E. C. The evolution of life. New York: Mentor; 1965: 302.
10. Tasch, P. Paleobiology of the invertebrates. New York: Wiley; 1973.
11. Lemche, H.; Wingstrand; K. G. Galathea report. Vol. 3. Copenhagen: Danish Science Press; 1959: 9–57.
12. Romer, A. S. Vertebrate paleontology. Chicago: Univ. of Chicago Press; 1966.
13. Grimmer, J. L. National Geographic. 122 (3):391; 1962.
14. Colbert, E. H. Evolution of the vertebrates. 2nd ed. New York: Wiley; 1969: 71–78.
15. Sibley, C. G.; Ahquist, J. E. Auk. 90:1; 1973.
16. de Nouy, L. Human destiny. New York: American Library; 1947: 58. Cited by: Gish, D. T. Evolution, the fossils say no! San Diego: Creation Life; 1973: 63.

2.3 Evidence from Physical Anthropology

To trace the *presumed* evolutionary lineage of humans, one has to start with living and fossil members of the superfamily *Hominoidea*. This group consists of all the great and lesser apes and all humans. Table 2.9 represents a summary of the members of superfamily *Hominoidea* and their known and related fossils.

As shown in Figure 2.14, the evolution of *Hominoidea* can be traced by three separate lines. Each can be represented by an extinct genus,

Table 2.9. Superfamily *Hominoidea*.

SUPER FAMILY	FAMILY	GENUS	COMMON NAME	KNOWN FOSSILS
Hominoidea	*Hylobatidae*	*Hylobates* *Symphalangus*	Gibbon Siamang	*Pliopithecus* (Limnopithecus) (Propliopithecus [?])
	Pongidae	*Pongo* *Pan* *Gorilla*	Orangutan Chimpanzee Gorilla	*Dryopithecus* (Aegyptopithecus) (Oligopithecus)
	?	?	?	*Ramapithecus* (Kenyapithecus) (Graecopithecus) (Rudapithecus)
	?	?	?	*Australopithecus*
	Hominidae	*Homo*	*Humans*	Homo erectus Homo neander- thalensis Homo sapiens (Modern man)

namely, *Pliopithecus, Dryopithecus,* and *Ramapithecus.* All three fossil lines were definitely more like apes than humans. However, there have been speculations that *Ramapithecus* is more humanlike and was the remote ancestor of modern humans (1). Assessment of evolutionary relationships of the fossils above has been based mainly on available anatomical features such as posture, brain size, and dentition (kind, number, and arrangement of the teeth). For example, Table 2.10 summarizes the cranial capacities of several forms within the superfamily *Hominoidea.*

Table 2.10. Cranial capacities of humans and some presumed relatives.*

Species	Range † of brain size in cubic centimeters
Modern chimpanzee	350–450
Modern gorilla	?–700
Fossil australopithecines	425–775
Fossil *Homo erectus*	815–1067
Fossil Neanderthal	1200–1500
Modern human	<1000–2102

†Excluding where possible, pathologically abnormal individuals.

*NOTE: Reprinted, with permission, from Lerner, I. M.; Libby, W. J. Heredity, evolution, and society. San Francisco: W. H. Freeman and Co. © 1976.

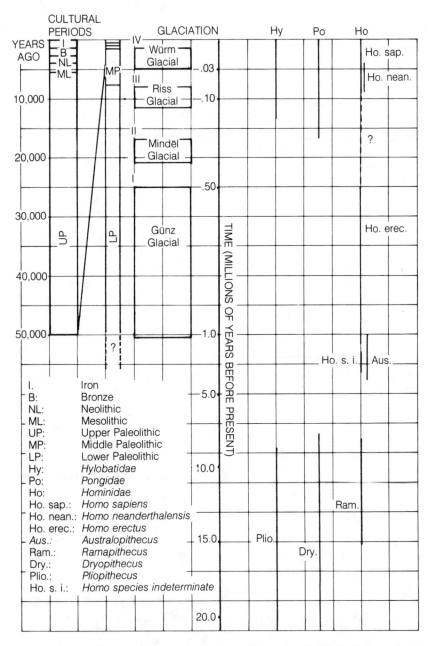

Figure 2.14. Time scale of *Hominoidea* ancestry as correlated with glaciation and cultural periods.

2.3.1 Pliopithecus *and* Dryopithecus. *Pliopithecus* was discovered in Europe from rocks dated between the Miocene (25 million years ago) and Pliocene (6 million years ago) eras. There were several fossil finds assigned to this genus, including an almost complete skull. Remains of a fossil discovered in East Africa in Miocene rocks included parts of the postcranial skeleton and the limbs. This form was known as *Limnopithecus*. *Pliopithecus* and *Limnopithecus* are very similar and both seem to be related more to the family *Hylobatidae* than to *Pongidae* and *Hominidae*.

Dryopithecus (2) was found both in Oligocene (38 million years ago) and Miocene rocks and is related to the family *Pongidae*. The dryopithecines have been divided into four genera, namely, *Aegyptopithecus*, *Oligopithecus*, *Propliopithecus*, and *Dryopithecus*.

Aegyptopithecus was found in North Africa and was especially important because in addition to five partial lower jaws, an almost complete skull was found. The teeth are low crowned (minimal development of enamel) and not specialized. The jaws protrude beyond the ridge of the upper part of the face, a feature shared by many primitive primates. Members of *Aegyptopithecus* seem to have made their abode in the forest canopy and probably had a herbivorous (plant-eating) or frugivorous (fruit-eating) diet.

In contrast, *Oligopithecus* is known only from a single jaw uncovered from an early Oligocene rock. The jaw is comparable in size to that of a squirrel monkey, but the teeth definitely resemble those of higher primates. Although only the lower jaw is available, the pattern of wear in the lower premolar is consistent with that of a higher primate in which the upper canine is commonly honed to a sharp edge against the first lower premolar. Because of the scanty record, the interpretation of the Oligocene evidence is only tentative.

Propliopithecus was found in 1908 in an Oligocene rock in Egypt. The find includes two half mandibles (bone of lower jaw) and some teeth that may or may not have come from the same skeleton. The dentition, with small canines comparable in size and form to the premolars and the low-crowned molars, has caused some anthropologists to link this fossil to the family *Hominidae*. However, its homology to the modern gibbon is more striking, and it seems more accurate to put *Propliopithecus* in the lineage of *Hylobatidae*.

The Miocene dryopithecines are abundant and widely distributed. *Dryopithecus* was found in Europe, Asia, and Africa and is represented by a large collection of jaws and teeth. This form is also known from Pliocene deposits. The dentition of *Dryopithecus* is more like that of modern apes than the other finds in the same period.

The African dryopithecine, *Dryopithecus africanus* (originally named *Proconsul*), left considerable remains, including limb bones, a skeleton of a hand, and an almost complete skull. There are three species ranging in size from a large gibbon through a chimpanzee to a small gorilla. As evidenced from the limb bones, these Miocene apes seemed to be of a lighter build than modern apes. They were most likely quadrupeds. The dentition varied in different species, with some resembling that of the modern chimpanzee; some, the orangutan; and still others, the gorilla. The canine teeth were moderately tusklike but not as pronounced as those of modern apes. In summary, *Dryopithecus* is thought to be an ancestral form of the apes and possibly of the family *Pongidae*.

2.3.2 Ramapithecus. In 1932, G. Edward Lewis, a young Yale University graduate student, discovered in Haritalyanger, a cluster of villages some 100 miles (160 km.) north of New Delhi, India, a single fragment of an upper jaw of a so-called manlike ape. Subsequently, many similar specimens have been found in Miocene and Pliocene rocks in Turkey, central Europe, and East Africa. The specimens include *Kenyapithecus*, *Graecopithecus*, and *Rudapithecus*. The finds were mainly teeth and jaws. The dentition of *Ramapithecus* differs from that of *Dryopithecus* and approaches that of *Australopithecus* (*see* I.2.3.3), the most humanlike fossil primate. The smaller teeth, less prominent canines, thicker enamel, and other differences induced anthropologists to give this find the status of a new genus, *Ramapithecus*.

E. L. Simons has postulated that *Dryopithecus* gave rise to at least three genera between 10 and 15 million years ago. Two of them, *Sivapithecus* and *Gigantopithecus*, were apes with faces as large as those of the modern chimpanzee or gorilla. However, the third genus, *Ramapithecus*, had a distinctly small face. On the basis of this and the comparison of the rearward divergence of the tooth arcade in the fossil primates (Figure 2.15), he concluded that *Ramapithecus* is part of the family *Hominidae* that may have given rise to the later hominid *Australopithecus*. However, the interpretation of *Australopithecus* itself is now in jeopardy. The recent discovery of a possible *Homo* fossil living at the same time with an early *Australopithecus* has suggested that *Australopithecus* may not be in the direct lineage of the genus *Homo* at all. Therefore, this uncertainty, the scanty evidence for *Ramapithecus* (only jaws and teeth), and the absence of intermediate fossils during the 4–5 million years between the most recent find of *Ramapithecus* and the oldest *Australopithecus* fossil have made many skeptical of Simons's interpretation.

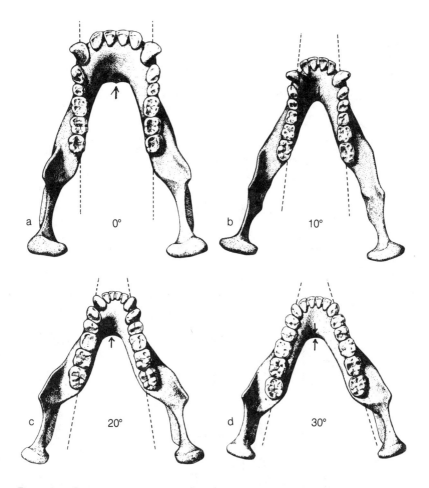

Figure 2.15. Four lower jaws show variations in the amount of rearward divergence of the tooth arcades in three fossil primates. For comparison, *(a)* is the mandible of a modern chimpanzee; its typically U-shaped dental arcade has parallel tooth rows; thus, the degree of divergence is zero. Next *(b)* is a reconstructed *Dryopithecus* mandible; the tooth rows show an angle of divergence (dotted lines) averaging some 10 degrees. Next *(c)* is a composite reconstruction of a *Ramapithecus* mandible. Its tooth rows, when preserved, show an angle of divergence averaging 20 degrees. Last *(d)* is a reconstructed *Australopithecus* mandible. Its typical angle of tooth-row divergence is 30 degrees. The tooth rows of later hominids show even greater angles of divergence. Arrows show differences in the two jaw-ridge buttresses known as the superior and the inferior torus. Modern apes possess a large, shelflike inferior torus; in *Dryopithecus* the superior torus was dominant. Both the ridges are developed in *Ramapithecus* and *Australopithecus*. Reprinted, with permission, from Simons, E. L. Ramapithecus. Sc. Am. 236 (May): 32–33; 1977.

Table 2.11. Sites yielding evidence of *Australopithecus*.*

Location	Date Found	Comment
1. *South Africa* Taung	1924	Almost complete skull and mandible of a child. This was the original discovery that some felt was a fossil chimp.
Sterkfontein	1936–57 1966–present	Site yielding an abundance of skull fragments, teeth, mandibles, and postcranial bones. Among the most interesting remains are an almost complete skull and pelvis. The material was originally identified as *Plesianthropus transvaalensis*.
Swartkrans	1948–52 1967–present	Apart from the *Homo erectus* remains, this site has produced several fragments of skulls, jaws, teeth, and postcranial bones. Original designation: *Paranthropus robustus*.
Kromdraii	1938–41	Compared with Swartkrans fewer and less complete remains but also identified as *P. robustus*.
Makapansgat	1947–62	An almost complete skull with fragments of others and mandibles, teeth, and postcranial bones, including pelvic fragments. Originally called *Australopithecus prometheus* (it was mistakenly thought that there was evidence for the controlled use of fire). These remains are recognized as similar to those from Taung and Sterkfontein.
2. *East Africa* Olduvai	1959–present	According to Leakey (5) these deposits indicate the coexistence of three hominids in early Pleistocene times: *Australopithecus* (originally *Zinjanthropus*). H. erectus, and *Homo habilis*. Le Gros Clark (6), among others, feels that *H. habilis* and *Zanjanthropus* are both australopithecines.
Lake Natron	1964	An almost complete mandible found about 50 miles (80 km.) from Olduvai Gorge.
Lake Eyasi	1938	Three teeth and a fragment of an upper jaw.
Omo Basin,	1966–72	Three complete mandibles (two without teeth), one partial jaw with two teeth, some cranial and mandibular parts, a number of postcranial bones, and several dozen isolated teeth. Some teeth are at least 3.5 million years old (7).

Location	Date Found	Comment
East Rudolph	1968–73	The 87 specimens include several complete or almost complete crania, a complete mandible with small teeth, a juvenile mandible with mixed dentition, and more than 30 postcranial bones (7, 8).
Koobi Fora, Kenya	1974–75	Several skull fragments, some with complete dentition; a left femur. They were discovered together with skulls similar to *H. erectus* (9). The 28 specimens include a complete cranium, three cranial fragments, 1 partial cranium, seven postcranial bones, and a host of dental remains (10).
Hadar, Ethiopia	1979	Skeletal remains of between 35 to 65 individuals with nearly all anatomical regions of the body represented (11).
Laetolil, Tanzania	1979	Primarily dental and gnathic remains. A new taxon *Australopithecus afarensis* was created for these Pliocene hominid fossils (11).
3. *Chad* Koro Toro	1960	The skull fragments here were identified by their discoverer as *Australopithecus*, but he and others now suggest that the remains may be more like those of *H. erectus*.
4. *Israel* Ubeidiya	1959	Fragments of two skulls and a tooth.
5. *Java* Sangiran	1939–53	There are three mandibles and some teeth of alleged australopithecine affinity.

*NOTE: Adapted, with permission, from Kelso, A. J. Physical anthropology. Philadelphia: J. B. Lippincott & Co.; 1970.

In surveying the fossil record pertaining to primate evolution, one point becomes obvious and has an important implication: many of the phylogenetic relationships postulated are based on very little fossil evidence. Most of the more credible conclusions are obtained not by logical deduction from the fossil finds but by imposing characteristics of modern representatives onto the fossil record (1). Moreover, Mixter (3) has pointed out that the origin of the distinct human feature of bipedalism (being two-footed) is not substantiated by any fossil finds. Therefore, although some primate paleontologists are dogmatic about their assertions of human lineage, evidence is not conclusive.

2.3.3 Australopithecus. The first *Australopithecus* (4) find was discovered in 1924 in Taung, a village about 80 miles (128 km.) north of Kimberley, South Africa. It was the fragmentary remains of a child's skull, five to seven years of age. The anatomist Raymond A. Dart judged it to be the remains of an extinct hominid, perhaps the missing link between humans and apes. He called it *Australopithecus africanus* or the South African Apeman.

The skull has a curious mixture of human and simian (apelike) features. It looks very much like that of an infant chimpanzee and is not consistent with the morphological pattern of later more positively identified hominid skulls. However, Dart, and later Robert Broom, argued that the Taung child's age was inconsistent with its being a pongid because the brain's size was too large for its age. They believed that if it were a chimpanzee, five to seven years old, it should have begun to show adult characteristics such as crests and ridges of the skull and they noted that its dentition resembles the teeth of humans rather than those of chimpanzees or gorillas.

The evidence presented by one specimen is not convincing, and the difficulties of the interpretation of this find are complicated since most comparisons with other finds are based on adult characteristics. However, the interest sparked by the find has prompted a diligent search for more *Australopithecus* remains. At present, a considerable number of additional skeletons, more mature and some nearly complete, have been collected from many places, including South Africa, East Africa, Chad, Israel, and Java (Table 2.11).

However, the attempts to categorize the various finds of *Australopithecus* have met with some difficulties. First, the early descriptions and interpretations, reflecting the dominant opinions of that time, tended to maximize the differences not only between *Australopithecus* finds and modern humans, but among the *Australopithecus* themselves. Secondly, the scattered *Australopithecus* finds and scanty geological stratigraphic evidence in most cases, except for the Tuang child, made a temporal correlation of the different finds a difficult task. Adding to the complication, the finds were cut out during excavation and later investigated. They should have been categorized chronologically according to climatic and faunal change evidence found along with them.

The recently discovered Plio-Pleistocene vertebrate assemblages in eastern Africa have been employed in correlating different sites in East and South Africa with important implications of hominid evolution (12) involving species of *Australopithecus*. *Australopithecus gracilis africanus*, the smaller form, apparently occupied an earlier phase, and *Australopithecus robustus*, the larger form, was found in a later phase. Some authorities regard the *A. gracilis africanus* as hominid and classified it as *Homo africanus* and *Homo habilis*.

Figure 2.16 compares *A. africanus* and *A. robustus* with modern humans. Tobias (16) thought that the morphological differences between the two species were not as great as those between male and female gorillas. R. E. F. Leakey (b. 1944) (13, 14) also alluded to the fact that *A. africanus* and *A. robustus* may not be separate species but are probably female and male forms, respectively, of a single species. He also suggested that some australopithecines were similar to extant long-armed, short-legged, knuckle-walking African apes while *H. habilis* walked upright (13, 15).

Starting in 1959, L. S. B. Leakey (1903–72) and Mary Leakey, his wife, uncovered important fossils ranging from about one million to two million years in age in East Africa in the Olduvai Gorge beds. The Olduvai formation consists of two beds, and Bed I was the deeper layer where Leakey uncovered two types of remains. He classified the two types as of a hominid nature and called them *Zinjanthropus* and *H. habilis* (5).

The *Zinjanthropus* fossil unearthed included the cranium, tibia, fibula, and two teeth. *Zinjanthropus* is grossly apelike, with a massive face and features strongly suggestive of a heavy musculature, including sagittal and occipital crests. The brain size is within 600–700 cc, a range closer to the upper limit of *Australopithecus*. Although Leakey classified this find into a new genus of hominid, it was later reclassified as *Australopithecus* (16). The potassium-argon radiometric dating technique put *Zinjanthropus* at an age of 1.75 million years.

H. habilis is the remains of an infant and was found at a lower level than *Zinjanthropus* but still at Bed I. Although L. S. B. Leakey claimed it to be more humanlike than apelike, LeGros Clark (6), among many others, has discounted *H. habilis* and grouped it together with *Australopithecus*.

L. S. B. Leakey also found *Homo erectus* remains in the upper layer of Bed II of the Olduvai Gorge and had evidence that *Australopithecus* was also found in the same formation and thus contemporary with *H. erectus*. Additional *Australopithecus* remains were found at Lake Rudolf in northeastern Kenya, in the Omo basin of Ethiopia, and other sites. These finds have pushed the fossil record of *Australopithecus* back to 5.5 million years ago if one accepts the more liberal estimate.

Australopithecus was found to be associated with toolmaking by the discovery of stone flakes struck off in the process of shaping pebble choppers in the vicinity of the 1.75-million-year-old fossil near Lake Rudolf (17). Stone tools of the most primitive type, the old Oldowan pebble tool (Figure 2.17), have been found with *Australopithecus* fossils in three of the other five South African sites. Since wild chimpanzees have been known to make crude tools (15, 17), the toolmaking capacity of *Australopithecus* was not entirely surprising. However, a circular stone

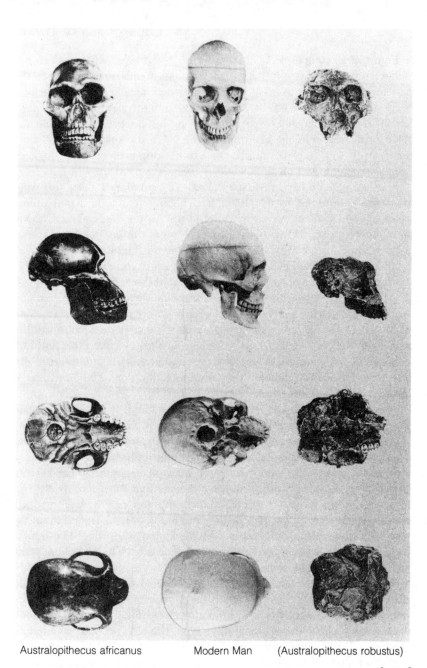

Australopithecus africanus   Modern Man   (Australopithecus robustus)

0   cm   5

Figure 2.16. Comparison of four views of two adult australopithecine skulls with a skull of modern humans. Reprinted; with permission, from Kelso, A. J. Physical anthropology. Philadelphia: J. B. Lippencott & Co.; 1970.

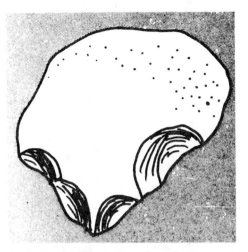

Figure 2.17. Oldowan pebble tool. Reprinted, with permission, from Kelso, A. J. Physical anthropology. Philadelphia: J. B. Lippincott & Co.; 1970.

structure, usually associated with shelter building, found at the base of Bed I in the Olduvai Gorge contemporary with *H. habilis* is still not well explained (18). It is very unlikely that the "artifact" was used for the manufacture of shelters since this venture is believed to be a late human accomplishment occurring within the last 100 000 years. However, the dissimilarity of this tool with the other crude pebble tools makes it most perplexing.

As indicated in Figure 2.16, *Australopithecus*, although resembling the chimpanzee, differs significantly in its cranial capacity of 400–600 cc and in having a much larger body size (about four feet tall, slender forms weighing around 50 pounds). The forehead is more rounded out, and the eyebrow ridges are less prominent than in the chimpanzee. The jaws also protrude less prominently than in apes. The dentition is quite similar to that of modern humans (Figure 2.18). The occipital condyles, by which the skull articulates with the spinal column, are set much farther forward toward the ventral surface on the skull, suggesting a relatively upright posture. The rest of the skeletal remains of *Australopithecus* generally corroborates the evidence of the skull.

Although the factual findings of *Australopithecus* are almost universally accepted, their interpretations have been controversial. It is difficult to establish definitive relationships of *Australopithecus* with hominids. The temporal, spatial, formal, and contextual information from each locality of the finds has to be considered, and a satisfactory means must still be established to relate with much certainty the time of South African *Australopithecus* deposits to the glacial sequence in the northern latitudes. Moreover, in contrast with *H. erectus* and *Homo neanderthalensis* (*see*

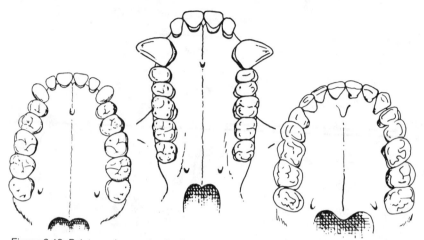

Figure 2.18. Palate and upper teeth of an australopithecine; a gorilla; and a human; from left to right, respectively. Reprinted, with permission, from Clark, 10th ed. The history of primate. British Museum (Natural History), by permission of the Trustees of the British Museum (Natural History). 1970.

I.2.3.4.b), which have some modern-day analogues or simulated analogues, *Australopithecus* has no modern-day counterpart. Although some scholars contend that these modern-day analogues have nothing to do with how a fossilized organism might have lived, others believe they would at least illuminate some ways of life of their ancestors. Therefore, the interpretation of the way *Australopithecus* lived is at best an educated guess.

In the earlier days of its discovery anthropologists were reluctant to accept *Australopithecus* into the lineage of human evolution. After the successful campaign of Dart, Broom, and Clark with more finds, most anthropologists placed *Australopithecus* in the direct line of human descent. However, several recent findings have placed doubt on this interpretation.

The first find was a living high-altitude Ethiopian baboon, *Theropithecus galada*. It was found to have incisors and canines that are small relative to those of extant African apes. Its cheek teeth are closely packed and heavily worn. In addition, it also possesses many features shared by *Ramapithecus* and *Australopithecus*, such as powerful masticatory muscles and a short, deep face (19, 20). Since the living baboon *T. galada* possesses some of the dental and facial characteristics of *Ramapithecus* and *Australopithecus*, a question is raised about the validity of classifying the two fossils as hominids. The baboon is living now, so presumably it is not directly related to man phylogenetically.

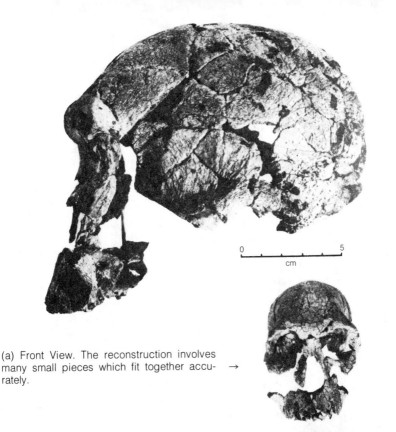

(a) Front View. The reconstruction involves many small pieces which fit together accurately. →

(b) Rear View. The sides of the vault are nearly parallel. →

(c) Top View. The brow ridges are moderate-sized by modern standards. →

Figure 2.19. Cranium KNM-ER-1470, a new *Homo* from East Rudolph. Reprinted, with permission, from Professor Birdsell, Department of Anthropology, UCLA. From Birdsell, J. B. Human evolution. Chicago: Rand McNally; 1975.

The second find was a recent discovery by R. E. F. Leakey at East Rudolf in northern Kenya of 150 fragments of a single skull (KNM-ER-1470) in one stratum dated by the potassium-argon method to be 2.6 to 2.9 million years old (21). The cranial capacity is 780–810 cc. This is much larger than that of *Australopithecus* and very similar to that of *H. erectus* (Figure 2.19). At the same time both *A. robustus* and *A. africanus* lineages were found at the same stratum although some australopithecines less than one million years old were also found. In addition, the Lake Rudolf skull is quite unlike, and possibly more advanced than, the skull of *H. erectus*. Therefore, Leaky classified it as *Homo sp. indet.* (species indeterminate). The antiquity of this *Homo* species is also corroborated by the possible remains of genus *Homo* found in the Laetolil Beds near the Olduvai Gorge in northern Tanzania. They were dated back to 3.59 to 3.77 million yeras ago (21, 22). It is of interest to note that the cranial capacity of KNM-ER-1470 is larger than that of some primitive *H. erectus* though the two *Homo* species are separated by almost two million years. The KNM-ER-1470 skull raises the question that the earlier *Australopithecus* was contemporary with *Homo sp. indet.* and thus the australopithecines may have had nothing to do with the evolution of the genus *Homo*.

2.3.4 Homo erectus *and* Homo neanderthalensis. *H. erectus* and *H. neanderthalensis* are the two better documented early human fossils that trace the history of human beings back to the glacial periods. In addition to the large cranial capacities of these two species, the cultural remains also lend much support to their being human fossils. *H. erectus* was found not only with tools made of chipped stone and bone but also charred deer bone, a fact that strongly suggests they had learned to cook with fire. *H. neanderthalensis* had better-quality stone tools and buried their dead. Figures 2.20, 2.21 and 2.22 compare *H. erectus* with *H. neanderthalensis*, *H. erectus* with modern humans, and *H. neanderthalensis* with modern humans, respectively.

a) Homo erectus *Discussed.* The original find of *H. erectus* was made in Java in 1890–91 and includes fragments of a skull and a femur. It was designated as *Pithecanthropus erectus.* Subsequently, various skulls and jaws were found in Java, China, Hungary, Germany, Algeria, Morocco, South Africa, and Tanzania (Table 2.12). The best documented among them was the *Sinanthropus pekinensis* with many fragments of 15 skulls and 11 mandibles found near Peking, China. It was renamed *H. erectus pekinensis* and dated by an amino acid racemization technique (23) to be around 300 000 to 500 000 years old. Analyzed fossil fauna associated with the human fossils are suggestive of the climatic change of

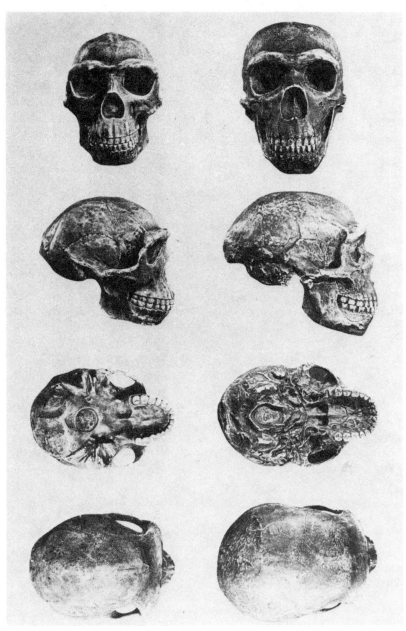

Homo erectus   Neanderthal

Figure 2.20. Comparison of four views of *Homo erectus* with a Neanderthal skull cast. Reprinted, with permission, from Kelso, A. J. Physical anthropology. Philadelphia: J. B. Lippincott & Co.; 1970.

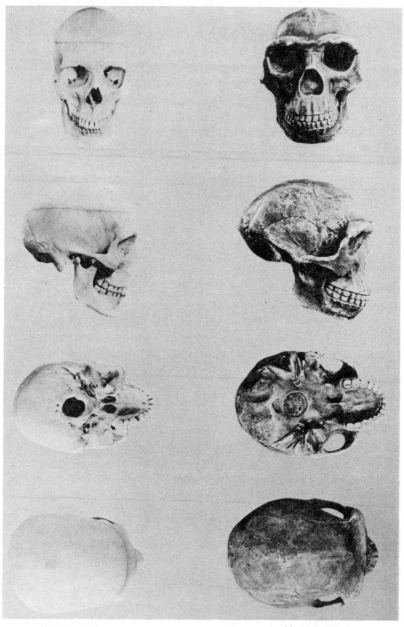

Modern Man   Homo erectus

0   cm   5

Figure 2.21. Comparison of four views of a modern human skull with a *Homo erectus*. Reprinted, with permission, from Kelso, A. J. Physical anthropology. Philadelphia: J. B. Lippincott & Co.; 1970.

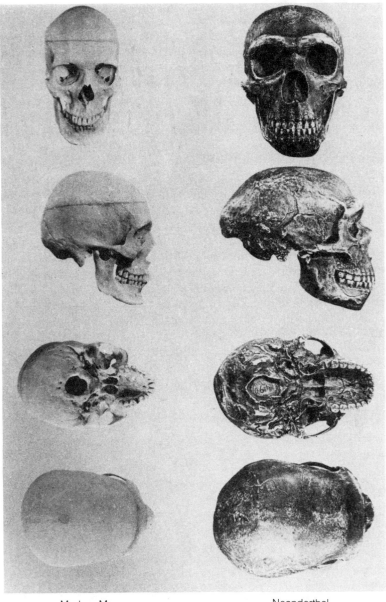

Modern Man   Neanderthal

                                              0   cm   5
                                              ┗━━━┻━━━┛

Figure 2.22. Comparison of four views of a modern human skull with a Neanderthal skull cast. Reprinted, with permission, from Kelso, A. J. Physical anthropology. Philadelphia: J. B. Lippincott & Co.; 1970.

the time and have helped to correlate *H. erectus* with the glaciation of the Northern Hemisphere. It is estimated that the period of time occupied by *H. erectus* appears to be a period spanning the first and second glacial period, and this is roughly from 1 million to 500 000 years ago (24). The absolute dating estimates on the materials uncovered from Africa, Java, and Europe also corroborate these dates.

The Java group of fossils seemed to be the most primitive, dating back to more than 710 000 years by the potassium-argon method. Their brain capacity averages less than 900 cc. Although cultural remains are not directly found in the original place with the Java fossils, circumstantial evidence indicates the oldest chopper-chopping stone tools recovered from central Java may be contemporaneous with the fossils.

The *H. erectus* found in a cave near Peking was the best studied because of the abundance of materials. The original find included 15 skulls and other bones representing some 40 individuals. Unfortunately the early discoveries were lost during World War II. Subsequent work from the same deposits was begun in 1949 and has yielded a humerus and tibia that can be attributed to modern man, as well as a jawbone and five teeth that are similar to the original find. An assemblage of chopper-chopping tools were uncovered in association with the fossil (Figure 2.23).

There is strong evidence indicating that *H. erectus* knew how to use and control fire. The evidence at the cave deposits includes fireplaces found at several locations and many burned or charred fossil bones of other animals presumably brought to the location by *H. erectus*. On the basis of this evidence, *H. erectus* was thought to be a hunter.

CHOPPERS

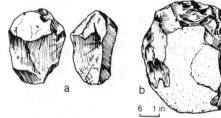

CHOPPING TOOLS

Figure 2.23. Comparison of choppers with chopping tools. Reprinted, with permission, from Kelso, A. J. Physical anthropology. Philadelphia: J. B. Lippincott & Co.; 1970.

112

Table 2.12. Locations yielding evidence of *Homo erectus*.

Location	Date Found	Comment
1. Java	1890–91	Original discoveries of skull fragment and femur. Originally designated as *Pithecanthropus erectus*.
	1936	Incomplete skull of an infant. Originally designated *H. modjokeriensis*.
2. China	1937–39	Three incomplete skulls found about 40 miles (64 km.) from original 1890 discovery. Also identified as *Pithecanthropus*.
	1927–37	Several fragments of 15 skulls and 11 mandibles. All were designated earlier as representative of *Sinanthropus pekinensis*.
	1949	A jaw bone, and five teeth that are similar to the original 1927 find were found in the same deposits. A humerous and tibia that can be attributed to modern humans were also found.
	1963–64	Mandible and skull fragments. Referred to as Lantian man.
3. Germany	1907	A mandible, also called Heidelberg jaw and *Homo heidelbergensis*.
4. Algeria	1954–56	Fragments of three mandibles that have been designated *Atlanthropus mauritanicus*.
5. Morocco	1954	From Sidi Abderrahman, a fragmentary mandible.
6. South Africa	1949	Some jaw fragments, teeth, and two bones of the postcranial skeleton. Designated originally as *Telanthropus capensis*.
7. Tanzania	1960	Skull fragments referred to as Chellean man.
	1964	Identified by Leakey as "George," a skull reconstructed from many small fragments.
	1976	Complete skull resembling *Homo sapiens*.

*NOTE: Adapted, with permission, from Kelso, A. J. Physical anthropology. Philadelphia: J. B. Lippincott & Co.; 1970.

The evidence of *H. erectus* in Europe is meager. No artifacts have been recovered in the sites where fossils were located. However, the associated fauna indicate that these beings may have lived during the first interglacial period.

Artifacts discovered with the African *H. erectus* are indicative of the advanced lower Paleolithic tradition. The Olduvai find in Tanzania is associated with early hand ax archaeological remains. The *H. erectus* fossil found near the bottom of Bed II is dated to one million years ago.

A recently unearthed cranium of *H. erectus* from Lake Ndutu in northern Tanzania indicates a link between *H. erectus* and *H. sapiens*. Both the cranial features of *H. erectus* and *H. sapiens* are represented in this skull. It was dated at 500 000 to 600 000 years by the amino acid racemization method. It is probably the transitional form between *H. erectus* and *H. sapiens* (25, 26).

Collectively, *H. erectus* can be described as of moderate but erect stature, as shown by the straight limb bones, broad hip bones, and the position of the occipital condyle. The relative proportions of arms and legs are like those of modern humans. The forehead is retreating, and the jaw is projecting, though both to a much lesser extent than in the ape. The dentition is essentially that of modern humans. *H. erectus* was distributed throughout the Old World from about 1 million to 500 000 years ago, although not without exception (i.e., it has been claimed that skulls buried merely 10 000 years ago in Australia showed typical *H. erectus* characteristics) (27). They made the chopper-chopping type or the hand-ax type of tool, both presumably having the same subsistence function. Their appearance in the fossil record seems to be associated with a shift of mammalian fauna toward a warmer and moister climate. *H. erectus* was essentially a hunter and cave dweller, and at least at one site found to date it appears he used fire for food preparation.

b) Homo Neanderthalensis *Discussed.* The first Neanderthal fossil was discovered in 1848 at Gibraltar but was not thought to be significant in the scientific community. Eight years later, a similar skull together with a few ribs and limb bones were found in a cave in the Neanderthal Valley of Germany. They were the first bones to draw the attention of anthropologists. Since that time a large collection of similar fossils, some of them quite complete, have been uncovered in the Republic of South Africa, Zambia, France, Belgium, Italy, Yugoslavia, Israel, Uzbekistan, and Java (Table 2.13).

From the skeletal remains a rather complete picture of Neanderthal beings can be constructed. Their skull was thick-boned, with prominent eyebrow ridges and receding forehead. The roof of their skull was flat. However, their average cranial capacity of 1450 cc exceeds that for some modern humans (Figure 2.22).

Table 2.13. Some fossil discoveries of Neanderthal varieties.*

	Name	Location	Head Length in mm.	Head Breadth in mm.	Date Before Present	Cultural Association
1. Temperate Glacial	Neanderthal	Germany	201	147	35,000–70,000	?
	Spy I	Belgium	200	146	35,000–70,000	Mousterian
	Spy II	Belgium	198	150	35,000–70,000	Mousterian
	La Chapelle	France	208	156	35,000–70,000	Mousterian
	La Ferrassie	France	209	158	>35,000	Mousterian
	La Quina	France	203	138	35,000–55,000	Mousterian
	Gibraltar	Gibraltar	190	148	35,000–70,000	Levallois-Mousterian
	Monte Circeo	Italy	204	156	35,000–70,000	Pontinian (Micro-Mousterian)
	Shanidar	Iraq	207	155–158	60,000–96,000	East Mousterian
2. Temperate Interglacial	Skhūl and Tabun	Israel	192	144	35,000–70,000	Levallois-Mousterian
	Ehringsdorf	Germany	196	145	60,000–120,000	Mousterian
	Steinheim	Germany	185	132	200,000?	—
	Fontechevade	France	194	154	70,000–150,000	Tayacian
	Saccopastore	Italy	181	142	60,000	?
	Krapina	Yugoslavia	178	149	?	Mousterian
	Teshik-Tash (child)	Uzbekistan	185	144	?	Mousterian
3. Subtropical to Tropical	Rhodesian	Zambia	208	144	35,000–70,000	—
	Saldanha	Republic of South Africa	200	144	40,000	Fauresmith
	Solo I	Java	196	143	?	Ngandongian
	Solo V	Java	220	147	?	Ngandongian
	Solo VI	Java	192	144	?	Ngandongian
	Solo IX	Java	201	150	?	Ngandongian
	Solo X	Java	203	155	?	Ngandongian
	Solo XI	Java	200	144	?	Ngandongian

*NOTE: Reprinted, with permission, from Kelso, A. J. Physical anthropology. Philadelphia: J. B. Lippincott & Co.; 1970.

The quality of the stone tools uncovered with the fossils is indicative of middle to upper Paleolithic culture. Since they were scattered through a period from approximately 150 000 years to 30 000 years ago, they can be categorized into three groups according to the climates where they lived: interglacial, glacial, and tropical. It can be safely concluded that the glacial group of Neanderthal beings were hunters, whereas it seems probable that the interglacial and the tropical groups were more vegetarians than hunters. The interglacial groups were known to practice burials and to place implements in the graves. The burials may have been in a single grave, but multiple burials resembling a family cemetery were also uncovered. A flint tool kit is frequently found buried with a dead male. One young Neanderthal child was found buried with the horns of four ibexes, the great mountain goat. The most impressive burial site was uncovered from the Shanidar cave in the Zagros Mountains in northern Iraq. The skull of the burial seemed to belong to a male around 30 years old who was killed by some strong blows that badly crushed his head. He was buried on a bed with a blanket made up of flowers, as evidenced by pollen analysis. This elaborate burial rite leaves the impression that *H. neanderthalensis* believed in life after death. It is also amazing to note that the man buried showed evidence of a withered right arm that had been amputated, reattached, and then healed.

Reconstruction from early finds depicted Neanderthal beings as persons with a stooped posture. The discoveries of more Neanderthal remains changed the picture. It is now apparent that the old conception of a Neanderthal being had been based on a misinterpretation of the study of an arthritic skeleton. Closer examination of the remains of other Neanderthal finds suggests that *H. neanderthalensis* was not much taller than five feet but stood with an upright posture.

Because of the advanced skeletal features of Neanderthal beings and their advanced stone tools and burial rites, *H. neanderthalensis* has been treated by many as a subspecies of modern humans—*Homo sapiens neanderthalensis*. This interpretation was substantiated by the discovery in caves of Mount Carmel in Israel of a possible intermediate between the two species.

Since modern humans *(Homo sapiens)* appear abruptly at around 40 000 years ago at the advent of Upper Paleolithic culture when the Neanderthal beings disappeared from Europe, it has been speculated that *H. sapiens neanderthalensis* is the direct ancestor of modern humans. Except for the recent find of a possible intermediate between *H. erectus* and *H. sapiens* (21, 22), there is no evidence against this interpretation. However, there are still unresolved questions raised in several finds (e.g., the Swanscombe skull and the Steinheim and Ehringsdorf skulls) concerning the antiquity of *H. sapiens*. Therefore, no conclusive human lineage can be established to date.

However, it seems reasonable to assume that the earliest fossil that can be placed in direct human lineage, according to the present evidence, is *H. erectus*, who lived around 1 million to 500 000 years ago, and possibly the KNM-ER-1470 skull. But the identity of this latter skull has to await excavation of similar remains and, more importantly, the excavation of cultural materials associated with this being so that the cultural capacity of the fossil can be evaluated.

In summary, *Ramapithecus* and *Australopithecus* are thought by many to be the ancestral stock of *H. erectus*. *H. erectus* is considered by many to be the forerunner of *H. sapiens* (modern humans). However, the presence of conflicting interpretations of the fossil material and the scarcity of cultural artifacts does not permit conclusive statements to be made about the evolutionary position of these forms.

References 2.3

1. Simons, E. L. Sc. Am. 236 (5):28; 1977.
2. Clark, W. E., LeGros. History of the primates. 10th ed. London: British Museum; 1970.
3. Mixter, R. Creation and evolution. Monograph. 2nd ed. Wheaton, IL: Am. Sc. Aff. 1967; 22.
4. Kelso, A. J. Physical anthropology, an introduction. Philadelphia: Lippincott; 1970 (chapter 5).
5. Leakey, L. S. B. Olduvai gorge 1951–1961. Vol. 1. London: Cambridge Univ. Press; 1965.
6. Clark, W. E., LeGros. Man-ape or ape-man: the story of discoveries in Africa. New York: Holt; 1967.
7. Tobias, P. V. Annual review of anthropology. Siegel, B. J.; Beals, A. R.; Tyler, S. A. ed. 2:311–34; 1973.
8. Leakey, R. E. F.; Walker, A. C. Am. J. Phys. Anthropol. 39:205; 1973.
9. Leakey, R. E. F.; Walker, A. C. Nature. 261:572; 1976.
10. Leakey, R. E. F.; Nature. 261:574; 1976.
11. Johnson, D. C.; White, T. D. Science. 203:321; 1979.
12. White, T. D.; Harris, J. M. Science. 1998:13–21; 1977.
13. Leakey, R. E. F. Nature. 231:241; 1971.
14. Science News. 100 (November):357; 1971.
15. Science News. 99 (June):398; 1971.

16. Tobias, P. V. Olduvai gorge, the cranium and maxillary dentition of *Australopithecus (Zinjanthropus) bosei*. Vol. 2. London: Cambridge Univ. Press; 1967.
17. Katz, S., editor. Biological anthropology: reading from Scientific American. San Francisco: Freeman; 1975: 14.
18. Kelso, A. J. Physical anthropology, an introduction. 223.
19. Philbeam, D. R. Nature. 225:516; 1970.
20. Philbeam, D. R. The evolution of man. New York: Funk and Wagnalls; 1970.
21. Leakey, R. E. F. Nature. 242:447; 1973.
22. Leakey, M. D. et al. Nature. 262:460; 1976.
23. Bishop, W. W.; Miller, J. A., editors. Calibration of hominoid evolution: recent advances. Isotopic and other dating methods applicable to the origin of man. Edinburgh: Scottish Academic Press; 1972: 177–85.
24. Katz, S., editor. Biological anthropology. 66.
25. Mturi, A. A. Nature. 262:484; 1976.
26. Clark, R. J. Nature. 262:485; 1976.
27. Katz, S., editor. Biological anthropology. 15.

2.4 Evidence from Biogeography

The study of biogeography is the categorization of the geographic distribution of fauna and flora. Careful studies of the biosphere reveal that each species of plant or animal has a certain range of existence on the earth. *Jordan's rule,* developed by David Starr Jordan, describes the distribution of ranges. In general, closely related species do not have identical ranges, but often their ranges are not very far apart. They are usually adjacent but sometimes separated by a barrier, such as a mountain, desert, or ocean.

Certain species of plants and animals are widely distributed throughout the world. In contrast, other species are confined to a certain location even though climatic conditions in other regions of the world seem well suited for their existence. The marsupial animals such as the opossum and kangaroo, found exclusively in North America and Australia, respectively, are examples of species with restricted distribution. In other instances, there are extreme discontinuities in the geographic distribution of a particular species or related species. The camel is found in Asia and Africa while their close relative the llama is only in South America. Other animals and plants are found in widely separated areas of the world: lungfish are known in Australia, Africa, and South America; alligators in the south-eastern United States and the Yangtze River of China; and magnolias in the eastern United States, China, and Japan.

The attempts to classify the patterns of distribution of living fauna have yielded six major biogeographic realms, namely, *Nearctic, Palearactic, Australian, Oriental, Ethiopian,* and *Neotropical* regions (Figure 2.24). The realms are separated by great physical barriers. However, diverse areas within the realms have been accessible to organisms found in them throughout geological time. The regions were originally classified according to the distribution of mammals, but later it was found that the regions are valid for other kinds of fauna and flora as well.

The Nearctic and Palearctic are sometimes grouped together as the *Holarctic* region that includes all of Europe and Asia (north of the Himalayan and Nan Ling mountian ranges), Africa (north of the Sahara desert), and North America (north of the Mexican Plateau). The animals found in the Nearctic (North America) and Palearctic (Old World) exhibit differences at the species and generic levels only. Representative animals found in the Nearctic realm are mountain goats, prairie dogs, opossums, skunks, raccoons, blue jays, and turkey buzzards. Some of the indigenous animals found in the Palearctic realm include goats, moles, deer, oxen, sheep, robins, and magpies.

The Australian region includes Australia and the associated islands. It is characterized by a predominantly marsupial fauna and the complete absence of any native placental mammals, other than bats and some rodents.

The Oriental region is separated from the Australian region by an imaginary dividing line known as *Wallace's Line.* It separates the islands of Bali and Lombok that are only 20 miles (32 km.) apart. It also goes through the Macassar Straits and passes to the east of the Philippines. The mammals found on both sides of this imaginary line are drastically different. The orangutan, black panther, tiger, water buffalo, Indian elephant, gibbon, and tarsier are characteristic animals of the Oriental region. However, the kangaroo, koala, and platypus are characteristic animals of the Australian region.

The part of Africa south of the Sahara and the island of Madagascar constitute the Ethiopian realm. Animals found exclusively in this region are the giraffe, aardvark, chimpanzee, gorilla, zebra, and hippopotamus.

Finally, the Neotropical region consists of South and Central America, southern Mexico, and the West Indian islands. The following animal's make up the distinctive fauna in this realm: the alpaca, tinamous puff bird, capybara, bloodsucking bat, sloth, llama, prehensile-tailed monkey, tapir, and anteater.

The distinctive habitats (ecological zones) within (e.g., lakes) and be-

119

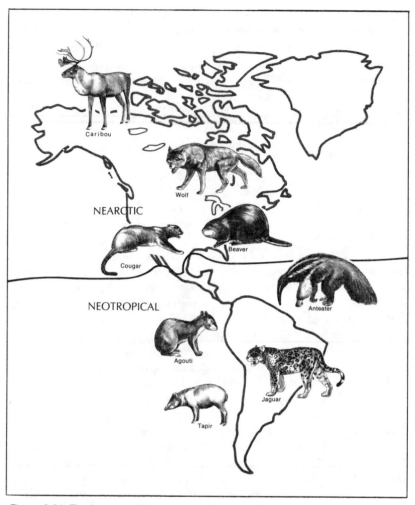

Figure 2.24. The biogeographic realms of the world. Reprinted, with permission, from Villee, C. A. Biology. 7th ed. Philadelphia. W. B. Saunders Co.; 1977. © 1977 by the W. B. Saunders Co.

tween (e.g., oceans) the biotic regions are barriers that affect the geographic distribution of fauna and flora. Because of the climatic difference in the altitudinal and latitudinal zones, plants are distributed according to their abilities to adapt to each habitat (Figure 2.25). Thus, ptarimigans and the varying hare are found in the higher mountains of the western United States as well as in the arctic and subarctic lowlands of Canada and

Alaska because the habitats are similar in each location. In Europe, the mountain hare is found in the mountains ranging from the east (Caucasus and Ural mountains) to the west coast and also in the arctic lowlands but not in the intervening lowlands.

Similarly, the different ecological zones (habitats) of the ocean each possess its own distinct flora and fauna (Figure 2.26). The narrow strand

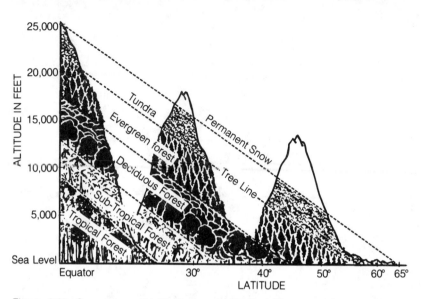

Figure 2.25. Comparison of latitudinal and altitudinal life zones of plants in North America. Reprinted, with permission, from Moore, J. N.; Slusher, H. S. editors. Biology. Grand Rapids, MI: Zondervan Publishing House; 1970.

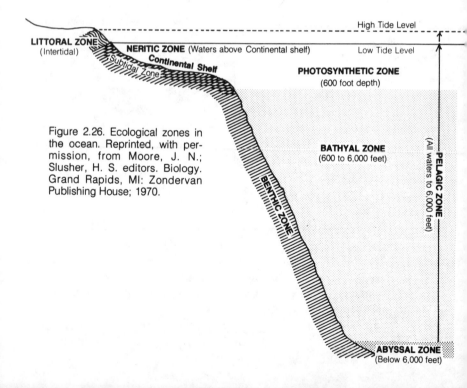

Figure 2.26. Ecological zones in the ocean. Reprinted, with permission, from Moore, J. N.; Slusher, H. S. editors. Biology. Grand Rapids, MI: Zondervan Publishing House; 1970.

on each shoreline that is alternatively covered and exposed by the tide is the *littoral* (intertidal) zone. The continental shelf usually slopes beyond this zone, forming continental islands at its higher portions. The shallow seas that cover the continental shelves, less than 600 feet deep, are the *neritic* zone. When the ocean floor drops off abruptly at the outskirt of the continental shelf, several zones of great depths are created. The surface layer of seas to a depth of as much as 600 feet is the *pelagic* zone where water is well aerated, lighted, and subject to wave action. The deeper seas, to a depth of 6000 feet, comprise the *bathyal* zone. The lowest part of the sea, the *abyssal* zone, is extremely cold, quiet, devoid of sunlight, and can sustain only a few profoundly modified and adapted organisms. This is in marked contrast to the littoral zone, which is the most richly inhabited area in the ocean. The deep sea basins form barriers that affect the geographical distribution of the marine fauna and flora found within the various continental shelves.

The distribution of animals in the six biogeographic areas has been an intriguing phenomenon for biogeographers ever since the inception of this branch of science. Many theories have been postulated to account for this phenomenon based on a uniform geological outlook with minor modification throughout the earth's history (1). However, these theories have not been very convincing. In exploring the migration theory, it is difficult to understand how the migration of reptiles and amphibians could have led to the deposition of the same amphibians and reptile fossils that are found on Antarctica, South America, South Africa, and the Indian continents when these areas are separated by the barriers of oceans and mountain ranges.

The continental drift theory has been put forth to account for some of the geographic distribution problems. This theory, which dates back to 1910 (10), states that from the Paleozoic era until late in the Mesozoic era only two major land masses existed, and the two, Gondwanda and Laurasia, were in contact. Gondwanda centered around the South Pole while Laurasia extended well into the northern hemisphere. During the Cretaceous era, Gondwanda gave rise to the southern continents by drifting away. Subsequently, the southern continents split to form Africa, South America, Australia, and Antarctica, as well as the Arabian and Indian peninsulas and the major Pacific islands such as New Zealand and Madagascar. Laurasia, on the other hand, broke up and formed North America, Europe, and Asia (Figure 2.27).

The continental drift hypothesis was unattractive when it was first proposed because no known mechanism could account for the drift. However, during the 1960s, the discovery of *terrestrial paleomagnetism*

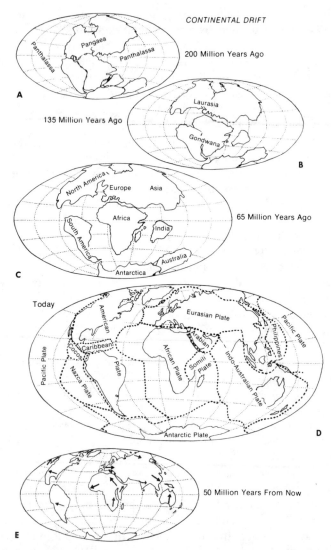

Figure 2.27. Continental drift. *A,* The supercontinent Pangaea of the Triassic period, about 200 million years ago. *B,* Breakup of Pangaea into Laurasia (Northern Hemisphere) and Gondwana (Southern Hemisphere) 135 million years ago in the Cretaceous period. *C,* Further separation of land masses, which occurred in the Tertiary period, 65 million years ago. Note that Europe and North America are still joined and that India is a separate land mass. *D,* The continents today. *E,* Projected positions of the continents in 50 million years. Reprinted, with permission, from Villee, C. A. Biology. 7th ed. Philadelphia: W. B. Saunders Co.; 1977. © 1977 by the W. B. Saunders Co.

sparked new interest in the continental-drift theory. Terrestrial paleomagnetism holds that the continents of the world have changed their positions relative to the earth's magnetic pole during its history (2). The plotting of Paleozoic paleomagnetic pole positions indicates that the southern continents and India were clustered together in the far south (9).

A mechanism based on circumstantial evidence, namely, plate tectonics, has been postulated to explain continental drift (3). The theory essentially states that the earth's crust is composed of a rigid outer shell—a lithosphere, resting on an underlying and less rigid asthenosphere. The outer shell is broken up into some 6 (4) or 10 (5) major plates. These plates and subplates of varying shapes and sizes are in a state of flux relative to each other, presumably as a result of the forces and processes occurring in the asthenosphere. The mechanisms by which plates move relative to each other is not clear. It is conceivable that they are being pushed, pulled, driven by gravitational forces, or carried by convection units into the mantle of the earth. The boundaries of the major plates coincide with the regions of major tectonic activities (e.g., San Andreas fault) of the lithosphere, such as earthquakes.

With the increasing popularity of the continental-drift theory, the biogeography of the world could be reinterpreted. Before the advent of evolutionary thinking, it was thought that similar fauna and flora in isolated areas of the world represented independent and unique creations. However, it was intriguing that animals and plants were in exclusively one region while equally suitable habitats in other areas were devoid of any trace of the same organism. No one was able to offer a satisfactory reason for the distribution patterns. However, a study of the distribution of bryophytes (mosses and liverworts) seemed to fit nicely into the scheme of continental drift (6). *Clasmatocolea vermicularis*, a species of leafy liverwort, was found to be distributed along the east coast of South Africa and the west coast of South America, as well as Central America and some islands (Figure 2.28). Since the plant is known to have a limited capacity of dispersal, it was next to impossible for it to cross the Atlantic Ocean in order to populate the two continents. Therefore, the distribution was most likely the result of scattering of the species at the south coast of Gondwanda when it split into the present continents.

In summary, the concept of natural selection, which gained popularity with the publication of *Origin of the Species* by Darwin, provides a good explanation of the diversification of species into the different habitats of the biosphere. Darwin's concept of natural selection emerged from his observations that began in 1831 when he became a naturalist on the *H. M. S. Beagle* that sailed from England to South America as part of a

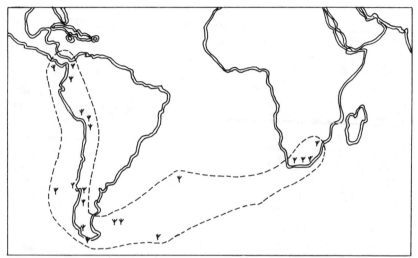

Figure 2.28. The distribution of *Clasmatocolea vermicularis* (¥) in South Africa, South and Central America as well as some islands.

survey of continental coastlines. Darwin visited the various isolated islands off the coast of Ecuador, and on these oceanic islands, he found a large number of endemic species of finches that are closely related with the finches on the South American mainland (Figure 2.29). Certain features of the birds are distinct and can be related to the habitats of the various populations. The most striking examples were the sizes and shapes of the beaks of endemic finches that seemed to be correlated with their diets. Darwin suggested that all these varieties of finches were descendents of an ancestral species that immigrated to the islands from the mainland. After the offspring of the ancestral species became numerous, they outstripped the food supply. By a process of natural selection, the variant individuals with slightly better-equipped beaks were able to survive in distinct parts of the islands, according to the type of food available. Over the course of time variant forms of finches came to occupy distinct niches in the environment (7, 8).

It was also intriguing for Darwin to observe that over half of the more than 300 plants in the Galapagos Islands were endemic. Yet, all of these plants show close relationship to South American plants. However, the mainland and the islands have totally different climatic and geological characteristics. Therefore, he postulated also that the varieties of plants on the islands descended from the introduction of the ancestral plants from the mainland, and the subsequent changes came by natural selection (7).

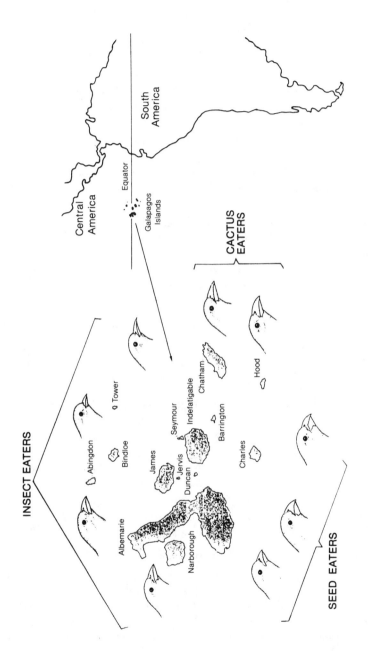

Figure 2.29. The location of the Galapagos Islands and their distribution of birds according to bill structures. Reprinted, by permission, from Dodson, E. O.; Dodson, P. 2nd ed. Evolution, process and product. New York: Van Nostrand Co.; 1976. © 1976 by Litton Educational Publishing, Inc.

On this basis, Darwin suggested that the biogeography of organisms can be explained by assuming each group of organisms after originating in the major regions of the world, spread to occupy as much space as it could, to be stopped only by the natural selective factors of physical and climatic barriers and competition with other organisms. Thus, he explained the similarities of the plants in different habitats by the assumption that they were from the same origin and underwent morphological changes after migration.

Theories of biogeography incorporate Darwin's assumption and further postulate that each species of fauna and flora originated only once at the "center of origin," and from there it diversified into different areas of the same region by natural selection. Thus, when the continents split apart, the species diversified separately by natural selection as the land drifted.

Based on the current assumptions of biogeographers, the occurrence of similar organisms in different biogeographical realms does not have to be attributed to separate creative acts of God. This could have resulted by continental drift, following the appearance of a species at the common "center of origin" through the creative act of God.

References 2.4

1. Dodson, E. O.; Dodson, P. Evolution, process and product. New York: Van Nostrand; 1976: 403–13.
2. Runcorn, S. K., editor. Continental drift. London: Academic Press; 1962: 1–40.
3. Dietz, R. S.; Holden, J. C. Nature. 229:309; 1971.
4. LePichon, S. J. Geophys. Res. 73:3661; 1968.
5. Dietz, R. S.; Holden, J. C. Sc. Am. 223:30; 1969.
6. Dodson, E. O.; Dodson, P. Evolution, process and product. 415.
7. Darwin, C. Voyage of the Beagle. New York: Dutton; 1957.
8. Darwin, C. Origin of species. New York: New American Library; 1958: 371.
9. Dodson, E. O.; Dodson, P. Evolution, process and product. New York: Van Nostrand; 1976: 403–13.
10. Holmes, A. Principles of physical geology. London: Nelson; 1965.

2.5 Evidence of Comparative Structure and Function

There are many similarities in comparative structure and function among all living organisms. These similarities have been used by evolutionists to support their thesis. This section reviews comparative structure and function evidence by dividing it as follows: comparative cellular structure and function, comparative gross anatomy, and comparative embryological development.

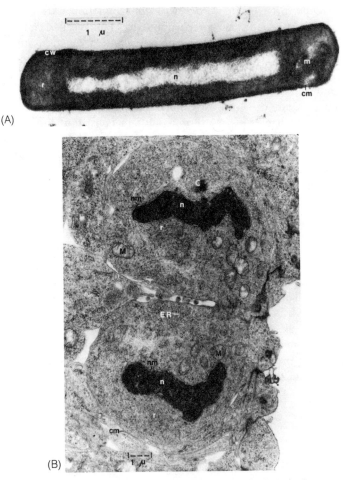

(A)

(B)

Figure 2.30. Electron micrographs of thin sections of procaryotic and eucaryotic cells. *(A)* A bacterium, *Bacillus subtilis,* that has a typical procaryotic cell structure. It is surrounded by a relatively dense cell wall *(cw),* enclosing the cell membrane *(cm).* Within the cell, the nucleus *(n)* is distinguishable from the cytoplasm, densely filled with 70S ribosomes *(r).* A membranous structure, mesosome *(m),* is also found at one pole of the cell. *(B)* Two dividing nerve cells from a three-day-old-chick embryo have a relatively undifferentiated eucaryotic cell structure. These nerve cells lack cell walls outside their cell membranes *(cm).* Recognizable structures in these cells that are not found in procaryotic cells are: mitochondria *(M),* endoplasmic reticulum *(ER),* centriole *(C)* (part of the mitotic apparatus), 80S ribosomes *(r),* and the nucleus *(n)* surrounded by a nuclear membrane *(nm).* These cells are in the terminal stage of mitosis that will be followed by the complete separation of the two cells and the reformation of the nucleolus in the nucleus. (Electron micrograph *(B)* is courtesy of Dr. John Sechrist, Department of Biology, Wheaton College, Wheaton, IL.)

2.5.1 *Comparative Cellular Structure and Function.* All living organisms are composed of small compartmentalized units called cells. Cells are units of life because they can perform essential functions that are indispensable for the survival of the whole organism. Cellular respiration provides the energy necessary for the activities of the organism. Cellular division and differentiation bring about the growth and development of the organism. Many cells can exist individually as free-living unicellular entities, such as bacteria or protozoa. Others constitute the building blocks of multicellular organisms. For example, in an adult human being, there are approximately one hundred trillion cells differentiated to form different parts of the body.

With the advent of electron microscopy, it was apparent that cells could be divided into two basic types according to the structure of the nucleus, namely, *eucaryotes* and *procaryotes* (Figure 2.30). Eucaryotes include mosses, liverworts, ferns, higher flowering plants, and all animals that are characterized by multicellular tissues and systems involving extensive differentiation of cells. Lower forms such as algae, protozoa, and fungi (many are microscopic) are also eucaryotic. Algae, protozoa, and fungi may be unicellular or multicellular. Multicellular forms may show little or no differentiation of cells and tissues. Procaryotes, on the other hand, consist of two main groups, the ubiquitous unicellular bacteria and blue green algae (Monera). Table 2.14 compares the basic differences between eucaryotic and procaryotic cells, and Figure 2.30 gives microscopic documentation of the differences.

Table 2.14. Comparison of eucaryotic and procaryotic cells.

	PROCARYOTIC CELL	EUCARYOTIC CELL
GROUPS WHERE FOUND AS UNIT OF STRUCTURE	BACTERIA, BLUE-GREEN ALGAE	MOST ALGAE, FUNGI, PROTOZOA, HIGHER PLANTS AND ANIMALS
Nuclear Membrame	−	+
Mitotic Division	−	+
Chromosome Number	1(?)	Always Greater Than One
Cytoplasmic Streaming	−	+ or −
Mitochondria	−	+
Chloroplasts	−	+ or −
Contractile Locomotor Organelles	Bacterial Flagella }in Some Axial Filaments	Multistranded }in Some Flagella or Cilia
Ameboid Movement	−	+ or −
Chromosomal Protein	−	+
Nucleolus	−	+
9 + 2 Structure in Cellular Appendages	−	+
Golgi Apparatus	−	+ or (−)
Endoplasmic Recticulum	−	+
Ribosomes	70S	80S (Cytoplasmic) 70S (Organellar)

Although cellular functions are basically the same in the two cell types (*see.* I.2.6), they are mediated in different ways. For example, cellular respiration in the procaryote occurs in the plasma membrane (cell membrane) while the corresponding reaction site in a eucaryote is in the inner membranes of the cytoplasmic organelle, the mitochondrion. The plasma membrane in some procaryotes is also the site of photosynthesis, whereas the process in eucaryotes occurs in the chloroplast, a cytoplasmic organelle. The similarities of the mitochondrial and chloroplast organelles in the eucaryotic cell to an entire procaryotic cell are striking. They are membrane-bound structures that contain DNA, RNA, and the same kind of ribosomes. This has led many biologists to speculate on the evolutionary origin of the two organelles. Figure 2.31 summarizes some of the current thinking. The prevailing hypothesis is that certain bacteria came to be permanently associated (in symbiosis) with precursor procaryotic amoeboid cells, thus establishing the first true eucaryote.

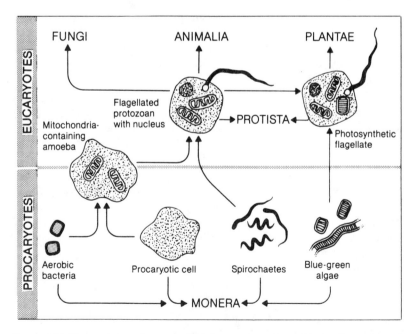

Figure 2.31. The evolution of eucaryotic cell types through symbiosis. The membrane-bounded organelles that characterize eucaryotic cells may have originated in symbiotic relationships among procaryotic cells. Reproduced, with permission, from Stephens, G. C. Biology. New York: John Wiley & Sons; 1974. © 1974 by John Wiley & Sons.

The evolutionary interpretation of the relationship between pro-caryotes and eucaryotes is, to say the least, strained. There is no direct evidence to link the two types of cells. It is also legitimate to suggest that the two types have separate and independent origins. Therefore, evidence for evolution based on cellular structure and function is purely circumstantial.

2.5.2 *Comparative Gross Anatomy.* The anatomical features of many vertebrates follow more or less similar patterns. These patterns are used as evidence for a common ancestor. Some of the frequently cited patterns are the development of *homologous structures*, the development of vertebra, the evolution of the heart, and the existence of *vestigial* organs.

a) *Homologous Structures.* Homologous structures are defined as those that can be traced to the same embryonic origin and are similar in basic structure and development. They may not be used for the same function, but their similarities are said to indicate a common ancestry. Figure 2.32 shows the bones of the forelimbs of the frog, lizard, bird, human, cat, whale, and bat. The homologous nature of the structures seem to be evident because of the similar arrangement of the bones in each member of the group. Structural variations represent adaptations of each member to a particular mode of life. Each structural variation is thought by evolutionists to be built from a common ancestral form by the process of natural selection.

Evolutionists have based their conclusions about the common genetic origin of the above organisms on the basis of anatomical similarities. However, after examining this evidence, we cannot eliminate the possibility that similar structures were created by God independently from a master design with variations suitable for each group of organisms, according to its mode of life.

b) *Development of Vertebra.* The vertebra of crossopterygian bony fish and some of the earliest amphibians, the so-called arch vertebrae (*see* I.2.5.2.b), consisted of a large anterior, medium wedge-shaped element that was incomplete dorsally, termed *intercentrum* (hypocentrum), and two smaller, intersegmental, posteriodorsal elements called *pleurocentra* (Figure 2.10). This configuration is also termed *rachitomous*.

The various types of vertebrae found in the different groups of vertebrates has been compared and schemes constructed to show possible evolutionary relationships. Figure 2.33 shows one possible evolutionary sequence of the vertebra from crossopterygians and amphibians to modern amniotes. The main line of evolution seems to involve the progressive reduction of the hypocentrum accompanied by the progressive enlargement of the pleurocentrum until finally the pleurocentrum takes over completely in the higher forms.

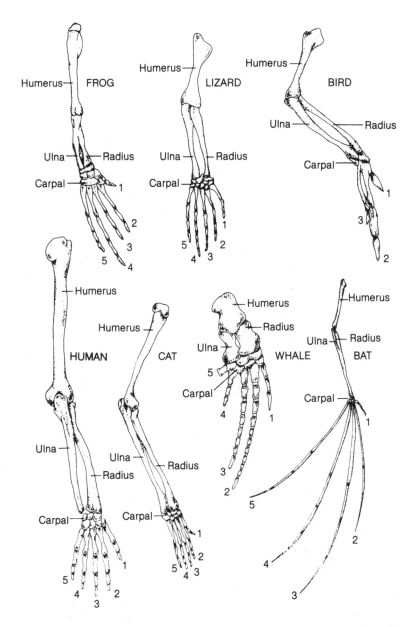

Figure 2.32. The bones of the forelimbs of a frog, lizard, bird, human, cat, whale, and bat, showing the arrangement of the homologous bones in these superficially different structures. Adapted, with permission, from Villee, C. A. Biology. 7th ed. Philadelphia: W. B. Saunders Co.; 1977. © 1977 by the W. B. Saunders Co.

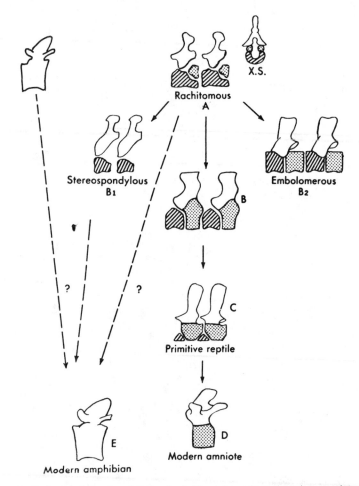

Figure 2.33. Comparison of vertebrae of primitive tetrapods and modern amniotes. The rachitomous type (shown also in cross section, X.S.) occurred in crossopterygians and in the earliest amphibians. *B* is from a labyrinthodont in the reptile line. *B1* and *B2* are from other labyrinthodonts. Whether the modern amphibian centrum represents a hypocentrum (diagonal lines) or a pleurocentrum (stippled) is not certain. The unmarked part of the vertebra is the neural arch. Adapted, with permission, from Kent, G. C. 4th ed. Comparative anatomy of the vertebrates. St. Louis: C. V. Mosby Co.; 1978.

Vertebral changes for *Stereospondyli* and *Embolomeri,* two extinct suborders of primitive amphibians, follow a different pathway. In *Stereospondyli* the pleurocentrum is lost, and the hypocentrum takes over completely. In *Embolomeri* both the hypocentrum and pleurocentrum are retained, each expanding to equal size (Figure 2.33).

134

The vertebral structure of modern amphibians, however, poses an interesting question to the evolutionists. It is the so-called husk-type vertebra and consists of a single structure somewhat spooled in shape and often pierced lengthwise in the upper part for the passage of the notochord. This type of vertebra was also shared by the extinct primitive amphibian subclass *Lepospondyli*, which existed during the Paleozoic time (Figure 2.10a, b). Since the commonly accepted sequence of vertebrate evolution is crossopterygian to amphibian and labyrinthodonts to modern tetrapods, it is difficult to see how the modern amphibian could have evolved in light of the similarities of its vertebra with an extinct subclass of primitive amphibian that did not enter the main stream of tetrapod evolution (1). (*See* discussion on fish-amphibian transition in I.2.2.2.) Therefore, the evolutionary interpretation of the vertebra is somewhat unsatisfactory.

c) *Evolution of the Heart.* The circulatory systems of all vertebrates are very similar. The principal differences reside in the heart. Figure 2.34 shows the heart structure of the fish, frog, reptile, bird, and mammal.

The fish heart is composed of four chambers aligned in series (linear configuration): sinus venosus, atrium, ventricle, and conus (Figure 2.34a). Veins collecting blood from the body drain into the sinus venosus. The contraction of the atrium and ventricle forces the blood into the ventral aorta that leads into the gills. Gas exchange occurs in the gills, and the now-oxygenated blood is distributed to the body via the dorsal aorta. Blood is circulated through the heart once during a gas-exchange cycle. The fish's blood circulation is presumably less efficient than that of land animals because blood passes only once through the heart for each complete cycle through the body. However, since the rate of exchange of dissolved oxygen in the water with the carbon dioxide in the blood is slow due to the meager solubility of oxygen in water, the linear configuration of the heart functions well for the fish.

The amphibian heart has a left and a right atrium separated by a partition (Figure 2.34b). Venous blood enters the ventricle via the right atrium, whereas blood oxygenated in the lungs enters the ventricle via the left atrium. There is a tendency for the oxygenated and less oxygenated venous blood to mix in the ventricle. However, venous blood from the right atrium tends to enter the ventricle first and is followed by the oxygenated blood from the left atrium. A spiral valve in the conus helps to guide the less oxygenated blood into the pulmonary arteries upon initial ventricular contraction. Continued ventricular contraction forces the more oxygenated blood into the aorta. The aorta then carries the oxygenated blood into the different parts of the body while the pulmonary

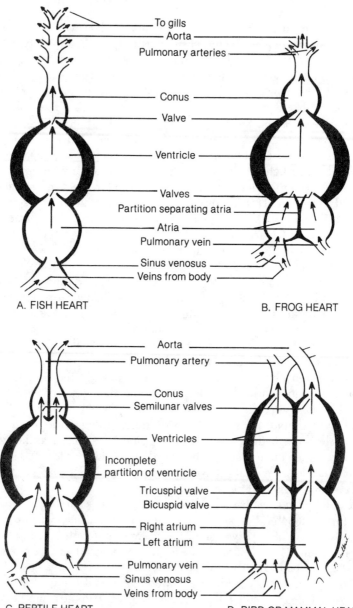

Figure 2.34. Diagram comparing the structures of vertebrate hearts. Adapted, with permission, from Villee, C. A. Biology. 7th ed. Philadelphia: W. B. Saunders Co.; 1977. © 1977 by the W. B. Saunders Co.

arteries deliver the blood to the lungs for gas exchange. Blood is returned to the left atrium via the pulmonary vein.

In the amphibian the circulatory system is more advanced than in the fish because contractions of the heart can deliver the less oxygenated blood to the lungs while pumping the more oxygenated blood through the aorta to the body tissues. Due to the mixing effect in the ventricle, a red blood cell could pass through the heart several times before completing a gas exchange cycle in the lungs. However, the respiratory capacity of the thin, moist amphibian skin helps to compensate for failure of all the deoxygenated blood to be shunted to the lungs after the first pass through the heart. Thus, the lungs and thin skin enable the amphibian to exist on land and in the water.

In reptiles a more efficient circulatory-gas exchange system is needed because of the thick cornified skin that prevents any significant skin respiration. Most reptiles have a partial partition in the ventricle so that the mixing effect of oxygenated and deoxygenated blood can be minimized (Figure 2.34c). Alligators and crocodiles have the thickest and most cornified skin and possess a complete ventricular partition. In all reptiles the sinus venosus is less prominent than in the amphibians.

Birds and mammals have the most specialized hearts with two atria and two ventricles; each chamber is completely separated from the others by thick muscular walls (Figure 2.34d). In contrast with the reptiles, the conus and sinus venosus are absent. Oxygenated and deoxygenated blood never mix. Deoxygenated blood enters the right atrium and passes to the right ventricle. It then goes to the lungs, is oxygenated, and returns to the left atrium. The blood then passes to the left ventricle and enters the systemic circulation via the aorta. The circulatory pattern is an efficient high-pressure system. This may account for the high metabolic rate in both birds and mammals and the maintenance of a regulated body temperature.

Evolutionists have attributed the development of the structural differences in vertebrate hearts to the creative role of natural selection, a process that selects genes that can produce the structures best adapted to the mode of living of each group of organisms. Alternatively, these structural patterns, reflecting a common design with variation, can equally be attributed to a divine Creator.

d) *Vestigial or Rudimentary Organs.* Many apparently functionless structures in advanced animals and plants are thought to be the remnants of once useful organs that have fallen into disuse because of natural selection. These structures are assumed to be in the process of being eliminated. At one point, there were thought to be up to 180 vestigial organs in

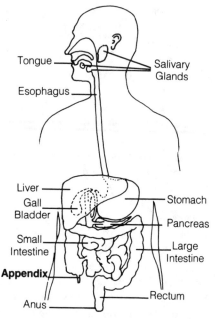

Figure 2.35. The appendix in the human digestive system.

humans alone; however, the number has been dwindling as the functions of these organs are slowly being discovered.

The most frequently cited vestigial organ in humans is the vermiform appendix (Figure 2.35). It can be surgically removed without any apparent ill effect to the body. However, there are good indications from the studies of the appendix in rabbits that this organ functions as part of the immune system. In one experiment using the rabbit, total body irradiation with shielding of the appendix resulted in restoration of normal antibody synthesis after a short initial lag of three to four days, whereas the irradiation on the appendix alone did not affect the antibody synthesizing capacity of the rabbits (2) (Figure 2.36). Appendectomy alone induced a slight suppression in antibody synthesis thought to be insignificant. Another set of experiments suggested that the appendix in rabbits may be responsible for the recovery of their capacity to manufacture blood-bound lympthocytes after neonatal thymectomy (3).

The structure of the appendix in rabbits is quite different from that in humans. However, it is reasonable to assume that the vermiform appendix in humans probably also has the function of a lymphoid tissue that is responsible for the replenishment of a damaged immune system. After all, most concepts in immunology are derived first from animal studies

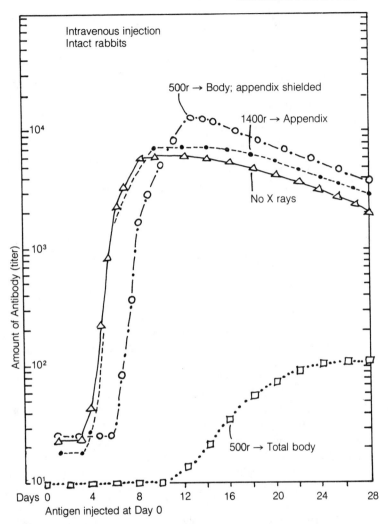

Figure 2.36. Mean antibody curves, showing the effect of shielding of irradiation of the appendix as compared to totally irradiated and nonirradiated rabbits. Note the complete protection to peak titer by appendix-shielding as compared to the nonirradiated rabbits. Adapted, with permission, from Sussdorf, D. M.; Draper, L. R. Journal of Infectious Diseases. 99:135; 1956. The University of Chicago Press.

before they are found to be applicable to humans. Therefore, the appendix in humans is probably an important secondary source of the immune response, and it cannot be treated as a useless vestigial organ without considering this possibility.

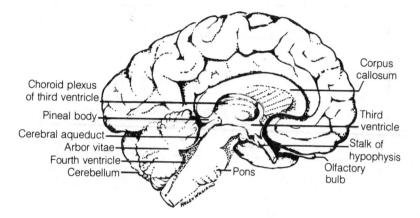

Figure 2.37. Human brain, left half, sagittal section. Reprinted, with permission, from Francis, C. C.; Martin, A. H. Introduction to human anatomy. 7th ed. St. Louis: C. V. Mosby Co.; 1975.

The pineal body in humans (Figure 2.37) was once thought of as a vestige of the mid-dorsal third eye found in the skull of extinct primitive chordates. It is now known that the pineal body is responsible in living primitive vertebrates for the synthesis of the hormone melatonin (4) that regulates the distribution of skin pigments. In mammals, however, it functions in the regulation of sex-hormone secretion. Studies of the time-measuring system of the sparrow indicate that the pineal body seems to affect the parts of the brain that may be involved in some aspect of the biological rhythm phenomenon (5). Thus, the pineal gland has been shown to be far from functionless in the body of vertebrates.

The plica semilunaris in humans (Figure 2.38) and other mammals, regarded as a vestigial structure of the nictitating membrane or third eyelid in birds, was found to be structurally and functionally different from the nictitating membrane (6). This fold in the human eye may serve as an added protective barrier to bar foreign substances from entering the eye. The sticky mass formed in the corner of the eye may be formed by the fatty substance secreted by the plica semilunaris to trap dirt, preventing it from damaging the eye.

The vestigial coccygeal vertebrae (Figure 2.39) of the coccyx in humans seems to serve the function of helping to support the abdominal viscera in light of its being bent forward toward the abdomen. It is also possible that the coccyx provides attachment for a muscle that controls the process of elimination of feces.

The status of other structures formerly thought to be vestigial is now

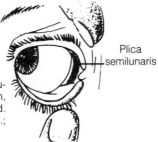

Figure 2.38. Plica semilunaris in humans. Reprinted, with permission, from Villee, C. A. Biology. 7th ed. Philadelphia: W. B. Saunders Co.; 1977. © 1977 W. B. Saunders Co.

Plica semilunaris

being challenged, including human male nipples, tonsils, and certain portions of the whale skeleton. The interpretation that the nipples in the human male are inherited from an ancestor in which they were functional is being questioned (6). The tonsils were once considered useless but are now known as part of the lymphoid mass that traps infectious agents (7, 8). Another doubted claim deals with the existence in whales of transitory teeth and small bones embedded in the flesh, the bones supposedly corresponding to the pelvis, femur, and tibia. However, the conclusion cannot be made from this evidence that the whale descended from a tetrapod ancestor with functional teeth and a normal skeletal structure (6). Some of these structures in the whale are believed to be important in the animal's developmental process.

In summary, although there are still body structures in higher animals and plants that appear to serve little if any function, further research is likely to show the importance of many of these structures. In order to demonstrate the vestigial nature of many structures with unknown func-

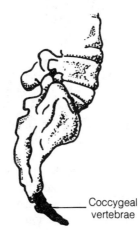

Figure 2.39. Coccygeal vertebrae in humans. Reprinted, with permission, from Villee, C. A. Biology. 7th ed. © 1977 W. B. Saunders Co.

Coccygeal vertebrae

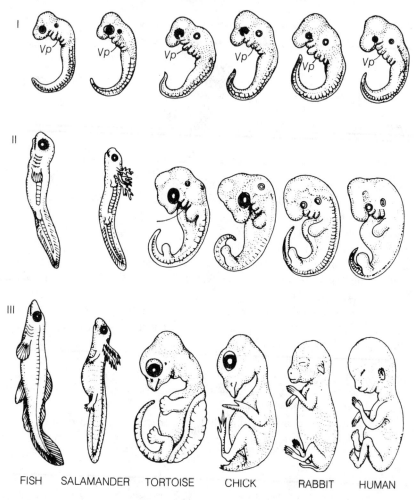

Figure 2.40. A comparison of vertebrate embryos at three stages of development. *Vp* (Visceral pouch). From Romanes, G. G. Darwin after Darwin. Open Court Publishing Co.; 1910.

tions in the higher forms of life, evolutionists are obliged to provide evidence that will link these structures to the *exact* counterpart that *was* functional in the presumed ancestors. At the same time they must establish the *functionless* status of the structures at present. The challenge as yet has not been well heeded, and the correlations often cited are tentative. Another interpretation of vestigial organs is that the basic homology in structure and the varying function of these organs indicates they were constructed (created) on the same fundamental plan for the different habitats where the organisms adapted.

2.5.3 *Comparative Embryological Development.* Modern embryology can be traced to the first systematic presentation of the characteristic development of animal embryos by Karl Ernst von Baer (1792–1876), who was a critic of the theory of evolution. His classical *Von Baer's law* (9) can be summarized as follows: (1) general characters appear in development before special characters appear; (2) the less general and then the specialized characters appear from the general characters; (3) as an animal develops, its appearance becomes progressively different from the form of other animals; (4) young or embryonic stages of an animal are very much alike, but the adult animals are different (Figure 2.40).

Muller (10) and Haeckel (11) incorporated von Baer's observation into what is known as the *biogenetic law.* The essence of this law is the assumption that ontogeny (the embryological development of an individual) recapitulates phylogeny (the evolutionary ancestry of the individual). In other words the embryo undergoes morphological changes that resemble the adult forms of its evolutionary ancestors. Muller cited as evidence of this thesis observations on the development of crustaceans (10). The larval forms of several stages of crustaceans closely resemble the adults in a sequence from primitive to advanced. The larvae were found to pass through these stages at successive molts, with larvae of primitive crustaceans stopping early in the series and advanced forms going through most of the stages.

This interpretation of the biogenetic law is not borne out, however, by subsequent observations. Most of the developmental stages in the embryo in higher organisms do *not* resemble the adult forms of their presumed evolutionary ancestors. Many of the presumed stages in the evolutionary lineages are missing in ontogeny. In fact, some of the presumed evolutionary sequence was observed to be reversed in ontogeny. For example, teeth were supposed to be developed from modified scales and were probably needed for biting before the tongue evolved. However, in mammalian embryos the tongue develops before the teeth (12).

Extensive studies in echinoderm embryology also suggested that the differences in the larval stages actually have adaptive values, for they contribute directly to the various distinctive features of the adult forms (13). In other words, the developmental stages resemble their adult stages more than the adult stages resemble their presumed ancestors (14). Therefore, the embryological development of each organism has more to do with the preparation for its own adult life than with the recapitulation of its phylogeny. The visceral pouches (pharyngeal clefts) of the embryos of reptiles, birds, and mammals closely resemble those of the fishes (Stage I, Figure 2.40) but they actually have no relationship with the gill slits of the adult fish that developed from these embryonic structures. In half of the vertebrates, none of the pouches ever bear gills. In the other half, gills develop only from some of the posterior pouches. No true internal gills are present in any vertebrate at the embryonic stage in which the pharyngeal clefts are seen (15).

In light of these difficulties, the biogenetic law has been reinterpreted to state that embryonic stages resemble *embryonic stages* of the ancestral forms and only incidentally do they resemble adult forms. This has reduced the law to barely stating the obvious since all vertebrate embryos are known to undergo essentially similar processes of earlier development that lead to the morphological similarities in Stage I (Figure 2.40). This pattern of development must be important to the subsequent adult life before differentiation of the tissues can occur. Consequently, theories of design *or* evolution are equally applicable to this evidence.

References 2.5

1. Romer, A. S. Vertebrate paleontology. Chicago: Univ. Chicago Press; 1966: 79.
2. Sussdorf, D. H.; Draper, L. R. J. Infect. Dis. 99:129; 1956.
3. Archer, O. K.; Sutherland, D. R.; Good, R. A. Nature. 200:337; 1963.
4. Wurtman, R. J.; Axelrod, J. A. Sc. Am. 213 (July):54; 1965.
5. Gaston, S.; Menaker, M. Science. 160 (June 7):1125; 1968.
6. Thompson, W. R. Introduction to the origin of species by C. Darwin. London: J. M. Dent and Sons; 1956: XIV.
7. Kent, G. C. Comparative anatomy of the vertebrate. 3rd ed. St. Louis: Mosby; 1973: 281.
8. Barrett, J. T. Textbook of Immunology. 2nd ed. St. Louis: Mosby; 1974: 65.
9. Von Baer, K. E. Uber Entwicklungsgeschichte der Tiere, Beobachtung und Reflexion. Konigsberg; 1828.
10. Muller, F. Fur Darwin. Leipzig; 1864.
11. Hackel, E. Naturliche Schopfungsgeschichte. Berlin; 1868.
12. DeBeer, G. Embryos and ancestors. 3rd ed. London: Oxford Univ. Press; 1958: 7.
13. Foll, H. B. Biograph. Rev. 23:81; 1948.
14. Olson, E. C. The evolution of life. London: Weidenfeld & Nicholson, 1965; reviewed by DeBeer, G. Nature. 206 (April 24):331; 1965.
15. Ballard, W. W. Comparative anatomy and embryology. New York: Ronald; 1964: 75.

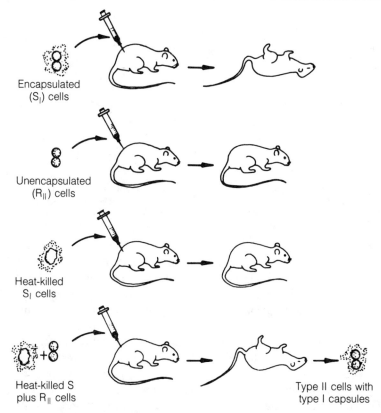

Encapsulated
(S$_I$) cells

Unencapsulated
(R$_{II}$) cells

Heat-killed
S$_I$ cells

Heat-killed S
plus R$_{II}$ cells

Type II cells with
type I capsules

Figure 2.41. Bacterial Transformation. Transformation was discovered by F. Griffith, who noted that encapsulated (smooth or S) diplococci cause a fatal infection in mice, whereas nonencapsulated (rough or R) cells do not. Heat-killed S cells are likewise harmless, except when mixed with live R cells. In the latter case, a fatal infection can occur, and live cells having capsules characteristic of the S strain are found. Reprinted, with permission, from Dyson, R. D. Cell biology, a molecular approach. 1st ed. Boston: Allyn and Bacon, Inc.; 1974.

2.6 Evidence from Molecular Biology and Genetics

2.6.1 DNA as Genetic Material. As was stated earlier (*see* I.1.4), genetic variability arising from mutation and recombination by natural selection serves as the raw material of evolution. Before the advent of molecular biology, very little was known concerning the nature and mode of action of the gene. Later, the identification of biological macromolecules in cells prompted many to explore the relationships between these substances and the Mendelian concepts (*see* I.1.3) of particulate genes.

The first experiment that paved the way for understanding the chemical

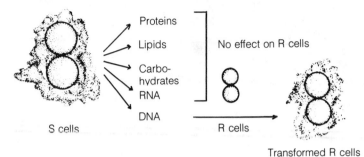

Figure 2.42. The Transforming Principle. When encapsulated diplococci were chemically fractionated, and the transformation experiment performed *in vitro* with each fraction one at a time, O. T. Avery and his colleagues found that DNA is the agent responsible for transformation. Reprinted, with permission, from Dyson, R. D. Cell biology, a molecular approach. 1st ed. Boston: Allyn and Bacon, Inc.; 1974.

nature of the gene was the discovery of *transformation* in the bacteria *Diplococcus pneumoniae* by F. Griffith in 1928 (1). The pathogenicity of the *D. pneumoniae* bacterium is associated with the existence of a *capsule*. The capsule is a slimy material that surrounds the cell and prevents phagocytosis by the white blood cells of the host organisms. A non-pathogenic strain lacks the capsule and is easily destroyed by host white blood cells. Griffith demonstrated that there were stable materials from the heat-killed pathogenic strain of *D. pneumoniae* (S form) that could be transmitted and incorporated into the nonpathogenic strain (R form). The materials could induce the latter to synthesize the capsule and thereby transform the bacterium from a nonpathogenic to a pathogenic strain (Figure 2.41). In 1944, Avery, Macleod, and McCarty (2) identified the material responsible for this genetic transformation of *D. pneumoniae* as DNA (Figure 2.42).

With the establishment of the chemical nature of the gene, the next important questions asked were (1) What is the chemical structure of DNA? and (2) How are genetic messeges encoded in DNA? The answers to these two questions were provided by J. Watson and F. Crick (3, 4) and made a great impact on modern biology. The answers opened up the new discipline of molecular biology that presently is advancing rapidly and is influencing every area of modern biological thinking.

For a chemical model to account for the functions of a gene, it must be able to show two characteristics: (1) the potential to duplicate itself with exact fidelity so that each of the daughter molecules will be a replica of itself and (2) the ability to carry coded information that specifies a particular set of traits characteristic of a certain line of descent. Watson and

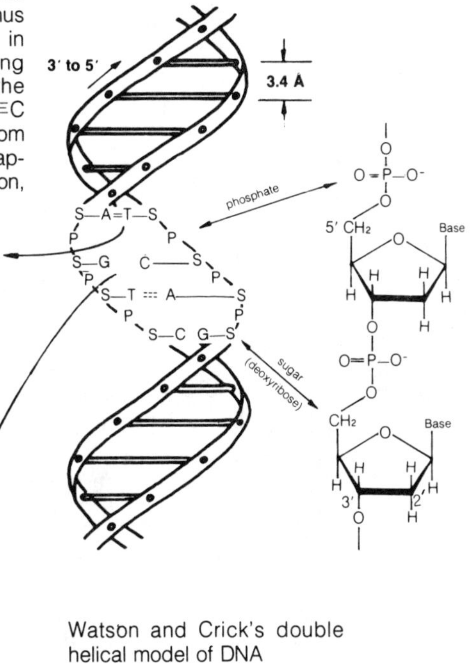

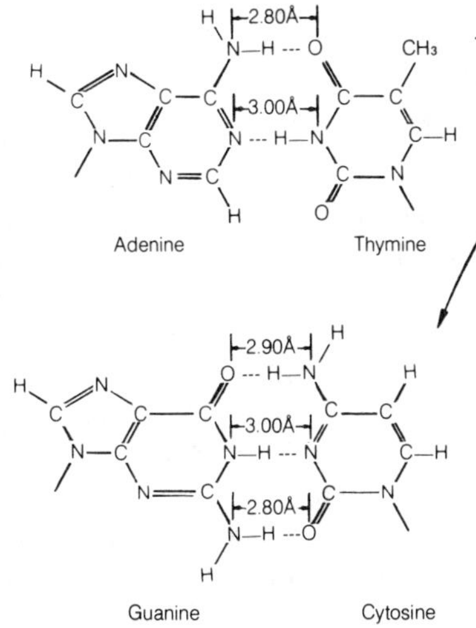

Figure 2.43. Base Pairing in DNA. A pyrimidine nucleotide (cytidine or thymidine) is always paired with a purine nucleotide (adenosine or guanosine), thus maintaining uniform overall dimensions in each pair. The hydrogen-bonding capabilities of the common form of the bases lead specifically to A═T and G≡C pairing. Reprinted, with permission, from Dyson, R. D. Cell biology, a molecular approach. 1st ed. Boston: Allyn and Bacon, Inc.; 1974.

Adenine   Thymine

Guanine   Cytosine

Watson and Crick's double helical model of DNA

Crick postulated a double helix model of DNA that satisfies both of these criteria (Figure 2.43).

The structure of the double helix (DNA) can be viewed from several levels. The first and most important level is the *bases*, namely, the pyrimidines thymine and cytosine, and the purines guanine and adenine (Figure 2.44). They can form metastable paired configurations by hydrogen bonding (i.e., adenine paired with thymine via two hydrogen bonds; guanine paired with cytosine via three hydrogen bonds) (*see* Figure 2.43). The second level is the *nucleoside*. This is the combination of a single base with a 5 carbon (pentose) sugar having a 5 membered furanose ring. The absence of an oxygen at the 2′ carbon position of the ring makes the sugar of the nucleoside deoxyribose. At the third level, there are *nucleotides* consisting of a nucleoside with an added phosphate group at the 5′ position of the sugar. The fourth level involves the joining together of nucleotides by hooking up the 5′ phosphate group of one with the 3′

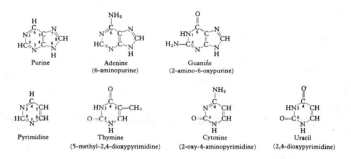

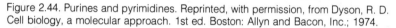

Figure 2.44. Purines and pyrimidines. Reprinted, with permission, from Dyson, R. D. Cell biology, a molecular approach. 1st ed. Boston: Allyn and Bacon, Inc.; 1974.

position on the sugar ring of another, producing a long chain of nucleotides called a polynucleotides (Figure 2.45). The fifth and highest level involves two adjacent polynucleotide chains bound together by a long series of hydrogen bonds between the complementary bases forming a double helical structure.

The double helical structure of DNA can readily account for replication. As soon as the double helix unwinds and separates, each strand serves as a template for the synthesis of the missing strand. Because of the specificity imposed on the pattern of hydrogen bonding between the adenine-thymine pair and the guanine-cytosine pair, DNA replication proceeds with high fidelity. During replication the parent strands of the DNA helix separate and a complementary daughter strand is synthesized on each parent strand. Thus two DNA molecules identical to the original molecule are produced (Figure 2.46).

2.6.2 *Gene Expression and the Genetic Code.* The action of the genetic material in an organism can be summarized in the central dogma of molecular biology: DNA→RNA→protein. The information in the DNA is transcribed into the messenger RNA that is then translated into protein (Figure 2.47).

The RNA's or ribonucleic acid transcribed from the DNA is single stranded and contains the bases adenine, guanine, and cytosine as in DNA, but a new base uracil substitutes for thymine (Figure 2.44; 2.47). Also RNA has an oxygen at the 2' position of each sugar ring (*see* Figure 2.45) that is not present in DNA. Each different RNA is transcribed on only one of the DNA strands by complementary pairing facilitated by hydrogen bonding between bases (Figure 2.47a).

There are three types of RNA that can be transcribed from the DNA: messenger RNA, transfer RNA, and ribosomal RNA. Each transfer RNA carrying an amino acid makes contact with a messenger RNA at the ribo-

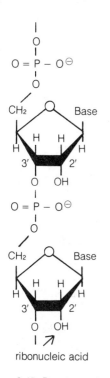
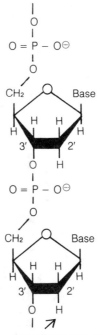

ribonucleic acid

deoxyribonucleic acid

Figure 2.45. Presence of an oxygen in the 2′ position of each sugar ring of the ribonucleic acid as contrasted with deoxyribonucleic acid.

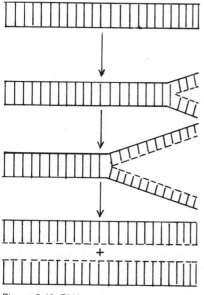

Intact DNA double helix. The two horizontal lines represent the sugar phosphate backbone. The vertical lines represent hydrogen bonding between complimentary bases (see Figure 2.43).

DNA unwinds and separates. New DNA (---) is synthesized using the unwound strand of the parental DNA as a template.

Two daughter DNA double helices with one strand contributed by the parental molecule and one newly synthesized strand.

Figure 2.46. DNA replication.

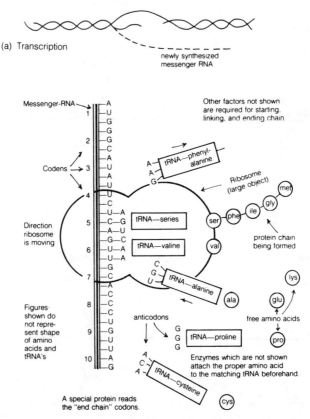

(a) Transcription

newly synthesized
messenger RNA

(b) *Messenger-RNA being translated into protein as it is traversed by a ribosome*

Figure 2.47. Transcription and translation. As each codon or triplet of letters is read, a transfer-RNA molecule approaches which has an anticodon that will base-pair with those letters. This tRNA carries its matching amino acid which has been attached to it by its interpreter enzyme. As the tRNA is processed by the ribosome, the amino acid is joined onto the forming protein chain in the order called for by the mRNA sequence of code letters, which in turn was transcribed shortly before from the DNA master copy. This complex process takes place with fantastic speed and precision, and is remarkably similar in all living things known, from amebas to human beings. Recent evidence indicates that both transcription and replication may often be associated with cell membranes, including the *endoplasmic reticulum.* Adapted, with permission, from Coppedge, J. F. Evolution: possible or impossible? Grand Rapids, MI: Zondervan Publishing House; 1973.

some through base pairing of a triplet base sequence (codon) of the messenger RNA and a complimentary sequence (anticodon) of the transfer RNA (Figure 2.47b). Peptide bonds are formed between adjacent amino acids at the ribosomal level. By a process of translocation or the movement of the ribosome along the messenger RNA, each successive codon of the messenger RNA binds with another transfer RNA that loses its amino acid to the growing amino acid polypeptide chain through peptide bond formation.

By the elegant experiments of Nirenberg and Mattaei (5); Nishimura, Jones, and Khorana (6); and others, the genetic code was deciphered. The 20 amino acids present in proteins (Table 2.15) are specified by 64 triplet *code* words in DNA. These code words pass on the information via the *codons* in the messenger RNA and the *anticodons* in the transfer RNA, thereby specifying the amino acid sequence of the gene product. Since there are more code words than amino acids, a phenomenon known as degeneracy was observed, i.e., each amino acid is specified by more than one code word. Table 2.16 lists all the possible combinations of the triplet codons on the messenger RNA and the corresponding amino acids they specify.

There are also *initiation* and *termination* codons that are involved in the punctuation of the genetic message. The initiation codons GUG and AUG specify a particular amino acid named N-formylmethionine, which starts every polypeptide chain. However, when GUG and AUG are found in the middle of a polypeptide message, they specify instead valine and methionine, respectively. The termination or nonsense codons are the UAA, UAG, and UGA codons that specify no amino acids. Thus the polypeptide chain falls off the ribosome as soon as it reaches one of these codons. Delimitated by the initiation and the termination codons, a gene is defined as the number of consecutive triplet codes on the DNA that determines the primary sequence of a polypeptide chain—the so-called one-gene, one-polypeptide concept. This concept has been well documented in the genetic systems of bacteria and bacterial viruses and has provided modern biologists with the first operational tool to examine the interaction of genes.

The genetic code is probably universally applicable. The codons UUU, AAA, and CCC have been found to specify phenylalanine, lysine, and proline, respectively, in cell extracts prepared from a variety of different organisms ranging from bacteria to mammals (7). Purified messenger RNA encoding the protein hemoglobin extracted from rabbits was shown to be able to direct the synthesis of rabbit hemoglobin in frog oocytes, suggesting the codons in rabbits and frogs are translated the same way (8).

The apparent universality of the genetic code has been cited as evidence that all living organisms arose from a single origin. After the early evolution of the genetic code in organisms, it is thought to have remained constant over a long period while other features of the organisms diverged

Table 2.15. The common amino acids.*†

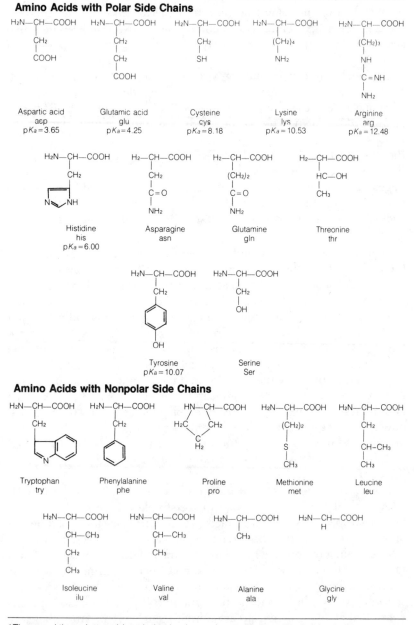

Amino Acids with Polar Side Chains

Aspartic acid
asp
$pK_a = 3.65$

Glutamic acid
glu
$pK_a = 4.25$

Cysteine
cys
$pK_a = 8.18$

Lysine
lys
$pK_a = 10.53$

Arginine
arg
$pK_a = 12.48$

Histidine
his
$pK_a = 6.00$

Asparagine
asn

Glutamine
gln

Threonine
thr

Tyrosine
$pK_a = 10.07$

Serine
Ser

Amino Acids with Nonpolar Side Chains

Tryptophan
try

Phenylalanine
phe

Proline
pro

Methionine
met

Leucine
leu

Isoleucine
ilu

Valine
val

Alanine
ala

Glycine
gly

*The usual three-letter abbreviation is given, along with the pK_a of side chain groups that may carry significant charge at physiological pH.

†NOTE: Reproduced, with permission, from Dyson, R. D. Cell biology, a molecular approach. 1st ed. Boston: Allyn and Bacon, Inc.; 1974.

in subsequent evolution. However, the constancy of the evolution of the genetic code may be challenged if examples of discrepancy are discovered in future research. The presence of odd guanosine triphosphate at the 5' end and polyadenosine monophosphate at the 3' end of the eucaryotic messenger RNA with obscure functions may suggest that there are new mechanisms of the expression of the genetic code yet to be discovered (9). Alternatively, the universality of the code could be attributed to a Creator's master design that enables all living organisms to operate under a similar set of physiological conditions.

Proteins are ubiquitous components in the cell. They serve as the building blocks of cellular structure, and in the form of enzymes they also catalyze chemical reactions in the metabolic pathways of the cell. The

Table 2.16. The genetic code.*†

5' BASE	MIDDLE BASE				3' BASE
	U	C	A	G	
U	UUU } Phe UUC UUA } Leu UUG	UCU UCC } Ser UCA UCG	UAU } Tyr UAC UAA ochre UAG amber	UGU } Cys UGC UGA opal UGG Try	U } pyramidines C A } purines G
C	CUU CUC } Leu CUA CUG	CCU CCC } Pro CCA CCG	CAU } His CAC CAA CAG Gln	CGU CGC } Arg CGA CGG	U C A G
A	AUU AUC } Ile AUA AUG* Met	ACU ACC } Thr ACA ACG	AAU } Asn AAC AAA } Lys AAG	AGU } Ser AGC AGA } Arg AGG	U C A G
G	GUU GUC } Val GUA GUG*	GCU GCC } Ala GCA GCG	GAU } Asn GAC GAA } Glu GAG	GGU GGC } Gly GGA GGG	U C A G

*Note that in all cases but two (Try, Met), the third position may be occupied by either of the two purines or either of the two pyrimidines without changing the coding specificity. The terminator codons—UAA, UAG, and UGA—stop amino acid incorporation and free the growing polypeptide chain. (The names ochre, amber, and opal refer to the mutant bacterial strains in which the action of these terminators were first studied.) Chain initiation begins with AUG or GUG, marked with an asterisk (*), either of which can code (in procaryotes) for N-formylmethionine in addition to the amino acid shown for it.

153

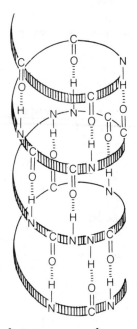

Figure 2.48. The alpha helix maintained by intrachain hydrogen bonding.

functions of proteins are controlled by their structure that can be described at four levels: primary, secondary, tertiary, and quarternary.

The primary structure is the linear sequence of amino acids that are joined together by peptide bonds to form a polypeptide chain. There are 20 naturally occurring amino acids in the living world—11 that are charged ionic forms (those with polar side chains) and 9 that are neutral (those with nonpolar side chains) under physiological conditions (Table 2.15). Each species of protein has a unique amino acid sequence that essentially determines its secondary, tertiary, and quarternary structure. One type of secondary structure is the α helix configuration of a polypeptide chain (Figure 2.48) (the envelope in Figure 2.49) formed by *intrachain* hydrogen bonding. The tertiary structure is the apparent globular shape of the polypeptide in solution when it coils together by intrachain, mostly noncovalent forces between amino acid side chains. Proteins with more than one polypeptide chain have quarternary structure, each chain being a subunit. The position of each subunit is stabilized by noncovalent forces between chains (Figure 2.49). Hemoglobin (Figure 2.49), the oxygen-carrying protein in vertebrate red blood cells, has a quarternary structure consisting of two α and two β chains.

The function of any protein depends on the nature of its three-dimensional structure that is a reflection of the tertiary and quarternary

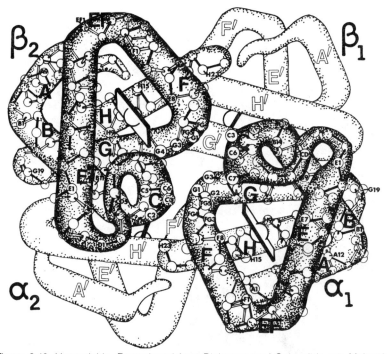

Figure 2.49. Hemoglobin. Reproduced from Dickerson and Geis, slide set, Molecular structure of protein. By permission from Dr. Richard E. Dickerson, Department of Chemistry, California Institute of Technology, Pasadena.

structure state. This can best be understood by the lock-and-key theory of enzyme function. The theory states that each enzyme (all enzymes are proteins) has a specific configuration that fits the substrate (Figure 2.50). If the functional three-dimensional structure of the enzyme is destroyed, the reaction catalyzed by the enzyme does not take place.

Many inheritable phenotypic traits can be attributed to abnormal structure of a single protein. The frequently cited example of a congenital disease is sickle cell anemia (*see* I.3.2.1.c). This disease is caused by the replacement of a single amino acid in the sixth position of the β chain of hemoglobin. This replacement distorts the three-dimensional structure of hemoglobin and causes the stacking of adjacent molecules in such a way that the red blood cells carrying these distorted hemoglobins will become sickle shaped and clump together in the absence of oxygen (Figure 2.51). The sickle red blood cells last only half as long as normal cells, and clumping of the sickle cells causes severe damage in vital organs. Therefore, sickle cell anemic patients seldom live beyond 30 years of age. This

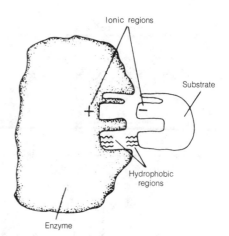

Figure 2.50. Enzyme-Substrate Interaction. According to the lock-and-key theory, enzyme and substrate have complementary configurations. In this diagram, matching spatial conformations permit ionic and hydrophobic interactions to take place between the enzyme and its specific substrate. Reprinted, with permission, from Dyson, R. D. Cell Biology, a molecular approach. 1st ed. Boston: Allyn and Bacon, Inc.; 1974.

Figure 2.51. Photomicrograph of normal (dislike) and sickle (crescent-shaped) blood cells. Reprinted, with permission, from Lehninger, A. L. Biochemistry. 2nd ed. New York: Worth; 1975. Reprinted by permission from Walter Dawn, National Audubon Society, New York.

has been called a *molecular disease* since the cause can be traced to the distortion of a single molecule induced by a simple amino acid replacement.

The production of enzymatic proteins is known to be a delicately regulated cellular process. The best-documented case of this type of gene expression is that of the *operon* model, which has been demonstrated in bacterial systems. An operon is a composite of several genes, usually clustering together in the bacterial chromosome and involved in similar functions. These genes are regulated by a single operator gene as the result of its interaction with the product of a regulatory gene.

EVIDENCE FOR EVOLUTION

The *OPERON* Model
OPERON: A single operator switches on a sequence of genes and it and the structural genes it controls comprise an integrated unit as both the physical and functional levels.

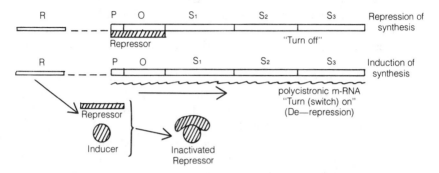

Figure 2.52. The Jacob-Monod operon model for control of the synthesis of lactose-metabolizing enzymes. The repressor produced by the regulator gene *(R)* normally binds to the operator gene *(O)* and stops the transcription of the structural genes (S₁, S₂, S₃) by blocking the RNA polymerase from binding to the promoter gene *(P)*. In the presence of the inducer (lactose), the repressor is bound by it, and a conformational change takes place that inactivates the repressor from binding to the operator gene. Transcription of the structural genes gives rise to polycistronic messenger RNA (m-RNA) that is a continuous piece of RNA spanning across several genes. This m-RNA is then translated to form the three enzymes required before lactose can be used as an energy source.

The best exemplified system of the operon is the *lactose operon* of the colon bacteria *Escherichia coli* (10) (Figure 2.52). The lactose operon is composed of three consecutive structural genes, each coding for a different enzyme: β galactosidase that hydrolyzes the sugar lactose to galactose and glucose, galactoside permease that enables the galactose sugar to enter the cell, and galactoside acetylase that puts an acetyl group on the galactoside. The expression of these structural genes depends on the action of three other genes, namely, the regulator gene that synthesizes a protein repressor; the operator gene to which the repressor protein binds; and the promotor gene on which RNA polymerase (the enzyme responsible for the transcription of the structural genes into RNA) binds and starts RNA synthesis.

The intriguing feature of this model is that the structural genes are expressed only when the operator gene is not bound by the repressor molecule. This can be brought about when an inducer, namely, lactose, is present and combines with the repressor to inactivate it. The enzymes encoded by the structural genes can thereby be synthesized and the inducer metabolized. As the lactose concentration decreases, more repressor is freed to interact with the operator gene again and shut off the transcription of the structural genes. The repressor molecule has been isolated and identified. It is a so-called allosteric protein that can undergo changes in its three-dimensional structure when it is combined with small molecules such as lactose. The altered configuration of the repressor molecule accounts for the inability of the repressor to bind to the operator gene.

Thirty-one operons have been identified in the *E. coli* linkage map (11); therefore, the operon model is one of the very important modes of regulation in bacteria. Some of these operons may act in ways different from that of the lactose operon. However, all of them involve the action of regulator and operator genes on the structural genes. Whether the operon mechanism exists in eucaryotes is not known. Understanding the gene expression control mechanisms is difficult because the eucaryotic chromosome is a complex structure consisting of chromosomal proteins and chromosomal RNA and DNA. Some data, though limited, suggest that a type of operon exists (12). Mutation in regulator genes in the eucaryotic chromosomes are thought by some to be the raw material for molecular evolution. This concept will be considered further in the following section.

2.6.3 *Molecular Principles of Mutation.* There are six distinguishable kinds of molecular mutations caused by changes in the DNA (13) (Figure 2.53).

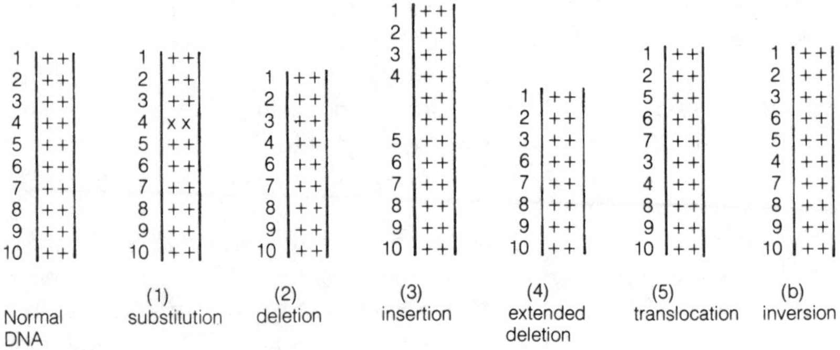

Figure 2.53. Six distinguishable kinds of molecular mutation. (++), normal base pairs; (xx), substituted base pairs. See text for explanation.

1. Substitution of one or several nucleotides
2. Nucleotide deletion
3. Insertion of one or several nucleotides followed by restoration of sugar-phosphate bonds in DNA

4. Removal of a segment of the polynucleotide chain (extended deletion)
5. Excision of a DNA segment and insertion of the segment at a different site (translocation)
6. Excision of a DNA segment and reinsertion of the segment at the same site of removal but with an 180° rotation (inversion)

a) *Nucleotide Substitution.* Even though there are six types of molecular mutations, it is likely that only nucleotide substitution is important in evolution. Most spontaneous mutations fall into this category. Many spontaneous mutations have little if any adverse effect on organisms, and sometimes they may even impart selective advantage.

Two ways that nucleotide substitutions come about is through *transversion* and *transition* (Figure 2.54). Transversion is the replacement of a pyrimidine with a purine or a purine with a pyrimidine. Transition is the replacement of a pyrimidine with a pyrimidine or a purine with a purine. Several mechanisms can account for these phenomena.

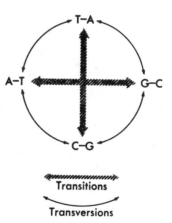

Figure 2.54. Classes of nucleotide replacement. When a mutation substitutes one nucleotide for another in a strand, at the next replication the new nucleotide is paired to its regular partner. The resulting pair is represented. Example: if in the upper TA pair, T is replaced by C, the result is the lower CG pair. Note that each base pair can undergo one kind of transition and two kinds of transversions. Reprinted, with permission, Davis, B. D. et al. Microbiology. Hagerstown, MD: Harper & Row, Publishers; 1973.

(1) *Tautomeric Shift.* Depending on the pH ($-\log[H^+]$) of the medium, the bases in the DNA can exist as two or more forms by internal rearrangement of hydrogen atoms. The process of internal rearrangement is called *tautomerization.* For example, thymine normally exists in the keto form, allowing it to pair with adenine. Occasionally, tautomerization produces the enol form of thymine allowing it to pair with guanine instead (Figure 2.55). If tautomeric shift of thymine occurs during a round of DNA replication, the resulting daughter strand of DNA will have acquired a guanine in place of adenine. This is a transition mutation.

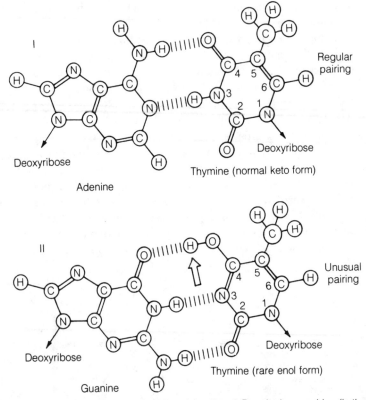

Figure 2.55. Regular and unusual base pairing of thymine. *I*. Regular base pairing (in the common keto form) with adenine. *II*. Base pairing (in the rare enol form) with guanine. The heavy arrow in *II* indicates the displacement of the proton in the tautomerization of thymine. Reprinted, with permission, Davis, B. D. et al. Microbiology. Hagerstown, MD: Harper & Row, Publishers; 1973.

(2) *Base Deamination*. Many side products or intermediates of cellular metabolism, such as peroxides, nitrous acid, formaldehyde, and purine analogues, may be mutagenic and can cause transition mutation. For example, nitrous acid can deaminate adenine, cytosine, and guanine to hypoxanthine, uracil, and xanthine, respectively (Figure 2.56). Hypoxanthine and uracil pair with different bases than adenine and cytosine. Deamination of guanine does not affect the pairing specificity.

(3) *Mutator Gene Effect*. There is a mutation in the bacteria *E. coli* and *Salmonella typhimurium* that causes an increase in the spontaneous mutation rate for all detectable genetic loci by a factor of 100 to 1000. A region of DNA called the *mutator gene* is responsible for this event (14).

The mutations caused by the mutator locus are all transversion mutations. The product of the bacterial mutator gene has not been identified, but a similar mutator gene in the bacterial virus coliphage T4 (15) has been known to produce DNA polymerase, the enzyme responsible for the replication process of DNA. Thus, a mutation in the mutator locus apparently alters the behavior of DNA polymerase in such a way that the

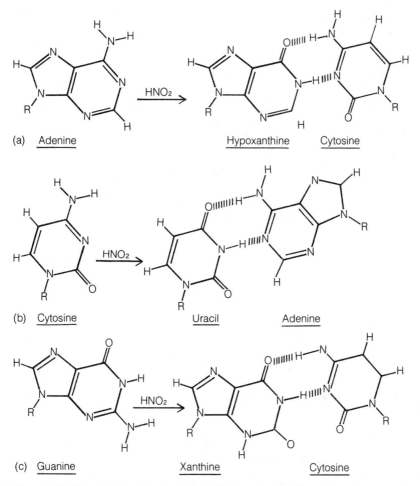

Figure 2.56. The oxidative deamination of DNA by nitrous acid, and its effect on subsequent base pairing. (a) Adenine is deaminated to hypoxanthine, which bonds to cytosine instead of to thymine. (b) Cytosine is deaminated to uracil, which bonds to adenine instead of to guanine. (c) Guanine is deaminated to xanthine, which continues to bond to cytosine. R is the sugar-phosphate backbone of DNA.

fidelity of DNA replication is diminished, leading to transversions attributed to base mispairing. Although there remains a possibility that mispairing can occur in the presence of normal enzymes, it occurs at a very low rate (16).

The gene *mu* located in the third chromosome of the fruit fly *Drosophila melanogaster* may be the counterpart of the procaryotic mutator gene. It increases the rate of lethal mutations as well as mutations having morphological effects by suppressing mechanisms of chromosomal repair (17, 18).

(4) *Irradiation Effect*. Mutations caused by irradiation may occasionally be important in evolution. The best documented sources of irradiation are ultraviolet light and x-ray. Ultraviolet light is known to cause dimerization in adjacent pyrimidine bases in the DNA (Figure 2.57). The dimerized thymines will lose their pairing specificity. During subsequent DNA replication, gaps will be formed opposite to the thymine dimer in the DNA duplex that is not functional. Pairing up of the daughter duplexes may lead to recombination that will repair the gaps left by the dimers. But frequently, mistakes in base pairing may occur resulting in nucleotide substitution in the recombinant molecule (Figure 2.58). X-rays can also induce breaks in the DNA molecules as well as cross-linking within and between duplexes (Figure 2.59).

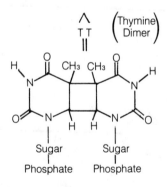

Figure 2.57. Thymine dimers produced by ultraviolet irradiation.

b) *Nucleotide Deletion*. Besides nucleotide substitutions, a few spontaneous mutations have been identified as *deletions* of DNA segments. The deletions may involve one or more genes. A good example is the tryptophan dependent *E. coli* mutants that are also resistant to T1 coliphage (16). Genetic studies indicate that the DNA of these mutants has a deletion of the segment containing the receptor site for T1 coliphage and also the genes encoding the tryptophan (an amino acid) biosynthetic

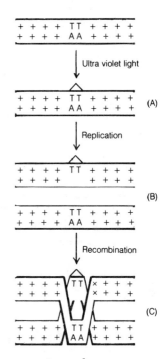

Figure 2.58. Ultraviolet-induced mutation. (A) Irradiation produces thymine dimers at random sites in the DNA molecule. (B) Replication produces a nonfunctional duplex with a gap opposite the dimer and a functional duplex from the strand with no thymine dimer. (C) Sister strand recombination reconstitutes an undamaged duplex. Base-pair changes or mutations (x x) occur as a result of errors in the recombination process. (++) are normal unmutated base pairs.

enzymes. The cause of the *E. coli* deletion mutants is not known.

2.6.4 *Interrelationship of Molecular Mutations.* It is often said that mutations are mostly harmful and are usually eliminated by selection; therefore, they cannot serve as the raw material for evolution. In most of the mutations involving drastic changes in the DNA, the mutants are lethal. Deletion, insertion, translocation, and inversion involving large segments of DNA will induce such massive alteration that all the triplet codes starting from the point of mutation will be changed, causing an

$$H_2O \xrightarrow{\text{x-ray}} H_2O^* \longrightarrow H\cdot + \cdot OH$$

$$\text{excited} \quad \text{free}$$
$$\text{state} \quad \text{radicals}$$

Figure 2.59. Possible mechanism by which cross-linking of the double helex of DNA can occur after x-ray irradiation. R_1 and R_2 are any organic molecules located on the opposite sides of the double helix. Thus a covalent linkage between R_1 and R_2 represents the cross-linking of the DNA molecule.

$$R_1H + H\cdot \longrightarrow R_1\cdot + H_2$$
$$R_1H + \cdot OH \longrightarrow R_1\cdot + H_2O$$
$$R_2H + H\cdot \longrightarrow R_2\cdot + H_2$$
$$R_2H + \cdot OH \longrightarrow R_2\cdot + H_2O$$

$$R_1 + R_2\cdot \longrightarrow R_1 + R_2$$
$$\text{covalent}$$
$$\text{cross-link}$$

163

Wild-type lysozyme	—	Thr	Lys	Ser	Pro	Ser	Leu	Asn	Ala	—
Wild-type mRNA		ACX	AAY	AGU	CCA	UCA	CUU	AAU	GCX	

Delete   Insert

| Pseudo-wild mRNA | | ACX | AAY | GUC | CAU | CAC | UUA | AUF | GCX | |
| Pseudo-wild lysozyme | — | Thr | Lys | Val | His | His | Leu | Met | Ala | — |

Figure 2.60. The effect of two compensating frame-shift mutations in the gene coding for lysozyme in the bacteriophage *T4*. Only a fraction of the messenger RNA is shown. A nucleotide deletion has occurred in the third codon, and an addition in the seventh codon. As a consequence, the amino acid sequence is changed from the third to the seventh amino acid, but the normal sequence is restored after the seventh amino acid shown. X = A, G, C, or U; Y = A or G. Reprinted, with permission, from Dobzhansky, T. et al. Evolution. San Francisco: W. H. Freeman and Co.; 1977. © 1977 W. H. Freeman and Co.

almost complete revamping of the amino acid sequence of the gene product. The mutated protein will usually be nonfunctional, and the mutants will die.

If the mutation changes only a small segment of the amino acid sequence that does not affect the function of a protein, the mutation is selectively neutral. For example, if the amino acid replaced due to nucleotide substitution has similar ionic properties as the original amino acid, the effect to the overall structure of the protein may be minimal, and the mutation will also be almost neutral.

Many potentially harmful mutations are suppressed by some interesting mechanisms. Translation mistakes can correct for mutation caused by nucleotide substitution by bringing in the right amino acid for the wrong codon, resulting in phenotypic suppression of the mutation. Finally, two mutations may restore the reading frame of the DNA and thus enable the gene product to become functional again if the segments changed by the two mutations only code for the nonessential part of the protein (Figure 2.60). Some examples that demonstrate the apparently beneficial effects of some mutations will be reviewed in the following section.

2.6.5 *Nature of Chromosomal Mutation.* Multiplication of eucaryotic cells occurs by mitosis except for production of gametes that are produced by meiosis (Figure 2.61; 2.62). During the early phases of mitosis and meiosis, chromosomes are doubled (replicated) and then become visible as the nuclear material condenses. Mitosis involves a single chromosomal separation event to assure that each daughter cell receives the same genetic material as the parent cell. In contrast, the events of meiosis

164

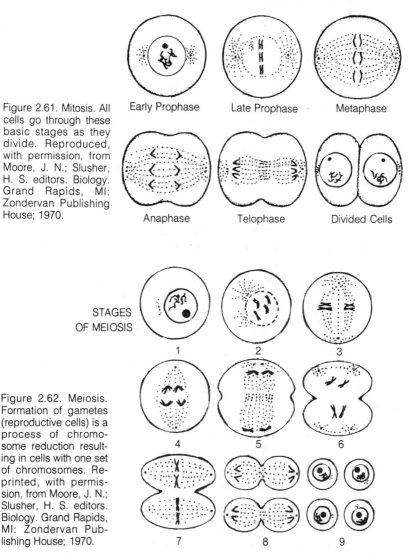

Figure 2.61. Mitosis. All cells go through these basic stages as they divide. Reproduced, with permission, from Moore, J. N.; Slusher, H. S. editors. Biology. Grand Rapids, MI: Zondervan Publishing House; 1970.

Early Prophase Late Prophase Metaphase

Anaphase Telophase Divided Cells

STAGES OF MEIOSIS

1 2 3

Figure 2.62. Meiosis. Formation of gametes (reproductive cells) is a process of chromosome reduction resulting in cells with one set of chromosomes. Reprinted, with permission, from Moore, J. N.; Slusher, H. S. editors. Biology. Grand Rapids, MI: Zondervan Publishing House; 1970.

4 5 6

7 8 9

result in genetic variability among the newly formed cells. Following the synapsis of homologous chromosomes in meiosis, chromatid arms become entwined, leading to recombination of genetic material through chance chromatid breakage and reunion with the wrong partner (Figure 1.5). This process, called crossing over, produces new genetic combinations in the daughter cells.

The process of chromosomal replication and crossing over occasionally leads to chromosomal mutations. These mutations can be classified as *structural chromosomal changes* that affect the arrangement of genes in the chromosomes, and/or *numerical changes* that affect the number of chromosomes (19). The first category can be further subdivided into (1) changes due to loss or reduplication of some of the genes on the chromosome and (2) changes due to altered arrangements of the genes. *Deletion* and *duplication* involve chromosomal loss and gain, respectively. When the genes ABCDEFG carried by a normal chromosome have been cut to only ABEFG, a *chromosomal deletion* of the region containing genes CD has occurred. On the other hand, if the chromosome has acquired two additional genes and carries instead ABCDCDEFG, duplication has added the extra CD gene to the chromosome.

Translocation, inversion, and *transposition* are patterns of altered arrangement of genes in the chromosome. Translocation involves the exchange of genes between two chromosomes. If chromosome 1 with genes ABCDEFG exchanges some of its genes with chromosome 2 with genes HIJK, a "new" set of chromosomes with genes ABCDJK and HIEFG may result. Inversion changes the location of several genes on the chromosome by rotating them 180° such that genes ABCDEFG will become AEDCBFG. Transposition simply moves the genes on the chromosome from one location to another as in the case of ABCDEFG to ADEFBCG.

There are several conditions that result from numerical changes in chromosome number. *Aneuploidy* results when the chromosome number is not an exact multiple of the single set of chromosomes in the sex cells. *Polyploidy* results from an even-numbered multiplication of chromosomes beyond that of the diploid configuration of most cells.

Chromosomal mutations are observed in natural populations, but they are usually harmful to the organisms. Although Goldschmidt proposed that systematic chromosomal rearrangement (20) can give rise to a "hopeful monster" under certain environments, his thesis has not been confirmed by experimental observations.

Polyploidy is commonly found in plants and constitutes rare examples of speciation that can be directly observed (*see* I.3.3.1.c). However, its significance in the evolution of animals is doubtful because the majority of the animals that have been reported to be polyploids are parthenogenetic, i.e., they developed from unfertilized eggs. Thus, polyploidy fails to account for the evolution of bisexualism and the genetic diversity in animals, for it cannot be established in species with separate sexes and regular outcrossing.

Translocation can give rise to chromosomal duplication and deletion during meiosis (Figure 2.63). In plants, pollen grains and ovules with duplicated or deleted chromosomes are usually nonfunctional, though there is evidence that translocation is regularly tolerated in some species.

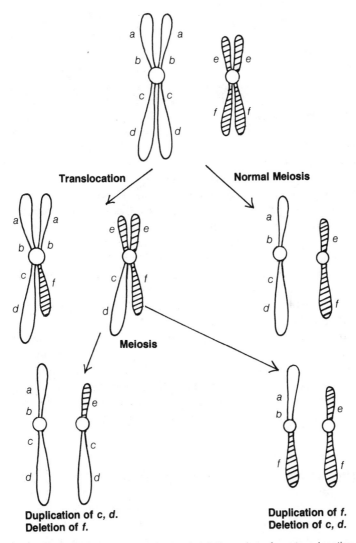

Figure 2.63. Chromosome duplication and deletion arisen from translocation during meiosis. Genes *a*, *b*, *c*, *d*, and *e*, *f* are genes on two separate pairs of homologous chromosomes.

167

Animal gametes with duplicated or deleted chromosomes may function, but the zygote formed by the union of a normal gamete and one of these defective gametes will usually die or develop into an abnormal individual. Therefore the possibility that chromosomal mutations can provide the raw material for evolution is very much in doubt.

2.6.6 *Evolution and Genetic Equilibrium.* The Mendelian concept of dominant and recessive genes raises an interesting question when dealing with a population of interbreeding individuals with different genotypes. Will the recessive genes be eventually replaced by the dominant genes? The search for the answer to this question led G. H. Hardy, an English mathematician, and G. Weinberg, a German physician, to develop the Hardy-Weinberg model of genetic equilibrium. They defined the relative proportions of genes and genotypes in a population as the gene frequency and the genotype frequency, respectively. The principle of genetic equilibrium is that gene frequencies and genotype frequencies will stay constant in a population under the following conditions:

1. The population must be large enough to make it highly improbable to alter the gene frequencies significantly by chance alone. The lower limit of such a population is estimated to be around 10 000.
2. Mutations must not occur or the forward mutation rate must equal the backward mutation rate (mutational equilibrium).
3. The population is stable with no genetic exchange caused by immigration or emigration.
4. There must be no selection of any kind in the patterns of mating and reproduction.

Hardy and Weinberg used a mathematical formula to represent their observations. Let p and q be the gene frequencies of a dominant character and recessive character, respectively. Then p^2, $2pq$, and q^2 will represent the genotype frequencies of the homozygous dominant AA, heterozygous Aa, and homozygous recessive aa individuals. The Hardy-Weinberg model then can be expressed by two equations:

$$p + q = 1 \tag{1}$$
$$p^2 + 2pq + q^2 = 1 \tag{2}$$

Equation (2) is actually the binomial expression of $(p + q)^2$, and thus, it is an expansion of equation (1).

Let us consider an example of a hypothetical population that is composed entirely of heterozygous individuals *(Aa)*. Assuming random mating, the proportion of the genotypes in the F_1 offspring will be ¼AA : ½Aa : ¼aa, (*see* I.1.3). The gene frequencies of A and a in the parental generations are both 0.5. However, the gene frequencies in the

F_1 generation are less obvious. To calculate the gene frequency of $A(p)$ in the F_1 generation proceed as follows:

$$p = \frac{\text{number of } A \text{ alleles in population}}{\text{total number of } A \text{ and } a \text{ alleles in the population}} \quad (3) \text{ or}$$

$$p = \frac{\frac{1}{4}(AA) \times 2 + \frac{1}{2}(Aa) \times 1}{\frac{1}{4}(AA) \times 2 + \frac{1}{2}(Aa) \times 2 + \frac{1}{4}(aa) \times 2}$$

$$= \frac{\frac{1}{2} + \frac{1}{2}}{\frac{1}{2} + 1 + \frac{1}{2}} \qquad = \qquad \frac{1}{2} \qquad = \qquad 0.5$$

Substituting q and a in the above equation gives the frequency of the a allele.

In the second generation, random mating will give rise to the results listed in Table 2.17 with the genotype distribution of 4/16 AA : 8/16 Aa : 4/16 aa. The gene frequencies of A and a can be again calculated by using equation (3) to be 0.5 and 0.5.

Thus, we have demonstrated that the gene frequencies of A and a remain constant in the parental, F_1 and F_2 generations. The genotype frequencies of AA, Aa, and aa also remain the same in the first and second generation as predicted by equation (2):

$$p^2 = AA = (0.5 \times 0.5) = 0.25$$
$$2pq = Aa = (2 \times 0.5 \times 0.5) = 0.50$$
$$q^2 = aa = (0.5 \times 0.5) = 0.25$$

Table 2.17. The Offspring of the Random Mating of a Population Composed of 1/4 AA, 1/2 Aa, and 1/4 aa Individuals.*

Mating MALE FEMALE	Frequency	Offspring
AA x AA	1/4 x 1/4	1/16 AA
AA x Aa	1/4 x 1/2	1/16 AA + 1/16 Aa
AA x aa	1/4 x 1/4	1/16 Aa
Aa x AA	1/2 x 1/4	1/16 AA + 1/16 Aa
Aa x Aa	1/2 x 1/2	1/16 AA + 1/8 Aa + 1/16 aa
Aa x aa	1/2 x 1/4	1/16 Aa + 1/16 aa
aa x AA	1/4 x 1/4	1/16 Aa
aa x Aa	1/4 x 1/2	1/16 Aa + 1/16 aa
aa x aa	1/4 x 1/4	1/16 aa
		Sum: 4/16 AA + 8/16 Aa + 4/16 aa

*NOTE: Reprinted, with permission, from Villee, C. A. Biology. 7th ed. Philadelphia: W. B. Saunders Co.; 1977. © 1977 by the W. B. Saunders Co.

The gene frequencies will remain constant for an infinite number of generations as long as the four basic conditions listed earlier are maintained.

Therefore, Hardy and Weinberg predicted that there will be no change in gene frequencies and genotype frequencies regardless of the dominant or recessive characters of the genes as long as the four basic conditions are met. The principle of genetic equilibrium has provided a useful tool to monitor the most fundamental step of evolution—the change in gene frequencies (microevolution). Since there are very few natural populations that have maintained all of the four conditions of the Hardy-Weinberg law, it may be predicted that evolution is constantly occurring.

Several factors may contribute to the change of gene frequencies, among them are *mutation pressure, selection pressure,* and *genetic drift.*

a) *Mutation Pressure.* Mutation pressure is the difference in rate of forward mutation verses backward mutation. Since spontaneous mutations are always occurring and mutation equilibrium is seldom achieved in the natural population, mutation pressure tends to cause a slow "shift" in the gene frequencies in the gene pool favoring the more stable alleles over the more mutable alleles.

In spite of the popular belief that mutation is the raw material of evolution, since the mutation rate is so slow (on the order of 10^{-6} per generation), it alone seldom exerts much influence on evolution with the following exceptions: (1) microorganisms that have short generation times, (2) some higher plant groups in which polyploidy contributes to rapid speciation, and (3) small populations subject to genetic drift. In all the above cases, mutations are random and appear to influence only slightly the nature and direction of evolution.

b) *Selection Pressure.* Selection pressure is by far the most important factor directing the change of gene frequencies in a population. It can change the frequency of a particular gene drastically by selecting for or against it in every generation. Consider a hypothetical population in which the initial frequencies of alleles A and a are 0.9 and 0.1 and the genotype frequencies AA, Aa, aa are 0.81, 0.18, and 0.01, respectively. If A is selected against by a selection pressure such that its frequency is reduced to 0.8 in the same generation, then the frequency of a becomes 0.2 and the genotype frequencies of $AA, Aa,$ and aa will be changed correspondingly to 0.64, 0.32, and 0.04 (Table 2.18). If the same selection pressure against A is maintained throughout subsequent generations, the frequencies of A and AA will be reduced drastically to a barely detectable level. Such selection will lead to the wholesale revision of the frequencies of the genes and genotypes in the population. It can change the genetic

		No Selection			Selection		
First Generation	Genotype frequency	AA : 0.81	Aa : 0.18	aa 0.01	AA : 0.81	Aa : 0.18	aa 0.01
	Gametes	A = 0.9 (No Selection)	a = 0.1		A = 0.8 (After Selection)	a = 0.2	
	Possible Gamete Combinations		0.9A	0.1a		0.8A	0.2a
		0.9A	AA 0.81	Aa 0.09	0.8A	AA 0.64	Aa 0.16
		0.1a	aA 0.09	aa 0.01	0.2a	aA 0.16	aa 0.04
Second Generation	Genotype frequency	AA : 0.81	Aa : 0.18	aa 0.01	AA : 0.64	Aa : 0.32	aa 0.04

Table 2.18. Comparison of genotype frequencies under selection and no selection. See text for explanation.

structure of the population in the absence of mutation. However, if new competing alleles are produced through mutation, they may be selected for by a changing environment. Eventually the new genes and genotypes may be established by natural selection. Examples of evolutionary change brought about by selection are found both in laboratory studies and in natural populations (DDT resistance, antibotic resistance, sickle cell anemia). They will be discussed in 3.2.1.b, c. The three types of selection—stabilizing, directional, and disruptive (see I.1.4)—interact with each other constantly and probably account for most of the micro-evolutionary changes observed in nature.

c) *Genetic Drift*. Sudden random change of gene frequencies can occur in a population of any size, but it will produce the greatest fluctuations in small populations characterized by little or no migration.

The effect of genetic drift can be illustrated by a simple example. We can compare the ability of individuals in two hypothetical populations to taste the chemical phenylthiocarbamide (PTC). One population consists of 100 persons and the other 10 000. If the frequencies of the dominant nontaster allele T and the recessive taster allele t are *0.6* and *0.4*, respectively, in the parental generation of both populations, then the genotypic frequencies of *TT, Tt,* and *tt* will be 0.36, 0.48, and 0.16, respectively. This means that 16 individuals in the small population and 1600 individuals in the large population will have the homozygous recessive genotype *tt*, the taster phenotype. If by accident eight individuals from each population die in a car crash, the gene frequency of the t allele will be

171

changed significantly in the small population but not in the large population. This can be seen by tabulating the gene frequencies as follows:

For the small population, the genotype distribution after the trauma will be:

$$\frac{p^2}{36} + \frac{2pq}{48} + \frac{q^2}{8} = 92$$

The gene frequency of t (q) after the trauma is calculated from equation (3) as:

$$q = \frac{8 \times 2 + 48 \times 1}{92 \times 2} = \frac{16 + 48}{184} = 0.348$$

The corresponding frequency of T (p) is

$$p = 1 - q = 1. - 0.348 = 0.652$$

By the same token, the gene frequencies of t and T in the large population after the trauma will be 0.3995 and 0.6005. Thus, only the small population experiences a significant change in gene frequencies caused by the chance event.

Genetic drift can also be caused by inbreeding in a small population that can be represented by the *founder effect*. If a population is founded by a few individuals being isolated from the rest of the outbreeding population, it is possible that the isolated individuals may have unusually high frequencies of one or more harmful alleles. These alleles presumably result from previous inbreeding. Founder effect may plague also the surviving members of a population that suffers a famine or other catastrophes. The expansion of such a small population could lead to the establishment of harmful genes, the so-called *bottle neck* effect.

Examples of genetic drift can be found in laboratory and natural populations (21). It has been shown that the variability of chromosome arrangement of experimental populations of *Drosophila pseudoobscura* raised in isolated conditions depends on the number of founding individuals carrying different chromosome gene arrangements. The genetic homogeneity of certain human populations can also be traced to the few founders. For example, the Ramah Navaho Indian tribe began their population after isolation from an outbreeding population.

Finally, one must consider the interplay of neutral mutations and genetic drift resulting in gene frequency change. Mutations that are neither beneficial nor harmful to organisms are termed neutral and are the source of new genes that will be established eventually in the population by random drift. In other words, there is no selection exerted on the mutations by the environment or from intrinsic factors within the population.

Recently it has been hypothesized that a large amount of genetic variability may be attributed to genetic drift acting on neutral alleles formerly produced by a substantial number of neutral mutations. Aspects of this hypothesis will be explored in I.3.3.2.a.1.

References 2.6

1. Griffith, F. J. Hyg. Camb. 27:113; 1928.
2. Avery, O. T.; MacLeod, C. M.; McCarty, M. J. Exp. Med. 79:137; 1944.
3. Watson, J. D.; Crick, F. H. C. Cold Spring Harbor Symp. Quant. Biol. 18:123; 1953.
4. Watson, J. D.; Crick, F. H. C. Nature. 171:464; 1953.
5. Nirenberg, M. W.; Mataei, J. H. Proc. Natl. Acad. Sci. USA. 47:1588; 1961.
6. Nishimura, S.; Jones, D. S.; Khorana; H. G. J. Mol. Biol. 13:302; 1965.
7. Watson, J. D. Molecular biology of the gene. Menlo Park, CA: Benjamin; 1976: 374.
8. Lane, C. D.; Marbaix, G.; Gurdon, J. B. J. Mol. Biol. 61:73; 1971.
9. Watson, J. D. Molecular biology of the gene. 482–83.
10. Jacob, F.; Monod, J. J. Mol. Biol. 2:318; 1961.
11. Bachmann, B. J.; Low, K. B.; Taylor, A. L. Bacteriol. Rev. 48:116; 1976.
12. Davidson, E. H.; Britten, R. J. Q. Rev. Biol. 48:565; 1973.
13. Soyfer, V. N. In: Evolutionary biology. Dobzhansky, T.; Hecht, M. K.; Steere, W. C. eds. Vol. 8. New York: Plenum Press; 1975: 123.
14. Stanier, R. Y.; Adelberg, E. A.; Ingraham, J. The microbial world. 4th ed. Englewood Cliffs, NJ: Prentice Hall; 1976: 414.
15. Hall, Z. W.; Lehman, I. R. J. Mol. Biol. 36:1321; 1968.
16. Springgate, C. F.; Loeb, L. A. Proc. Natl. Acad. Sci. USA. 20:245; 1973.
17. Green, M. M. Mutat. Res. 10:353; 1970.
18. Green, M. M. J. Genet. (Suppl.). 73:187; 1973.
19. Dobzhansky, T. Genetics of the evolutionary process. New York: Columbia Univ. Press; 1970: 44.
20. Goldschmidt, R. The material basis of evolution. New Haven, CT: Yale Univ. Press; 1940.
21. Strickberger, M. W. J. Genet. 2nd ed. New York: Macmillan; 1976: 777–79.

CHAPTER 3

A Critical Evaluation
of the Biological Theory
# of Evolution

3.1 Criteria to Evaluate the Biological Theory of Evolution

In order to evaluate the scientific theory of evolution, we must have some ideas about the *nature* of science. According to Webster's dictionary, the simplest definition of science is "a branch of study concerned with observation and classification of facts, especially with the establishment of verifiable general law, chiefly by induction and hypotheses." However, there are many different opinions among the philosophers of science concerning the nature of science.

The two extreme viewpoints of science can be represented by the positions of *naive realism* and *idealistic realism* (1). Naive realism (positivism) maintains that scientific knowledge is the most positive knowledge and involves the literal description of observations as well as the collection of objective facts. Subjective interpretations are totally dependent on objective facts. Idealistic realism, on the other hand, sees science as entirely the product of human activity, involving tentative models set up in the minds of scientists. Therefore, observations and data are collected by scientists according to presuppositions. However, the objective *facts* are subject to the interpretation of the scientists, the so-called *theory-laden data*. Thus, acquisition of scientific knowledge is based on objective and subjective activity.

The scientific method that involves verification or refutation of a theory by empirical observations (provable by experience or experiment) has played an important role in ushering in the modern technological era. Although this method can help man to arrive at only a partial understanding of the nature of reality, the empirical approach is constantly

cus aureus, a bacterium known to cause numerous infections in humans such as boils and absesses. Higher and higher doses of penicillin must be administered in order to kill the bacteria. These resistant bacteria are a serious problem in hospitals.

The problem that developed after using penicillin is a clear example of a change in the frequency of a gene bringing about drug resistance under strong selective pressure. The drug-resistant bacteria that were derived presumably by spontaneous mutation must have existed at a very low frequency before the widespread use of penicillin. However, penicillin has been so effective in wiping out drug-sensitive bacteria that rare drug-resistant mutants in the natural population have increased rapidly. Of course, as demonstrated earlier (I.1.3), the penicillin-resistant mutation is independent of the presence or absence of the drug.

Selection brought about by insecticides is another interesting example of evolutionary change caused by selection. Resistant strains of parasitic insects soon became known after the use of insecticides. For years, the citrus trees in Southern California have been infested by parasitic scale insects. In order to combat the insects, the trees were covered with tents and then fumigated with a cyanide poison—hydrocyanic acid. Later it was observed that cyanide-resistant varieties of scale insects had replaced the original cyanide-sensitive varieties.

The development of DDT resistance in household pests was also caused by selection after widespread use of the insecticide DDT. When DDT first came into general use in 1945, it was very effective in controlling the proliferation of houseflies, but soon resistant varieties of flies appeared. Under the strong selective pressure of DDT, resistant strains of flies quickly became well established and completely replaced sensitive strains in certain localities.

One of the best-established cases demonstrating the effect of natural selection in changing the gene frequency of a population is *industrial melanism* in the peppered moth *Biston betularia,* which flies by night and rests on tree trunks by day. Since the middle of the nineteenth century, the numbers of light and dark pigmented varieties of *B. betularia* have been compared in rural and industrial regions of England. In the latter areas the vegetation had been blackened by pollution, and the frequency of light-colored moths was very low; however, the frequency of the light varieties was high in the unpolluted rural areas. In some heavily polluted localities the dark varieties almost totally replaced the light varieties. A similar phenomenon was observed in 100 other species of moths in England.

Professor H. B. D. Kettlewell demonstrated that the basis of the

Figure 3.3. *Left: The peppered moth, Biston betularia,* and its melanic form, *carbonaria,* at rest on a soot-covered oak trunk near the industrial city of Birmingham, England. The *carbonaria* form is much less conspicuous than the typical peppered form, which is very conspicuous. *Right:* The same forms resting on a lichened tree trunk in unpolluted countryside. The typical form is much less conspicuous than the melanic. Reprinted, with permission, from Kettewell, H. B. D., Department of Zoology, South Parks Road, Oxford, OX1 3PS.

change in frequency of the gene controlling the moth's pigmentation was their need for protective coloration against their natural predators such as birds (6). In rural areas he noticed that dark pigmented moths resting on tree trunks with light colored lichens (a fungus and alga growing together) were conspicuous to birds while the light varieties were camouflaged. In the industrialized areas lichens were scarce, having been killed by pollutants. In these regions the dark varieties of the peppered moth matched the color of the polluted tree trunks, making it difficult for predators to detect them. This phenomenon was very striking in the industrialized city of Birmingham. In contrast, the presence of any light colored moth resting on a tree trunk in the Birmingham area was obvious (Figure 3.3).

Kettlewell theorized that birds selectively pick out the conspicuous varieites in both the polluted and nonpolluted environments, thereby contributing to the change in the frequency of the genes, controlling pigmentation. In order to test this hypothesis, he raised thousands of light- and dark-pigmented peppered moths, marked each with a dot of paint, and released them into the polluted (industrialized) and nonpolluted (nonindustrialized) areas of England. He then set out to recapture these moths. In the nonindustrialized areas, he managed to recapture 14.6% of the light varieties but only 4.7% of the dark varieties. In the industrialized areas, he was able to capture only 13% of the light varieties; however, 27.5% of the dark varieties were recovered.

In another series of experiments Kettlewell was able to photograph birds preying on moths that he placed on tree trunks. He demonstrated unequivocally that birds eat more light varieties in the polluted areas and more dark varieties in the nonpolluted areas.

Direct experimental tests, as well as the discovery of dark varieties in regions far away from the industrialized areas, suggested that the dark varieties did not arise from mutations induced by particulate matter, such as heavy metals, emitted from industrial plants. Industrialization apparently changed the environment, resulting in natural selection favoring survival of dark varieties and loss of light varieties. Thus the natural selective force of predation in a changing environment caused by industrialization was responsible for microevolution in moths.

c) *Balancing Selection.* Natural selection is not only capable of inducing changes in gene frequencies, it can also maintain the frequency of a harmful gene in a population, provided that this gene is advantageous for its carriers. This phenomenon is called *balancing selection.* If two or more alleles are maintained at a single genetic locus, the phenomenon is called *balanced polymorphism.*

An excellent example of balanced polymorphism is the distribution of the gene responsible for *sickle cell anemia.* As already discussed in I.2.6.2, the substitution of a nucleotide in the gene encoding for the β chain is called hemoglobin molecule changes the configuration of the protein reducing its solubility and causing the stacking of adjacent molecules. Hemoglobin containing this aberrant β chain is called hemoglobin S (*HbS*) and is distinguished from the normal hemoglobin A (*HbA*).

Sickle cell anemia patients are homozygous for the S gene (*SS*). Individuals heterozygous (*AS*) for the S gene are called carriers, having no apparent symptoms of the disease under normal levels of atmospheric oxygen. Therefore, the S gene is recessive and is lethal only when it is expressed in the homozygous (*SS*) state. Normally, if a gene is harmful, it will be selected against, and its frequency will diminish. However, in large areas of the world, the gene frequencies of S are much higher than would be expected on the basis of the selection against a lethal trait. This can be seen in Figures 3.4 and 3.5.

After much research it became apparent that the distribution of the S gene has strong correlation with the occurrence of malaria. The reason behind this correlation is that individuals heterozygous for the S gene (AS genotype) are resistant to malaria. When the malaria parasite in the red blood cells consumes all the oxygen carried by the cell, the AS cells become sickle shaped. (Red blood cells in normal individuals never sickle except at high altitudes where oxygen is limited.) The malaria parasite becomes trapped in the sickle cells, which in turn attract phagocytic cells of the defense system of the body that destroy both the cells and parasites. Thus, the AS genotypes makes a carrier resistant to malaria.

Since the heterozygote of a harmful gene becomes advantageous to its carrier, this phenomenon is also called *positive heterosis (overdominance)*. In Africa where malaria is prevalent, the frequencies of genes A and S are in equilibrium. This is achieved by balancing the disadvantage of the A gene with the disadvantage of the S gene through comparable selection pressure against each trait. If the gene frequency of S falls, due to the early death of SS individuals who fail to reproduce, the number of

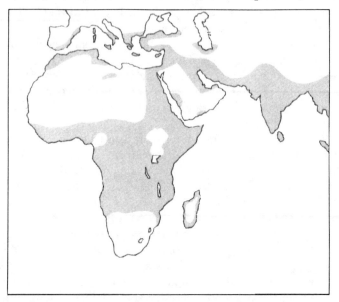

Figure 3.4. Distribution of the sickle-cell gene in Africa, the Middle East, and India. Sickle-cell gene is commonest in populations of tropical Africa; in Zaire, for example, the S gene frequency is about 18%, which means that some 30 % of the population carry the AS trait. The sickle-cell gene is also found in the Mediterranean, particularly in Greece and Turkey, and in northwestern Africa, southern Arabia, Pakistan, India, and Bangladesh. Individuals who carry the AS trait are more resistant to malaria than others. Reprinted, with permission, from Cavalli-Sforza, L. L. The genetics of human populations. Sc. Am. (Sept.) 83; 1974.

AA individuals (normal) increases, and they are highly susceptible to malaria. Malarial deaths of *AA* individuals lowers the frequency of the *A* gene in the next generation. The lowered *A* gene frequency means a rise in the frequency of the *S* gene resulting in more *SS* individuals who are likely to die of sickle cell anemia. Thus, the sequential increase and decrease in frequency of both genes results in a stable frequency over many generations in a malaria environment.

In America the *A* and *S* gene are not in equilibrium. The presence of an *S* gene is disadvantageous because malaria has been eradicated due to aggressive public health programs, and the frequency of the *A* gene continues to increase as the environment selects against the *S* gene. This is *directive selection* (*see* I.1.4.5.).

3.2.2 *Rational Coherency.*

a) *Domestication.* Domestication of animals and plants has been practiced from early human civilization, and breeders have been able to produce altered and improved breeds of both domestic animals and culti-

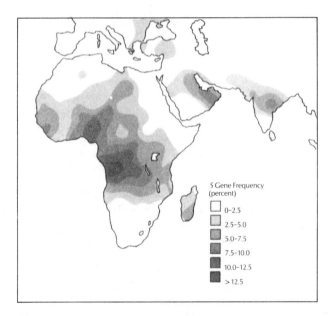

Figure 3.5. Distribution of malignant malarias caused by the parasite *Plasmodium falciparium*. Malaria was common in the 1920s in the parts of the Old World indicated on this map. Overlap with sickle-cell gene distribution is extensive. In many regions where malaria is prevalent but *HbS* is not, other mutant hemoglobins are commonly found. Reprinted, with permission, from Kirk, D. Biology today. 2nd ed. New York: Random House, 1975.

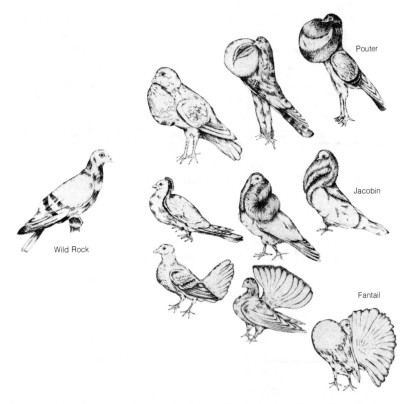

Figure 3.6. Variation among the breeds of domestic pigeon, a subject of investigation by Darwin that confirmed for him the strong influence on variation that can be exerted by natural selection. Reprinted, with permission, from Stebbins. The pigeon. Levi Publishing Co., Inc. (n.d.).

vated plants. In the 1800s Darwin became interested in these alterations. He noted the changes in the anatomical features in many domesticated pigeons as compared with wild pigeons. He found that some features of domestic breeds differed from each other to a greater degree than differences between species or even families of wild birds (Figure 3.6). Although the process of change of these features that must have occurred during the history of domestication cannot be observed, it is reasonable to assume that the artificial selection pressure imposed on the breeds by the breeders contributed to changes in anatomical features. It is also possible that changes were brought about by *inbreeding depression* (the selection of homozygous genotypes when heterozygotes are mated with each other in an inbreeding population) that could lead to reduction in the diversity of the breeds. Nevertheless, the breeders' experience at least provides a rational basis for the theory that selection can bring about changes in gene frequencies.

b) *Speciation in* Drosophila. The formation of new species (speciation) cannot be observed in the laboratory or in nature, because of its presumed slow pace. Yet the fact that speciation is occurring or has occurred is a reasonable inference that can be drawn from experimental models and natural populations. The four stages of speciation are believed to be: (1) division of a single population into two identical populations isolated from each other by a physical barrier, (2) the formation of a reproductive barrier between two populations, (3) the encounter of the two reproductively isolated populations, and (4) the independent evolutionary development of each population.

The evidence for the above stages of speciation is sparse, especially for the first stage. However, a rare case of reproductive barrier formation in natural populations of the fruit fly *Drosophila* was reported by Prakash (7). He collected flies of *Drosophila pseudoobscura* in Bogotá, a city located in the highland of Colombia, South America. When the females from the Bogotá population were crossed with males from any other location, the males in the first filial generation (F_1) were completely sterile. The reciprocal cross produced normal male offspring. These results are similar to that of the cross between two species of *Drosophila–D. pseudoobscura* and *D. persimilis*. The cross produces F_1 mates with very small testes when the cross is made in one direction but not when made in the other direction. Thus the sterility of the male offspring produced by the females in the Bogotá population with the males from other populations may be the first stage of speciation.

The above interpretation is strengthened by the fact that *D. pseudoobscura* was believed to be scarce in Colombia before 1960 after an intensive search located very few examples. However, they were found to gradually appear and increase in frequency from 1960 to 1962. The populations used for Prakash's studies were collected in late 1967. Thus *D. pseudoobscura* may have been introduced into Bogotá from North or Central America before 1960 where they later proliferated and populated the Colombian highland. However, it is possible that population numbers of *D. pseudoobscura* were at a low level in Colombia for a long time and thus went undetected. The evidence strongly suggests that *D. pseudoobscura* in Bogotá was undergoing speciation due to the isolation from the main region of its distribution. Furthermore, the process of speciation seemed to be accompanied by minimal genetic differentiation. Thus, this example provides support for the view that isolation and selection contribute to the evolution of a new species.

c) *Distribution of Skin Color.* The distribution of skin pigments among different human populations is also an important demonstration of the effects of natural selection on phenotypic traits (8). The distribution around the world of human skin color is shown in a very generalized way in Figure 3.7. The map is plotted in terms of skin color based on minimal exposure to the sun.

The adaptive values of each skin color is readily observable. The melanin particles, which are responsible for dark pigmentation, are distributed throughout the outer layers of the skin to protect the deeper layers from damage by ultraviolet irradiation from the sun. Dark-skinned people are native to the tropics and have thicker skin that contains more melanin than light-skinned Europeans.

In the United States, the frequency of skin cancer is seven to eight times greater in whites than in blacks living in the same urban areas in various latitudes. Although white skin tends to reflect more sunlight, the thicker dark skin is more resistant to damage by sunburn. Furthermore, the fact that dark skin absorbs heat faster means that the individual having it sweats more. The turning on of the evaporative cooling mechanism may also be an evolutionary advantage. Although the complete evolutionary significance of skin pigmentation is not known, the distribution of skin color as shown in Figure 3.7 is suggestive of its adaptive values.

The two darkest categories of skin color are concentrated around the equator in the Old World. This is to be expected because dark skin color protects against intense tropical solar radiation. People of Caucasoid origin living near the tropical zones differ from their Caucasoid relatives in the temperate zones by having much darker skin. Mongoloids living in temperate zones, presumably the place of their origin, have light brown skin that contrasts with the much darker skin of equatorial Mongoloids.

In areas below the tropics of Africa where the dense rain forests have top canopies as high as 200 feet and multilayered stories of foliage, the amount of sunlight reaching the ground is greatly reduced. Living in perpetual shade, the Negroid people in these areas show yellowish to reddish brown skin color, with much less melanin than is found in other Negroid races.

People with the least skin pigmentation are found in extreme northwestern Europe. This region is believed to have been covered by a glacier approximately 12 000 to 15 000 years ago. The inhabitants must have migrated to this area after the retreat of the glacier. Today the area has an oceanic climate characterized by cloudy and rainy summers with little intense sunlight. It has been theorized that the light skin of the northwestern Europeans is an adaptation that allows maximum absorption of

Fair-White
Light Brown
Medium Brown
Dark Brown
Very Dark Brown ("Black")

Figure 3.7. Unexposed skin color. Reprinted, with permission, from Birdsell, J. B. Human evolution. Chicago: Rand McNally; 1975. Reprinted, with permission, from Professor Birdsell. Department of Anthropology, UCLA.

sunlight needed for the synthesis of vitamin D, a necessary compound that allows the body to absorb dietary calcium. Natural selection may have favored a reduction of melanin in these people to a point that almost amounts to partial albinism.

The above hypothesis is highly plausible in view of the correlation of skin color with the weather. The skin color of the vast majority of humanity is light brown, presumably due to the fact that they live outside of the tropics. There is evidence to show that the light brown skin pigmentation does adequately protect these people against solar radiation in the areas where they live.

Before the recent immigration from the Old World, natives of North and South America were intermediate in skin color. Sometimes they had a reddish or ruddy component, hence the term *red man* (commonly used for Indians). It is believed that native Americans are descendants of a certain Mongoloid race who migrated to North America through the Bering Strait more than 10 000 years ago. The Indian populations also show some selective gradients of pigmentation despite their recent arrival in the Americas. The darkest pigmentation seems to have developed in the Indian population living along the Colorado River where it flows through the hot desert valley on its way to the Gulf of Mexico. Other dark varieties of the Indian race can be found in tropical areas of South America, except for the dense shady forest environment of the Amazon Basin. In contrast the Eskimos of the Arctic and Alaska are lighter in skin tone, experiencing the least exposure to solar radiation.

It is sufficient to conclude that the selective force of solar radiation for protective skin color apparently has produced the spectrum of skin pigmentation in the Old World. However, the relatively recent habitation of the New World has not allowed sufficient time for selection to produce a total regional adaptation.

In summary, microevolution is supported by evidence from studies on the positive effects of bacterial mutation, selection of traits in artificial breeding of domestic animals, fertility changes in insect populations, directive selection against sickle cell anemia in U.S. blacks, and adaptation of selected skin color patterns to specific environmental areas. These examples are both empirically adequate and rationally coherent.

References 3.2

1. Pun, P. P. T.; Murray, C. D.; Strauss, N. J. Bacteriol. 123:346; 1975.
2. Novick, A.; Szilard, L. Proc. Natl. Acad. Sc. USA. 36:708; 1950.
3. Fitch, W. In: Evolutionary biology. Dobzhansky, T.; Hecht, M. K.; Steere, W. S. eds. New York: Appleton-Century-Crofts: 1970; 68.

4. Gibson, T.; Schoppe, M. L.; Cox, E. C. Science. 169:686–88; 1970.
5. Hayes, W. The genetics of bacteria and their viruses. New York: Wiley; 1969.
6. Ford, E. B. Ecological genetics. 3rd ed. London: Chapman and Hall; 1971.
7. Prakash, S. J. Genet. 72:143; 1972.
8. Birdsell, J. B. Human evolution. Chicago: Rand McNally; 1975:490–97.

3.3 Evaluation of Macroevolution

Despite the systematic unity and comprehensive scope of macroevolution (synthetic or general theory of evolution), it has serious weaknesses when evaluated.

3.3.1 *Empirical Inadequacy.*

a) *Demise of the Theory of Spontaneous Generation.* The theory of spontaneous generation states that life arises continually from the nonliving, and this idea was accepted by most medieval scholars as a mechanistic explanation of the origin of life. Aristotle, Newton, William Harvey, Descartes, and van Helmont are but a few of a long list of learned men who accepted certain forms of the theory of spontaneous generation. Some scientists with a more naturalistic outlook of life chose to accept the theory as an alternative to the belief in a single primary act of a supernatural Creator.

The theory of spontaneous generation had its formal beginning after Anton von Leeuwenhoek (1632–1723) revealed to the scientific world the vast number of microscopic organisms in nature. The ancient thought that many plants and animals can be generated spontaneously under special conditions immediately took up a new dimension and presented itself in the form of the *abiogenesis of microscopic organisms.* This theory was the predominant view among scientists at that time because of its apparent consistency with the interpretation of observations that many organisms sprang from apparently nonliving material of various kinds.

There were always skeptics who questioned the popular view and ventured to test the theory of spontaneous generation experimentally. Francesco Redi tested the theory that maggots were derived from putrid meat by spontaneous transformation of some of the meat's components (*see* I.3.1). Redi proved this hypothesis untenable by demonstrating that maggots appeared to arise from meat only if flies had laid eggs on the meat. Redi's results and other studies of the origins of plants and animals weakened the theory of spontaneous generation considerably. However, since microorganisms were difficult to handle because of the primitive microbiological techniques used at the time, the proponents of the theory focused their attention on the origins of these microscopic "beasts" in organic infusions.

Louis Joblot paved the way for the eventually successful refutation of the theory of spontaneous generation by demonstrating that a heated hay infusion in a closed vessel did not give rise to microorganisms, but an unheated infusion in an open vessel was teeming with them. Lazzaro Spallanzani later showed that the same phenomena could be observed in heated meat broth. However, his results differed from those of another scientist John Needham, who had earlier found that life developed in broth in a heated closed vessel as well as in an open unheated vessel.

Needham, a proponent of the abiogenesis of life, criticized Spallanzani's experiment by alluding to the effect of prolonged heating that might have destroyed the "vital force" in the broth that was necessary for the abiogenesis of microorganisms. Spallanzani answered Needham's challenge by showing that the heated broth could support the growth of microorganisms after it was reexposed to air. However, the supporters of abiogenesis persisted in their criticisms by arguing that it was the exclusion of oxygen, which they believed was essential for the growth of the microorganisms, from the air in the closed vessel that prevented the abiogenesis of life in Spallanzani's experiments. They concluded that the appearance of microorganisms in the heated broth after it was reexposed to air was simply the result of the reintroduction of oxygen into the vessel.

Although Spallanzani's interpretation of his experimental results was not accepted by many of his contemporary scientists, the finding enabled Francois Appert to develop a canning method to preserve perishable organic materials. Appert enclosed food in airtight cans, heated the containers, and found the food could be preserved indefinitely. At the same time, the argument of the exclusion of oxygen continued to be used by the proponents of the theory of spontaneous generation to explain away Appert's results. Furthermore, proponents continued to amass erroneous data from poorly controlled experiments to support their contention.

It was not until 1861, when Louis Pasteur (1822–95) presented unequivocal empirical evidence, that the theory of spontaneous generation was finally discredited. Pasteur first demonstrated that air *does* contain microorganisms. He filtered air through a tube plugged with a piece of guncotton. The guncotton was then dissolved in a mixture of ether and alcohol. Microscopic examination of the sediment of the guncotton solution revealed the presence of microorganisms. Pasteur showed also that the introduction of heated air into a boiled sterile infusion in a closed system did not cause microbial contamination. However, if germ-laden

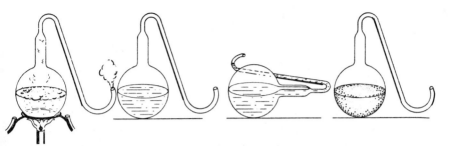

Figure 3.8. Pasteur demonstrated that bacteria were trapped in the curved neck of the flask by showing that as long as the flask with the boiled broth remained upright no decay occurred. But when the flask was tipped causing the broth to enter the neck and then set upright, the broth quickly showed signs of bacterial growth. Reprinted, with permission, from Moore, J. N.; Slusher, H. S. editors. Biology. Grand Rapids: Zondervan Publishing House; 1970.

guncotton obtained by filtering air was added to it, the infusion soon teemed with microorganisms.

Pasteur designed a specialized set of growth chambers, the *swan-necked flasks*, to show that filtration through cotton was not necessary to eliminate microbial contamination (Figure 3.8). The long curved neck prevented dust particles carrying microorganisms from entering a flask. Although air exchange between the broth chamber and the outside atmosphere could occur through the neck, heated broth was free from microbial contamination because microorganisms from the air were trapped on the inside walls of the necks by gravity. Interestingly, the broth could be contaminated by tilting the flask allowing the broth to wash the inside of the neck and then drain back into the flask or by breaking off the neck near the body of the flask, allowing contaminated air to enter.

John Tyndall gave the final death blow to the classic version of the theory of spontaneous generation. Using a box similar to that depicted in Figure 3.9, Tyndall demonstrated that dust-free air would not contaminate sterile broth. The entire interior of Tyndall's box was coated with glycerine to trap microorganisms. The box was practically sealed off from the atmosphere except for the two openings on either side of the box connected to convoluted tubings that allowed air to enter but trapped dust. After standing several days, the dust particles, floating in the air inside the box settled on the bottom, and air became "optically empty" (or revealed no suspended articles in the beam of light shone through the window) (*see* Figure 3.9). Then a pipette was inserted through a rubber stopper on the top of the box, and meat broth was introduced through the pipette into the tubes. The tubes were then boiled by immersing them for long periods in boiling brine. Tyndall found that after broth in the tubes had been cooled down to room temperature, it could be kept free of microbial growth indefinitely. Thus, his experiment eliminated the theory of spontaneous generation.

However, since the *mechanistic* outlook of life has never recognized any essential qualitative difference between the inorganic world and living organisms, the direct transformation of the inorganic world to the living world through some sort of spontaneous generation is necessary for this point of view. This apparently motivates the ardent supporters of the theory of spontaneous generation to fight to the very end.

Against the completely insurmountable wall of facts, some proponents of the mechanistic view gave up their ideas of spontaneous generation and

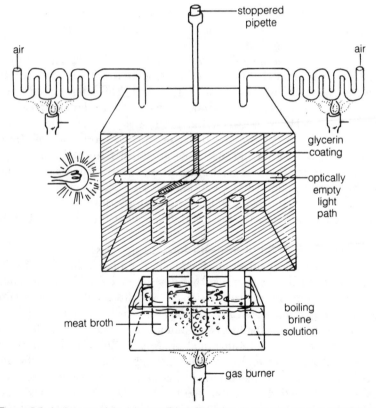

Figure 3.9. A diagram of the box that Tyndall used to demonstrate that "optically empty" air contained no microorganisms.

instead claimed that life emerged on earth by the transport of seeds from another torld *(panspermia)*. Proponents of panspermia believe that life forms were brought to earth by meteorites and/or *cosmic dust*. Numerous attempts to isolate microbes from meteorites have failed. Pasteur also tested this hypothesis by trying to isolate viable bacteria from a carbonaceous meteorite, but he was unsuccessful (1). Alleged success in isolating microbes from meteorites cannot be verified. Improper experimental techniques were used, including failure to avoid outside microbial contamination.

Transfer of living spores by cosmic dust from one heavenly body to another under the pressure of stellar rays is also an untenable theory to account for the origin of life on earth. The energetic irradiation penetrating interplanetary and interstellar space is destructive to all life, and it is inconceivable to maintain the viability of living spores or seeds on cosmic dust particles.

Finally, there is the speculation that life might have been brought to earth some time ago by interplanetary or interstellar travelers similar to our cosmonauts and astronauts. This remains at the level of science fiction, for it has no factual basis.

The majority of scholars who hold to a mechanistic origin of life have turned their attentions to a modified version of the theory of spontaneous generation. Their reasoning is as follows: Since life existed during only part of the earth's history, and since a divine act of creation is untestable and thus unscientific, life must have originated early in the earth's history by spontaneous generation under a different set of conditions, but this no longer happens. The idea of spontaneous generation under a different physical environment provides a way out for the mechanists. They can simulate the presumed *primordial conditions* of the earth in the laboratory and then test the possibility of the abiogenesis of life.

The mechanists believe that the last missing element of the general theory of evolution linking the first cell to inorganic matter has been supplied by the currently popular theory of spontaneous generation. However, the stipulation of the abiogenesis of life under conditions *different* from the present has removed the theory from the realm of empirical sciences, for it can neither be verified nor falsified by experiments done under present earth conditions (2). In addition, there are difficulties in the experimental documentation of the spontaneous generation of the first cell. These problems will be discussed in the following section.

b) *Difficulties in Accounting for the Abiogenesis of the First Cell.* The most commonly held theories of abiogenesis of life assume three stages of chemical evolution (Figure 3.10). The first stage involves the *accumulation* of certain organic molecules due to the random processes of collision and irradiation in the primeval "soup" of the ocean. The second stage is the *selection* of certain thermodynamically stable organic molecules existing in clusters or the formation of macromolecules, such as proteins and nucleic acids. In the final stage of chemical evolution some of the macromolecules *acquire* the capacity to reproduce (replicate), using some type of *template* mechanism that is the beginning of the first cell. Mechanists believe all of these chemical reactions were carried out in a reducing atmosphere devoid of oxygen since an oxidizing atmosphere would quickly destroy large molecules that formed.

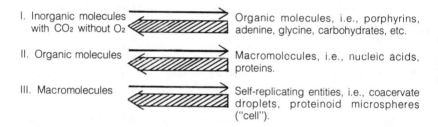

I. Inorganic molecules with CO_2 without O_2 → Organic molecules, i.e., porphyrins, adenine, glycine, carbohydrates, etc.

II. Organic molecules → Macromolecules, i.e., nucleic acids, proteins.

III. Macromolecules → Self-replicating entities, i.e., coacervate droplets, proteinoid microspheres ("cell").

Figure 3.10. *THREE STAGES OF CHEMICAL EVOLUTION.*

The above stages are thought possible for the following reasons: (1) The earth and solar systems are thought to be the results of the condensation of a cloud of cosmic dust rich in hydrogen; therefore, the primeval atmosphere of the earth must have contained this gas. Furthermore, the reducing atmosphere of hydrogen, methane, and ammonia observed on several planets of the solar system such as Jupiter, Saturn, Uranus, and Neptune supports this assumption. (2) It is assumed that the composition of meteorites is similar to that of the primeval earth. All the elements analyzed exist in meteorites in reduced form; therefore, the primitive earth may also have been devoid of the oxidizing agent oxygen. (3) Under the primordial conditions, many experiments designed to synthesize bio-organic molecules failed when molecular oxygen was present; however, they succeeded when oxygen was removed. Due to these stipulations, it has been suggested that the first living cell resulting from chemical evolution was an anaerobic cell existing deep in the ocean, removed from ultraviolet solar irradiation that would destroy it. However, Donald England (3) has made potent criticisms on the experiments supporting each of these stages of chemical evolution. Furthermore, an alternative model for the primitive atmosphere with ingredients similar to today's atmosphere except minus oxygen has been proposed (4). This model also necessitates the stipulation of an anaerobic cell.

The most famous example of abiogenesis of organic compounds in stage one is the experiment performed by S. L. Miller. He synthesized amino acids by passing an electric discharge for seven days through a closed system (Figure 3.11) containing methane, ammonia, water, and hydrogen. Porphyrins, important structural components of the photosynthetic and respiratory apparatus of living cells, were also obtained in a similar manner. Adenine, an important base in nucleic acids, was formed by chemical polymerization of hydrogen cyanide and ammonia. Carbohydrates, including the sugar backbones of nucleic acids, were also synthesized by incubating formaldehyde with an inert polar polymer, alumina, in the presence of some naturally occurring minerals.

Miller's results show that carefully controlled experiments in a closed system do result in the synthesis of a large variety of bio-organic compounds identical to those found in the living cell. However, compounds were synthesized only when sufficient starting materials were incubated with the right kind and right amount of energy in a *closed* system. On the other hand, in the primordial earth's *open* system with all processes random, the synthesis of these bio-organic compounds by *chance* alone is extremely improbable.

The second stage of chemical evolution involving the spontaneous origin of macromolecules seems contrary to the second law of thermodynamics. The law states that structures within a closed system tend toward a state of maximum disorder or randomness (increase in entropy). Thus a structure cannot become more complex (decrease in entropy) without the concomitant dismantling of another structure (increase in entropy) such that the resulting entropy of the whole system (i.e., the complex structure plus the dismantled structure) is increasing.

A living cell can order its amino acids and nucleic acid bases into proteins or nucleic acids, respectively. It does so by the efficient mechanisms of gene expression and replication fueled by a large expenditure of energy that has to be supplied by the breakdown of complex molecules acquired as nutrients from the environment. Carbohydrates represent one such energy source. During this process, the entropy of the universe increases slightly; therefore, the cell does not violate the second law of thermodynamics.

During the earth's primordial condition, such an intricate energy conversion machine as the cell did not exist. In isolated cases, energy may have been expended from the surrounding to fuel the ordering of certain organic molecules into bio-macromolecules. Yet the overall tendency in

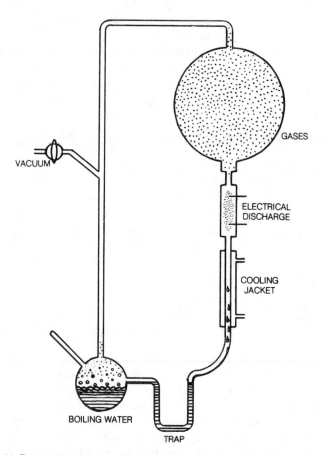

Figure 3.11. Experiment of S. L. Miller made amino acids by circulating methane (CH_4), ammonia (NH_3), water vapor (H_2O), and hydrogen (H_2) past an electrical discharge. The amino acids collected at the bottom of apparatus and were detected by paper chromatography. Reprinted, with permission, from Wald, G. The origin of life. Sc. Am. August 1954.

the primeval condition must have been such that spontaneous *dissolution* of transient macromolecules was much more probable than spontaneous *sustained* synthesis. These stipulations are represented in Figure 3.10 by the heavy backward arrows as compared to the slender forward arrows. In other words, the conditions that are presumably necessary for the synthesis of bio-organic and macromolecules are even more effective in *decomposing* them. Ultraviolet irradiation that was assumed to be a primary energy source for abiogenesis cleaves bonds of carbon compounds and causes their decomposition. Therefore the amino acids formed by processes analogous to Miller's experiment would be subject to the forces of dissolution right after their synthesis. The reason life can exist presently with these harmful solar irradiations is that ozone in the upper atmosphere filters out most ultraviolet radiation from sunlight before it reaches the earth. However, the ozone is formed from molecular oxygen that was presumably absent in the primeval atmosphere.

The lack of protection of the primitive earth's surface from solar irradiation by atmospheric gases prompted mechanistic evolutionists to suggest that life-requiring organic compounds were synthesized in the stratosphere where gases were diffused. This would allow organic compounds to be scattered right after their synthesis and minimize the dissolution effects of ultraviolet light.

It has been calculated that the rate of decomposition of glycine, the most abundant amino acid synthesized in Miller's experiment, is much greater than the rate of its formation, assuming the primordial conditions of the earth as proposed by Miller and his collaborator Urey. Thus 97% of the glycine synthesized in the atmosphere would be decomposed before it could reach the earth's surface (5). The minute quantity of glycine reaching the earth then must diffuse to a depth of at least 30 feet beneath the ocean's surface in order to escape the potential decomposing effects of ultraviolet light. Therefore, it is easily seen that the amount of organic compounds that could finally accumulate in the ocean would be much less than what the evolutionists would expect in the "rich primordial soup of organic nutrients," if they were accumulated at all.

The instability of covalent linkages in proteins, nucleic acids, and carbohydrates also adds to the seemingly insurmountable barriers that have to be overcome by advocates of abiogenesis. A. L. Lehninger stated: "In order for primordial polypeptides, polysaccharides and polynucleotides to accumulate in any amount in the primordial sea or in localized aqueous systems, the rate of their formation must have exceeded the rate of their degradation" (6). However, this stipulation is contrary to what is expected from the second law of thermodynamics. Therefore, a serious paradox exists in stage two of chemical evolution and cannot be easily ignored.

The commonly cited examples of self-replicating and metabolizing prebiotic systems (7) consist of *coacervate droplets* and *proteinoid microspheres*. Coacervate droplets are made up of bio-organic compounds of cell size in which organic macromolecules (amino acids, sugar, and bases) are entrapped in polymeric forms in aqueous (watery) droplets. The tendency to undergo coacervation is primarily a function of the molecular size and the matrix structure of the polymer that allows the penetration of water molecules. The droplet may increase in size to its physical limit and

199

then break into two smaller droplets just as oil breaks into smaller droplets when it is shaken in an aqueous environment.

Coacervate droplets are thought to be able to entrap a catalyst as well as a substrate and thus become a site for a primitive one-reaction metabolism. The droplets have been made in the laboratory from gelatin gum arabic, ribonucleic acid, nuclear protein, and serum albumin. However, coacervate droplets are unstable and lack the rigid template mechanisms that are typical of the genetic material of a living cell. Therefore, it is far from an adequate model of the first cell.

Proteinoid microspheres are synthesized when a high concentration of aspartic and glutamic acids in a nearly anhydrous (waterless) condition are heated to 170°C. Peptide bonds are formed, and proteinlike compounds with molecular weights of 3000 to 11 000 are generated. When these compounds are cooled slowly over a period of one or two weeks at the right pH and salt concentration, spherical droplets about 2.0 μ (μ = micron) in diameter appear. If the pH is adjusted properly, the outer boundaries of these microspheres show double-layered structures resembling a cell membrane. However, the outer boundary contains no lipid, an organic molecule always found in cell membranes. On the other hand, the microspheres have been observed to undergo "budding" or "cleavage" (processes common to living cells) when they are allowed to stand for a long period, or if exposed to Mg^{++}, or if there is a shift in pH.

The major deficiency of proteinoid microsphere formation as a model of the first cell is the absence of genetic material in the form of nucleic acid capable of self-reproduction through replication. Proteinoid microspheres would somehow have to be led to the formation of primitive nucleic acids for the propagation of the first cell if the model is valid (8). This process is difficult to accept since no present-day counterpart has been observed.

Dr. Peter T. Mora, a leading authority in research on the origin of life, has made some salient observations on problems faced by advocates of the theory of chemical evolution (9). His remarks are summarized in four points. The first point is that polymerization of chemical monomers under simulated primordial conditions contains no more than "information" input defined by physical and chemical means such as in experiments of organic chemistry, and it does not start new life processes capable of self-reproduction. Therefore, the results are analogous to the self-assembling process of a computer that operates only to the extent of information it is given. Mora's second point states that it is difficult to account for the switch to a self-reproducing *internal* control characteristic of the cell when chemical polymerization in the chemical evolution models is thought to be triggered by *external forces*.

In Mora's third point he deals with selectivity. Used in the physiochemical sense, selectivity does not parallel Darwinian selection that can explain only *how* a "living system" with a capacity to adjust to its changing environment reproduces persistently.

Selection, as used by Horowitz, Oparin, and other proponents of the theory of chemical evolution, includes the assumption that the more probable, less complex chemical events led to the acquisition of the more complex, less probable events having increased stability. In the physiochemical sense, selectivity can only mean the in vitro chemical reaction that operates only when the "selective" conditions exist, i.e., the reactants are in the right energy state, reactants collide, and catalysts are available. None of the above conditions persist and thus cannot lead to a consistently self-maintaining and self-reproducing system. The conditions produce only a temporary metastable order or function that will cease and tend to disperse more and more as its complexity increases. Therefore, natural selection in the Darwinian sense cannot be applied at the molecular level.

Mora's last point states that living systems require an increase in complexity and interaction of molecular aggregates. However, the presence of random physiochemical forces operate to decrease the formation and interaction of the above complexes. Therefore, there is a low probability that interacting chemical systems will reproduce persistently and overcome disruptive changes. The logical conclusion suggests that the origin and continuance of life on earth is not controlled by the above principles.

c) *Weak Empirical Documentation of Evolution Above the Species Level (Macroevolution, Transpecific Evolution).* Macroevolution (transpecific evolution) above the species level rests quite heavily on the concept of speciation. Although a rational explanation can be formulated to account for diversification of species in nature by microevolution (*see* I.3.2.2), it has not been observed in a controlled laboratory setting.

Experiments with the chemostat (*see* I.3.2.1) can allow the observation of numerous generations of bacterial evolution in a relatively short period of time. However, only varieties within a species do interchange genetic materials, and no new species have been detected. Ernst Mayr (10) pointing out the difficulty stated, "Knowing that there are alternative modes of speciation, the student of evolution is faced by a methodological difficulty. Speciation is a slow historical process and except in the case of polyploidy, it can never be observed directly by an individual observer."

Polyploidy is a major phenomenon in plant evolution, and it can be observed empirically. This phenomenon of plant speciation will be considered more carefully (11) in the following discussion.

201

Polyploidy was discovered 60 years ago when the chromosome numbers of some plants were analyzed. The diploid numbers of plant chromosomes range from 4 to well over 200. However, the most frequent number was 12, while 8 was the next frequent. About 50% of all plants have chromosome numbers below 12. Plants with higher chromosome numbers usually have multiples of the lower ones. Within a single genus, there is usually a series of species in which the chromosome numbers of some are multiples of that of another species. This condition in which the number of chromosome sets in the nucleus is a multiple (greater than two) of the haploid numbers is called polyploidy. This could happen in two ways, either a single set of haploid chromosomes is present more than twice (autopolyploidy) or two or more sets of chromosomes from different species are present, making a total of more than two genomes (allopolyploidy). Allopolyploidy is more frequent in plant speciation.

Autopolyploids are known both in nature and in experimental materials. One of the bases of de Vries's mutation theory was an autopolyploid mutant strain of *Oenothera lamarckiana* (evening primrose). It is a tetraploid containing 28 chromosomes instead of the diploid number of 14, and other tetraploid plants species exhibit features similar to those of this plant. First, it is considerably larger than the diploid *O. lamarckiana*, and de Vries named this autopolyploid plant *Oenothera gigas* because of its size and regarded it as a new species. Second, the stems are thicker, and the leaves are shorter, broader, and thicker than those of the diploid plant. Third, it seems to have a slower growth rate than the diploid *O. lamarckiana*. However, this is not typical, because most tetraploids can adapt to more severe environments. This is due to tetraploids usually being more vigorous than their diploid counterparts.

An autopolyploid produces offspring that can be mated to the diploid parent. Therefore an autopolyploid is not considered a new species. But there is considerable reproductive isolation between a diploid and its autotetraploid because the hybrid between them is a triploid (three haploid genomes in each cell). Triploids are highly *sterile* because they usually do not form regular gametes during meiosis. Many autopolyploids with odd numbers of the haploid genome are *nonviable*. Therefore the role played by triploids derived from autopolyploidy in plant speciation is minimal.

Allopolyploidy also has been produced experimentally and observed in nature. Two mechanisms are advanced to account for the occurrence of allopolyploidy in plants and are based on the occasional failure of reduction division during meiosis observed in plants and especially frequent in plants with chromosome complements that do not synapse readily.

In examining allopolyploidy, A and B will each represent a different haploid chromosomal set. Thus the chromosomal segregation and assortment in the cross of AA x BB will result in a hybrid F_1 of AB. In subsequent generations, if there is insufficient homology between A and B to permit synapsis, a significant percentage of AB gametes may be produced in meiosis, due to the failure in reduction of chromosomes. In a self-fertilized plant, some AB ovules will be fertilized by AB pollens. Thus an allotetraploid $AABB$ is formed at once. This allotetraploid has two sets of homologous chromosomes, and there is little tendency for synapsis to occur between A and B (a condition that leads to this formation in the allotetraploid in the first place). Also, there is little chance to have a complex and irregular segregation pattern during meiosis. Therefore the allotetraploid is perfectly fertile.

There is another mechanism by which allopolyploids can be formed. This mechanism involves a two-step utilization of the failure of reduction during meiosis. If a hybrid AB is backcrossed with one of its parent AA, an occasional nonreduction may occur, and AB fails to segregate during meiosis. Thus the offspring becomes AAB. If AAB is then mated with BB and fails to segregate during meiosis, then the allotetraploid $AABB$ is formed. Allotetraploid may also be formed by accidental doubling of the chromosomes in the zygote of the original hybrid AB, in a manner analogous to the experimental induction of chromosomal doubling by treatment with the drug colchicine. This drug blocks the assembly of the mitotic spindle apparatus.

Allotetraploids show characteristics of both parental species, in addition to new tetraploid characteristics. The species are good because they can propagate indefinitely without any apparent defect in their reproductive machinery. They are also reproductively isolated from their parent by the sterility or inviability of the hybrid produced by the cross between the allotetraploid and either of the parent species. This can be visualized by examining the meiotic pattern of the hybrid AAB obtained from mating $AABB$ and AA. The two A chromosome sets can form a synaptic pair and can undergo reduction in meiosis. However, the B set does not synapse, and it will be distributed randomly to each gamete. Thus it has meiotic difficulties and is highly sterile.

Allopolyploidy is commonly observed in nature and is one of the major mechanisms of plant speciation. It is a good example of sympatric speciation (see I.1.5). The evolution of bread wheat is a classic example of sympatric speciation through allopolyploidy. Modern wheat (Triticum aestivum) is a hexaploid represented by $AABBDD$ (Figure 3.12). Its lineage can be traced to the tetraploid wheat Triticum dicoccum with an

AABB genome that is produced by the intergeneric cross between the diploid wheat *Triticum monococcum (AA)* and goat grass *Aegilops speltoides* (BB). Later, a second intergeneric cross between *T. dicoccum* and *Aegilops squarrosa*, the latter contributing the *D* genome, occurred to produce modern bread wheat.

Although polyploidy plays a major role in plant speciation, it is considered to be of minor significance in animals. The majority of the animals that have been reported to be polyploids are parthenogenetic (reproduction without fertilization) or hermaphroditic (having both sexes in the same individual). All of the parthenogenetic organisms are arthropods such as the water flea, brine shrimp, "walking stick" insects, psychid moths, and some beetles. Flatworms and earthworms are representatives of polyploids among the hermaphroditic animals. Very few bisexually reproducing animals are polyploids. These include a nematode parasite of horses, several species of starfish and sea urchins, and the golden hamster. But the overall rarity of polyploids in animals makes them the exceptions rather than the rule.

Muller has suggested that the reason why polyploidy plays a greater role in plant evolution is that the sexes are usually separate in animals whereas plants are often hermaphroditic. Random segregation of several pairs of sex chromosomes in a polyploid animal would result in sterile combination whereas polyploids with even pairs of the haploid genomes (tetraploids, hexaploids, octaploids, etc.) in plants are perfectly fertile. For example, a male tetraploid animal of sex chromosome constitution *XXYY*, and a female tetraploid *XXXX* would produce gametes *XY* and *XX*, respectively. The union of these gametes gives rise to a zygote *XXXY*, and in some species this is neither completely male nor female; therefore, it is sterile. This explanation seems to be supported by observations and is widely accepted. Thus we can see that the above mechanism for speciation in plants is insufficient to explain speciation in animals.

Mayr (10) maintained that by postulating different stages a population has to go through during speciation and finding natural populations in each of these stages, the slow past events of speciation could be reconstructed and "proved." This approach was taken by Darwin and other early evolutionists, but their studies were not fruitful because of their poor definition of species. Today some of the difficulties in defining a species have been removed by the *interbreeding population* concept (*see* I.1.2), but this concept is not always easily applicable to natural populations. Therefore, species distinction is often arbitrary. Since there is more than one proposed mechanism to account for speciation, the attempt to categorize natural populations according to one's presupposition may at

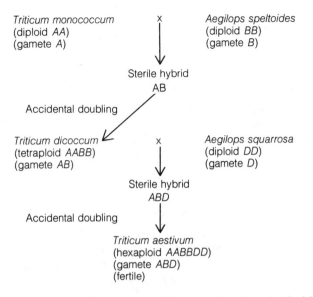

Figure 3.12. Evolution of bread wheat *(Triticum aestivum)* by allopolyploidy.

most yield circumstantial evidence of a highly inferential nature.

In summary, empirical documentation of evolution above the species level is not yet forthcoming. It can be argued that since macroevolution happened over a long period of time, it cannot be observed empirically in one's lifetime. Nonetheless, the phylogenetic developments in the higher categories have to be extrapolated from the well-defined processes of microevolution. The theory of organic evolution will be without a firm foundation if it is divorced from the empirical documentation of microevolution.

For years Neo-Darwinists have asserted that natural selection, a mechanism operating very nicely in microevolution, is equally applicable in the evolution of the higher categories. However, it will be seen that this assertion is seriously challenged, and some modern evolutionists maintain that natural selection plays a minimal role in transpecific evolution, if at all. This will be dealt with in I.3.3.2. The need to be anything but dogmatic in one's assertion based on the evidence is immediately apparent.

d) *Inconsistency of Molecular Biological Data With Data Supporting Macroevolution.* G. G. Simpson, a renowned taxonomist and paleontologist, predicted a few decades ago the relationship between morphological changes and genetic changes in evolution as follows (12):

205

Morphological and taxonomic rates [of evolution] have a decided, even though indirect, relationship to genetic rates. If this were not so, their bearing on evolutionary theory would be quite different. It has become commonplace that changes in morphology or phenotype may be induced by factors other than changes in genotype and therefore may not reflect the latter accurately. More recently it has been recognized that changes in genotype may not be accompanied proportionately, or at all, by changes in phenotype. Nevertheless, there can seldom be any doubt that well-defined morphological changes in phenotypes of successive populations, particularly as these occur over considerable periods of time in the fossil record, run parallel to genetic changes in those populations. It is therefore a proper assumption in such cases that morphological rates do reflect genetic rates, even though they are probably not exactly proportioned to the latter. The assumption is even more reliable for taxonomic rates because the concepts and usages of modern taxonomy are in part genetical even when the observed data are morphological.

As Simpson made clear, it has been held as the most reasonable assumption by most evolutionists that the rate of morphological evolution reflects the rate of genetic evolution. This was true until the advent of molecular techniques and their use in the analysis of the genetic differences of natural populations.

Lewontin delineated four required criteria for estimating genotypic frequencies in populations in order to classify individuals into genetic classes unambiguously (13): (1) Phenotypic differences caused by the substitution of one allele for another at a single locus must be detectable as an unambiguous difference between individuals. (2) Allelic substitutions at one locus must be distinguishable in their effects from allelic substitution at other loci. (3) All, or a very large fraction of, allelic substitutions at a locus must be detectable and distinguishable from each other, irrespective of the intensity or range of their physiological effects. (4) The loci that are amenable to attack must be a random sample of genes with respect to the amount of genetic variation that exists at the locus. He concluded that the methods of classical genetics that try to decipher the genotypes by examining the morphological and visible changes in the organisms fail to fulfill these criteria.

The best solution to detect genetic differences in populations appears to be the methods of molecular genetics. Since the sequence of nucleotides that makes up a structural gene is translated into the primary structure of a polypeptide chain with high fidelity (see I.2.6.2), the change in the amino acid sequence reflects the mutation in nucleotides with a high degree of colinearity. Therefore, the analysis of amino acid sequence of proteins is a method that can satisfy all the requirements listed above.

A single allelic substitution is detectable unambiguously since it results in a discrete change in the phenotype—a substitution, deletion, or addition of an amino acid. Every substitution is detectably different except for mutation within the degenerate codes. The gene effects of different loci cannot be confused with each other since they encode different proteins. The conflict between the discrete phenotypic effect demanded by Mendelism and the subtle phenotypic differences hardly detectable is resolved by looking at the gene product directly. By equating one gene to one polypeptide, the techniques in molecular genetics allow the examination of random samples of genes regardless of their variabilities or mutabilities.

There are several methods developed in molecular genetics to analyze genic differences among organisms.

(1) *Method of DNA Hybridization.* Since DNA carries the genetic information, the most direct method of detecting genetic differences of organisms is to measure the proportion of nucleotide pairs that are different in their DNAs. This can be accomplished by making hybrid molecules from single-stranded DNAs obtained by separating the double helices of the tested organisms by physical means. When the single stranded DNAs from different organisms are brought together, they will form hybrid duplex molecules according to their degree of DNA homology.

Two different measures of DNA differences can be obtained by hybridization: (1) the fraction of the DNA of two species that form hybrid molecules and (2) the proportion of nucleotide pairs that are complementary to each other in the hybrid molecules. The first measure can be obtained by selectively isolating the hybrid molecules from the single-stranded DNA. The second measure can be determined by monitoring the temperature at which these hybrid molecules separate into single strands again, which is proportional to the degree of nucleotide complementarity.

Since DNA hybridization is time consuming and the information obtained is too crude to be related to a single gene, it is largely used for preliminary analysis of genic differences among populations.

(2) *Immunological Techniques.* Immunological techniques depend on the specificities of the antigen-antibody reaction. Antibodies are proteins produced in vertebrates when they are exposed to foreign substances called antigens. The specificity of the immunological reaction can also be visualized by the *lock and key theory* (*see* Figure 2.50). The antibodies serve as a lock and the antigen the key. Most antigens are proteins. A single amino acid substitution in an antigen, reflected by the change in the configuration of the key, prevents it from fitting the lock as tightly.

Immunological comparisons of proteins from different species can be done easily. For example, blood albumin from a monkey is purified, and the purified protein is injected into another mammal, a rabbit. The rabbit will develop an antibody specifically against monkey albumin. One assesses how close any other protein not used to immunize rabbits comes to the monkey albumin injected into the rabbit by comparing the reaction between the uninjected protein and the antibody with the reaction between the injected antigen and the antibody produced. If the reactions are similar, the antigens are similar. The degrees of dissimilarity between a protein used in an immunization and a tested protein from another species is expressed as an *immunological distance* between the species. Since the immunological method is crude and produces indirect results, it is used only as a supplementary method for the analysis of genetic differences.

(3) *Electrophoretic Measurements.* Since all amino acids contain an acidic and a basic group, they behave as charged molecules under physiological conditions. Some common amino acids also have polar side chains that have a charge if ionized. Proteins formed by amino acids linked by peptide bonds also have as charged particles in solutions. At a given pH a protein has a certain defined net charge determined by the number and type of ionizable groups it possesses. A technique called electrophoresis is able to separate proteins according to the net charges of each protein at a given pH.

If an allelic change at a genetic locus results in the replacement of an amino acid having a nonpolar side chain with one that has a polar side chain or vice versa, the net charge of the protein will be altered. This can be detected when the protein is placed in an electric field, for it will migrate differently. For example, a single-step change in the codon AAC to AAA results in the substitution of the positively charged lysine for the neutral asparagine. An even more drastic single-step change is from AAG to GAG, which results in the substitution of a negatively charged glutamic acid for the positively charged lysine.

The apparatus of a typical gel electrophoresis experiment is depicted in Figure 3.13. It consists essentially of a slab of some jellylike material (starch, agar, or a synthetic polymer) whose two ends are in contact with the opposite poles of an electric potential. Material for electrophoresis is introduced into the wells at one end of the gel. Any charged molecules will move down the gel according to the force of attraction exerted by the electric field. The gel is surrounded by a cooling jacket to prevent overheating that may disrupt the three-dimensional structure of the proteins and thus adversely affect its mobility in the electric field. The proteins to be analyzed are extracted from tissue of an individual organism, subjected to several crude steps of a protein-purification scheme, and then applied to the electrophoretic chamber. The speed of migration (mobility) of each protein band will depend on its net charge and to a lesser degree its molecular size. After the proteins have migrated across the gel, the electrophoresis is stopped, and the proteins are stained and visualized.

Due to the relative ease of operation and the sensitivity of this method, it has been widely used to detect polymorphic forms of protein extracted from various individuals within a natural population. The identification of widespread protein polymorphism is in part the evidence that led to the formulation of the theory of neutral mutation. The occurrence of this phenomenon is poorly explained by the mechanism of natural selection. This will be discussed in more detail in the next section.

(4) *Amino Acid Sequencing of Proteins.* Amino acid sequencing of proteins is by far the most accurate method of estimating genetic differences among organisms. Proteins are extracted from tissues of animals or from whole organisms and exhaustively purified to remove contaminating proteins. The isolated protein is then subjected to amino acid sequencing. First, if the protein has quaternary structure, the individual polypeptide chains are separated and purified. Second, a sample of each polypeptide chain is subjected to total hydrolysis, and its amino acid composition is determined. Third, each polypeptide is broken into small peptide fragments by chemicals (some enzymes) that attack only specific regions of the polypeptide. Fourth, the amino acid sequence of each fragment is deter-

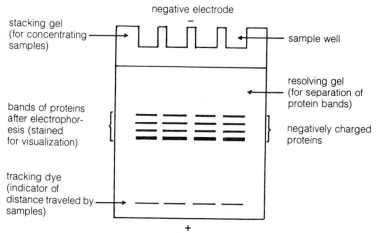

Figure 3.13. Diagram of a vertical slab gell-electrophoresis apparatus.

209

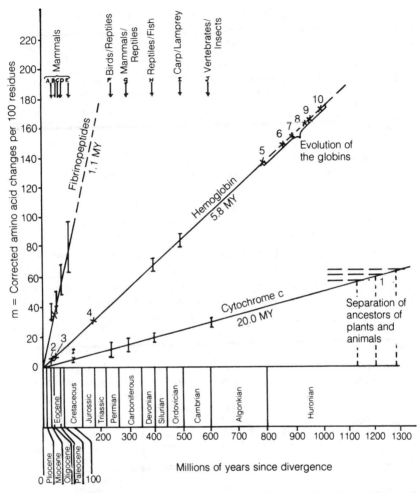

Figure 3.14. Rates of amino acid substitution in the fibrinopeptides, hemoglobin, and cytochrome c. Comparisons for which no adequate time coordinate is available are indicated by numbered crosses. Point 1 represents a date of 1200 ± 75 MY (million years) for the separation of plants and animals, based on a linear extrapolation of the cytochrome c curve. Points 2–10 refer to events in the evolution of the globin family. The δ/β separation is at point 3, γ/β is at 4, and α/β is at 500 MY (carp/lamprey). Reproduced, with permission, from Nei, M. Molecular population genetics and evolution. New York: Elsevier & N. Holland; 1975.

mined. Fifth, the amino acid sequence of each polypeptide is determined by analyzing the relationship of fragment overlap. Technological advances have enabled the procedures to be automated in a sophisticated apparatus known as an amino acid analyzer.

210

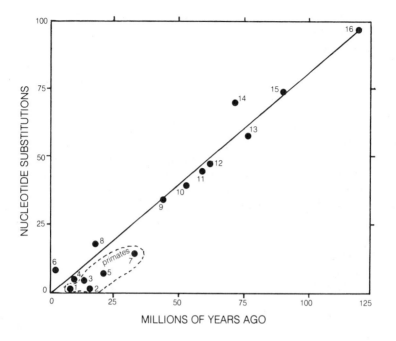

Figure 3.15. Assumed phylogeny of the species for which sequences were examined. The order of branching was assumed. The nodes depicting speciation are placed on the abscissa according to the maximum likelihood solution for the number of nucleotides substituted in all seven proteins. The upper scale does not give the true times of divergence but rather the estimated times of divergence if one placed the marsupial-placental divergence at 120 x 10⁶ years ago and time was directly proportional to the nucleotide substitution scale. Numbers are by increasing abscissal value. Reproduced, with permission, from Fitch, W. M.; Langley, C. H. Federation proceedings. 35:2093; 1976.

The results of amino acid sequencing are indisputably accurate, allowing one to determine relative similarity of sequences of proteins derived from different sources. Amino acid sequences have been studied extensively for the proteins cytochrome c, hemoglobin, and fibrinopeptides. This information has been used in studies of phylogeny. The results pose some serious problems for evolutionists who advocate the mechanism of natural selection.

When studying phylogeny using sequences of protein, the number of amino acid substitutions that differentiates the same protein extracted from two different organisms is plotted (14). This is plotted against the time that the lineages of the two organisms presumably diverged in the geological record. The results obtained are straight lines in the case of

211

each protein (14) (Figure 3.14). The number in millions of years (as obtained from the fossil record) listed parallel to and beneath each line represents the estimated time necessary for a single amino acid substitution to take place per 100 residues in the polypeptide chains. Thus, the rate of protein evolution is roughly constant over most of evolutionary time.

A comparison of the amino acid substitution rate of hemoglobins verses cytochrome c using sources such as the human, rabbit, snapping turtle, tuna, and rattlesnake shows them to be significantly different (15). Nevertheless, when the total nucleotide substitutions as calculated from the observed amino acid substitutions in seven proteins (cytochrome c, fibrinopeptides A and B, hemoglobin α and β, myoglobin, and insulin C' peptide) have been calculated by comparisons between pairs of mammalian species (Figure 3.15) and plotted against the time of presumed di-

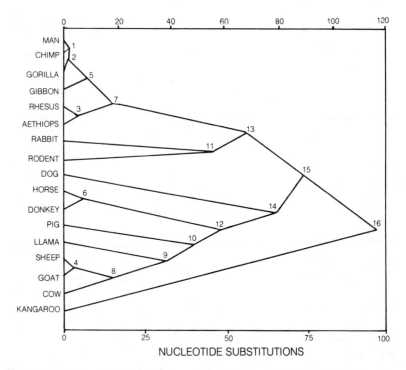

Figure 3.16. Linear relation between time elapsed and nucleotide substitutions. Numbers on points identify the nodes of Figure 3.15 that have been plotted according to the number of nucleotide substitutions expected from maximum likelihood solution. The line was simply drawn through the origin and point 16. Reprinted, with permission, from Fitch, W. M.; Langley, C. H. Federation proceedings. 35:2093; 1976.

vergence of the ancestors of the respective species, a straight line is obtained (Figure 3.16).

The presumed time of divergence of the lineages tested were constructed from protein sequence data. This was done independent of ac-

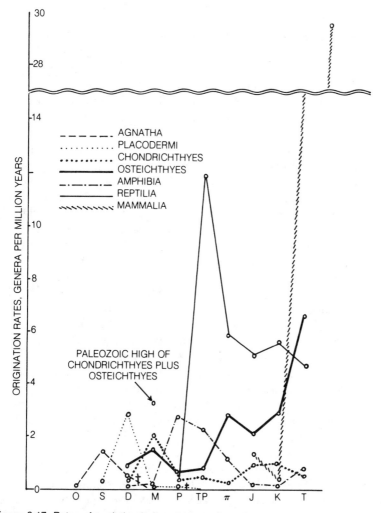

Figure 3.17. Rates of evolution in the classes of vertebrates (except birds). The time scale runs from Ordovician *(O)* to Tertiary *(T).* The abbreviations are as follows: *S* (Silurian), *D* (Devonian), *M* (Mississippian), *P* (Pennsylvanian), *TP* (Permian), *TT* (Triassic), *J* (Jurassic), *K* (Cretaceous). For the time scale in years, see Table 2.8. Reprinted, with permission, from Simpson, G. G. The meaning of evolution. New Haven: Yale University Press; 1949.

cepted phylogenetic schemes based on geological and fossil material. Therefore, the average rates of protein evolution over a period of time are constant and may be used as an approximate evolutionary clock. The overall correlation is fairly good except for the primates. They appear to have evolved at a substantially slower rate than the average of other organisms (16).

The rates of evolution as judged by structural changes and diversification of lines of descent, as expressed in the rate of origination of genera per million years measured in several classes of vertebrates throughout the geological eras, show an erratic pattern (17) (Figure 3.17). This evolution of morphological features and diversification of descent seems to be independent of genetic change as measured by the substitutions of nucleotides in the DNA.

An extensive comparison of 43 proteins extracted from humans and chimpanzees correlating the electrophoretic studies and protein sequencing with the techniques of DNA hybridization and immunological reactions were made. It was reported that the genetic distances among species from different genera within the same family are considerably larger than the genetic distance between humans and chimpanzees, and they are in different families (30). In other words, the anatomically and behaviorally distinct species of human and chimpanzee that are classified in different zoological families are found, according to these data, to be more closely related genetically to each other than are several sibling species or congeneric species of the frog, fruit fly, or mouse.

The rates of evolution at the molecular level among human and chimpanzee lines of descent seem to be equal to each other after the presumed divergence from a common ancestor. On the other hand, the biological evolution as measured by the organismic change in the two lines seems to indicate that the human has evolved much further than the chimpanzee after divergence (Figure 3.18). This evidence also indicates that genetic changes are independent of changes in morphological features during the course of evolution.

If the morphological and physiological features of an organism are the result of gene expression controlled by the messages carried by DNA, an assumption that is the working hypothesis for modern biologists, then the apparent independence of the two levels of evolution seems to indicate an inconsistency of molecular biological data with other data supporting macroevolution. Although several hypotheses are postulated to try to account for this inconsistency (*see* I.3.3.2), a solution that can be documented empirically is not yet in sight. This inconsistency will likely remain an enigma for evolutionists.

214

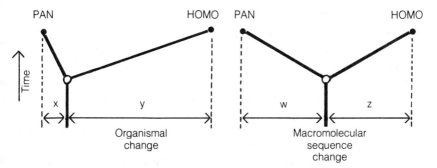

Figure 3.18. Contrast between biological evolution and molecular evolution since the divergence of the human and chimpanzee lineages from a common ancestor. As shown on the left, zoological evidence indicates that far more biological change has taken place in the human lineage *(y)* than in the chimpanzee lineage *(y ≫ x)*; this illustration is adapted from that of Simpson. As shown on the right, both protein and nucleic acid evidence indicate that as much change has occurred in chimpanzee genes *(w)* as in human genes *(z)*. Reproduced, with permission, from Science, 188 (April 11): 107–116; 1975. American Association for the Advancement of Science, Washington, D.C.

3.3.2 Rational Incoherency

a) *Insufficiency of Natural Selection to Account for Macroevolution.* Evolution above the species level has not been satisfactorily accounted for by the mechanism of natural selection even though it does explain nicely the phenomena of microevolution. This quote is from a recent text on evolution (18):

> The process of natural selection, acting upon the sources of genetic variability that reside in the gene pools of species, is clearly adequate to produce, preserve, and accumulate the sorts of changes that lead one species to another. There is a voluminous body of theory and evidence to explain the origin of species through microevolution.
>
> The differences between distantly allied species are profound, however. . . . The differences between such species are in fact so impressive that some investigators have suggested that they have arisen through mechanisms distinct from the microevolutionary processes of adaptation. This has led to some of the major controversies in evolutionary theory.

Various concepts have been proposed to account for macroevolution. The following sections will review the concepts of *neutral mutation, regulatory mutation, systematic mutation,* and *species selection.*

(1) *Concept of Neutral Mutation.* As mentioned earlier in I.1.4, the classical mutation theory was popular in the earlier part of the twentieth century until the elaborate work of Dobzhansky and others who presented a strong case for evolution by natural selection. The two theories predict different degrees of genetic variability in natural popula-

tions. The classical theory predicts that most individuals in the natural population are homozygous since natural selection serves to eliminate all but a few mutations that are in the form of heterozygotes. Therefore, genetic variability in natural populations, according to the classicists, is minimal.

The Neo-Darwinist, or the selectionist, on the other hand, predicts exactly the opposite results. Since natural selection works on gene mutations to cause changes in gene frequencies, many individuals in natural populations, which are presumably undergoing evolutionary change, would be heterozygotes that arise from mutations but are selected by overdominance (*see* I.3.2.1). According to selectionists then, genetic variability in natural populations is the rule instead of the exception.

Before the evidence from the studies of molecular evolution was available, only mutations that had drastic phenotypic effects were analyzed, and the phenomenon of genetic variability in natural populations could not be empirically detected. Therefore, although examples of polymorphism (i.e., situations where the members of a natural population can be sharply categorized into two or more relatively common phenotypes that are determined by commonly occurring alleles at a particular gene locus, such as blood types) were recognized in genetics early in the science, it was impossible to tell whether these represented special cases or a widespread phenomenon.

In the late 1960s, workers began to employ the technology of molecular biology to tackle the problem of genetic variability in natural populations. By the application of electrophoretic techniques, it was found that enzyme and protein polymorphism both in *Drosophila* (19, 20) and the human (21) is a common phenomenon. Similar studies have been carried out in plants (22, 23) and in animals, including protozoans, mollusks, arthropods, bryozoans, echinoderms, and vertebrates (24). It has become clear that this phenomenon is ubiquitous at least in the natural populations of animals. The discovery of the widespread polymorphisms together with the apparent constant rate of molecular evolution (*see* I.3.3.1.d) gave the classicists new impetus, and they postulated a new concept of *neutral mutation* in reformulating their theory. Presently, they are called the *neo-classicists* or *panneutralists* as contrasted with the Neo-Darwinian school of *selectionists*.

There are two parameters in the description of enzyme or protein polymorphisms in natural populations: (1) percentage of loci (alleles) that are polymorphic, and (2) percentage of loci (alleles) that are heterozygous. Each parameter can be accurately estimated by analyzing the gel-electrophoretic pattern (Figure 3.19) showing a typical analysis of enzyme polymorphism. The electrophoretic pattern can allow the differentiation of polymorphic alleles and can show if an organism is homozygous or heterozygous at a genetic locus.

The phenomenon of polymorphisms and heterzygosity is illustrated in a study of enzymatic differences within a single species. *Esterase-5* is an enzyme known to be synthesized by the gene locus 5 in a particular chromosome of *Drosophila pseudoobscura*. Sample 1 is a homozygous standard strain, as indicated by a discrete protein band synthesized by two identical alleles on locus *est-5[1.00]*. The superscript stands for the relative electrophoretic mobility of the protein specified by the allele. Samples 2, 3, and 6 have a slower migrating protein, while sample 5 moves faster than the standard. Sample 4 shows three bands, two identical with the fast- and slow-moving bands and one intermediate between

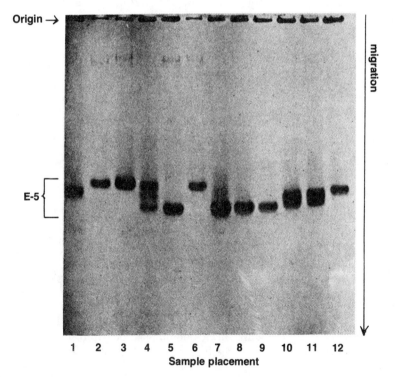

Figure 3.19. Adult esterases from *Drosophila pseudoobscura*. Sample 1, standard strain *est-5[1.00]/est-5[1.00]*; samples 2 and 3, *est-5[0.95]/est-5[0.95]*; sample 4, *est-5[0.95]/est-5[1.12]*; sample 5, *est-5[1.12]/est-5[1.12]*; sample 6, *est-5[0.95]/est-5[0.95]*. Reprinted, with permission, from Lewontin, R. C. The genetic basis of evolutionary change. New York: Columbia University Press; 1974.

them. Samples 7–12 contain other proteins that are irrelevant to the present discussion. By looking only at the mobilites and the discreteness of the protein bands in sample 5 and samples 2, 3, and 6, one can infer that the two homozygotes est-$5^{1.12}$ and est-$5^{0.95}$ are represented by the fast- and slow-moving bands respectively. Thus, we can conclude that the $esterase$-5 locus is polymorphic, because different homozygotes can be detected according to their electrophoretic mobilities from the natural population of $D.\ pseudoobscura$.

The three bands shown in sample 4 can be identified as a heterozygote est-$5^{0.95}/est$-$5^{1.12}$. The presence of the intermediate band in sample 4 indicates that $esterase$-5 is a dimeric enzyme (consisting of two polypeptides). Therefore, the heterozygote, est-$5^{0.95}/est$-$5^{1.12}$ can produce three dimers: (1) homodimer 0.95–0.95, with the same mobility as the dimer made by the homozygote est-$5^{0.95}$; (2) homodimer 1.12–1.12, with the same mobility as the dimer made by the homozygote est-$5^{1.12}/est$-$5^{1.12}$; and (3) a hybrid dimer 1.12–0.95, with a mobility halfway between. This heterozygosity of sample 4 is confirmed by the genetic analysis of individuals from the strain with extracted protein of sample 4 that segregates into two different alleles. Thus the electrophoretic pattern easily reveals the heterozygosity of a locus regardless of the dominance or recessiveness of the alleles because the product of each allele is examined.

Even when an enzyme is monomeric (consisting of only one polypeptide), the heterozygote is easily detected also for it makes two different forms of the enzyme. Each form corresponds to one of the homozygotes in mobility despite the absence of the "hybrid" molecule as seen in sample 4. The different enzyme forms produced by different alleles at the same locus are called *allozymes*. The difference of mobility in the various protein bands represents only one-third or one-half of the amino acid changes in the polypeptides that are responsible for the polymorphism. Many amino acid substitutions involve no change in net charge of the protein and are not detected by the change in electrophoretic mobilities. Therefore estimates of polymorphisms and heterozygosities are only for the "lower limits" of what the case actually is. From these data it is estimated that in sexually reproducing species of animals, one-third of their genes are polymorphic, and 10% of the loci of the individuals within the species are heterozygous (25).

The principles set forth by the neo-classicists to account for molecular evolution are fivefold (26): (1) For each protein, the rate of evolution in terms of amino acid substitutions is approximately constant per site per year, as long as the function and tertiary structure of the protein molecules remain essentially unaltered. (2) Functionally less important molecules or parts of molecules evolve (in terms of mutant substitutions) faster than more important ones. (3) Those mutant substitutions that cause less disruption in the existing structure and function of a molecule (conservative substitutions) occur more frequently in evolution than do more disruptive ones. (4) Gene duplication must always precede the emergence of a gene having a new function. (5) Selective elimination of definitely harmful mutants and random fixation of selectively neutral or very slightly harmful mutants occur far more frequently in evolution than the positive Darwinian selection of definitely advantageous mutants.

The first condition is somewhat substantiated by the development of the molecular clock (*see* I.3.3.1.d, Figure 3.16) and the apparent constant rate of evolutions in some proteins (*see* Figure 3.14). Despite some disparities in the rate of evolution in some proteins, the rate of neutral mutations is largely unknown because of limited data. However, it can be calculated that the rate of gene substitution for neutral genes is equal to the mutation rate, irrespective of population size (27, 13). Therefore, if mutation rate remains constant, the rate of evolutionary change for a given protein would also occur with constant probability. The second condition seems to be well documented by the fact that fibrinopeptide and proinsulinpolypeptide C, both relatively useless proteins, evolve 18 and 11 times respectively, faster than cytochrome c, which is an essential protein in the energy transport mechanisms (28). The evolution of hemoglobin α and β chain lends support to the third condition. The surface part of the molecules evolves nearly 10 times as fast as the functionally important heme pocket.

The fourth condition of gene duplication is a mechanism proposed initially to explain protein evolution of hemoglobins and myoglobins that share many common amino acid sequences and similar functions. It seems to be the most appealing mechanism to account for the evolutionary acquisition of a large amount of DNA in higher organisms (Figure 3.20). However, the theory of gene duplication has no empirical documentation. The lack of apparent selective values of most of the polymorphisms observed in natural populations are taken to be indicative of the failure of natural selection to maintain genetic variability of these loci. Last, natural selection is taken by panneutralists as the editor, rather than the composer, of the genetic message as claimed by the selectionists.

The controversies between panneutralists and Neo-Darwinian selectionists can be represented in their disagreements over the interpretation of two phenomena—the apparent constant rate of protein evolution and the widespread protein polymorphism. First, the panneutralists claim that the apparent constant rate of protein evolution (which may be subject to different interpretations) is strong evidence to support the hypothesis that it is the result of neutral mutation, the rate of which determines the rate of amino acid substitution by random genetic drift. However, the selectionists have to make very specific assumptions on mutation rates, selective advantages, and effective population sizes in order to explain the apparent constancy of protein evolution. On the one hand, selectionists question the constancy of protein evolution. On the other hand, they stress that amino acids in a protein sequence in a species have been selected in the course of evolution because they are best adapted to meet the particular features of external environment. Selection of an amino acid

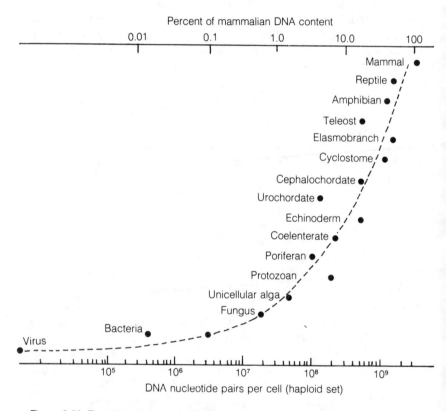

Figure 3.20. The minimal amount of DNA that has been observed for various species in the types of organisms listed. Each point represents the measured DNA content per cell for a haploid set of chromosomes. The ordinate scale and the shape of the curve is arbitrary. Reprinted, with permission, from Nei, M. Molecular population genetics and evolution. New York: Elsevier & N. Holland; 1975.

sequence of a protein also depends on the activities of the other genes present.

In considering the second phenomenon, panneutralists maintain that the widespread polymorphism in natural populations is the result of mutations that are neither beneficial nor harmful and are fixed by random genetic drift. Natural selection is mainly responsible for the elimination of harmful mutations and only occasionally establishes rare advantageous mutations. Selectionists argue that the heterozygotes are responsible for carrying the mutations and are selectively more advantageous (hybrid vigor or overdominance) than the homozygotes. Therefore, protein polymorphisms are the expressions of a stable genetic equilibrium maintained by balancing selection (see I.3.2.1.c).

Both theories seem to account for some of the observations of molecular evolution, but both have serious shortcomings. The panneutralists have to document their assertion of the constant rate of protein evolution more vigorously in light of the disparities observed in some known cases. In addition, the proportions of allozyme polymorphisms showing selective values are considerable and cannot be easily ignored.

The balancing selection theory is plagued with the conflict between "hybrid vigor" and "inbreeding depression." If a large percentage of natural populations are heterozygous as maintained by balancing selection, a significant percentage of homozygotes would be derived by the inevitable inbreeding of heterozygotes, and the genetic variability of the populations would be reduced accordingly. However, this was not observed. Moreover, heterozygotes produced by bisexual organisms seem not to be necessary for the maintenance of protein polymorphisms for self-fertilizing plants (22) and bacteria (29). Parthenogenic species of animals (24) are also shown to be polymorphic in many loci.

These data place severe strains on the selection theory. The rarity of observable hybrid vigor, except the well-studied sickle cell anemia (see I.2.6.2; 3.2.1.c), also does not aid the selectionist's position. At the present time the controversy between the selectionists and panneutralists goes on with no solution yet in sight. It is fair to conclude that the foundation of macroevolution based on natural selection is seriously shaken by the panneutralists.

(2) *Concept of Regulatory Mutation.* The concept that major anatomical changes are the result of mutations affecting gene expression (regulatory mutations) was proposed to account for the apparent inconsistency between molecular and organismal evolution (30) (see I.3.2.1.d). According to this hypothesis, small differences in the time of activation or in the level of activity of a single regulatory gene could in principle

influence considerably the systems controlling embryonic development. The organismal differences between chimpanzee and humans would then probably result chiefly from genetic changes in a few regulatory systems that are hardly detectable due to the difficulties involved in the purification and identification of regulatory proteins.

Regulatory mutations can occur in two ways. First, nucleotide substitution can affect a regulator gene that affects production but not the amino acid sequence of proteins in that operon (see I.2.6, Figure 2.52). Second, chromosomal rearrangements by inversion, translocation, duplication, deletion, or transposition may be responsible for the change in genetic expression without damaging the amino acid sequence of the gene products; however, the biochemical mechanisms behind these changes are obscure.

The regulatory mutation concept is purely speculative, for there is no empirical evidence to support it. The operon model is well documented in the bacterial system, but it has not been unequivocally identified in the eucaryotic genome due to the following four reasons:

1. DNA in the eucaryotic chromosome is wrapped in chromosomal proteins that may play important roles in the regulation of gene expression. The presence of these protein makes the identification of genes involved in the operon very difficult.

2. Genomes of higher organisms contain various classes of highly repeated DNA with virtually unknown functions.

3. A large part of the highly repeated DNA is apparently nonfunctional because it does not transcribe any RNA.

4. The nucleus of an eucaryotic cell contains heterogeneous nuclear RNA with high complexity (10 times that of cytoplasmic mRNA) that later becomes mRNA in the cytoplasm. Several other low molecular weight species of RNA with unknown function are also found in the nuclei.

Realizing the complexity of the eucaryotic genome (31), scientists have yet to work out the regulation of gene expression. Therefore, the concept of regulatory mutation can be treated only as a speculation that is difficult to test empirically. At the present time it is very much doubted whether the effects of regulatory gene mutation observed in bacteria (32) can be applied to the eucaryotic system.

(3) *Concept of Systemic Mutation.* The late Richard B. Goldschmidt (1878–1958), geneticist at the University of California, has expressed frustration in trying to account for the macroevolutionary development of many structures in higher organisms on the bases of the mechanisms of microevolution alone. He believed that the Neo-Darwinian mechanism (the accumulation of micromutations under the

influence of natural selection) was largely restricted to subspecific differentiation within species and that the decisive step in the formation of new species involves an entirely different genetic process called *systemic mutation* (33, 34).

Goldschmidt's reasoning on systemic mutation is threefold. First, if microevolution gives rise to new species according to different stages of geographic isolation, it should be possible to observe an entire series of geographically isolated subspecies with the terminal one representing the beginning of a new species. Goldschmidt expected to find these series of geographically isolated subspecies of closely related species blending into one another, but he cited many examples in which this blending did not occur. He treated a species as an interbreeding or potentially interbreeding population, and he claimed that many controversial cases of speciation depend in part on the purely morphological definitions of a species that do not take genetic aspects into account. Therefore he believed that good species are always separated from their nearest relatives by a bridgeless gap.

Goldschmidt's second point is that natural selection acting via geographical isolation is believed to cause the accumulation of enough genetic difference in the isolated subspecies so that it eventually becomes a new species and is distinct from the parent species. But Goldschmidt documented in many instances that long isolation did not produce more than subspecific variations. He cited a race of the gypsy moth *Lymantria dispar* that has been isolated on the island of Hokkaido (North Japan) since the early Tertiary period, yet in the intervening 60 million years only subspecific differentiation has occurred. He also pointed out that seasonal varieties within a race of the butterfly *Papilio* may be greater than the variation between races of *Papilio* butterflies at any one time.

Goldschmidt's third point is that the rate of evolution directed by natural selection is too slow and subtle to account for the existing varieties of plants and animals. Neo-Darwinian theory demands that only very minor mutants subject to very slight selection pressure are significant in evolution. If one defines selection pressure as the loss of survival value, then in a population with 1000 individuals of *AA* genotype and 999 individuals of *aa* genotype who reproduce, the selective pressure against *a* is 0.001. According to mathematics set up by J.B.S. Haldane (35), if a selection pressure of this magnitude is operating "in favor" of a new gene that arose by micromutation present in frequency of one in a million, it will take almost 12 000 generations to increase the gene frequency to 2 in a million if the favored gene is dominant, and 322 000 generations if the favored gene is recessive. Goldschmidt inferred also from the lack of genetic differentiation of natural populations above the species level such as in the case of *Lymantria*, which was under prolonged and complete isolation, that natural selection is ineffective in speciation.

Goldschmidt therefore advocated a wholesale chromosomal rearrangement that he called "the systemic mutation" as the novel genetic process to account for speciation. Such a drastic chromosomal rearrangement is supported by observations of *Drosophila* chromosomes. While natural selection usually eliminates such individuals who arise from systemic mutation, occasionally it may allow them to propagate as "hopeful monsters" under special circumstances.

The concept of systemic mutation lacks sufficient empirical documentation. The only observable example seems to be polyploidy in plant speciation, and this cannot be generalized to represent all living organisms. However, the body of highly pertinent evidence amassed by Goldschmidt to support his contention that the mechanisms of microevolution fail to account for macroevolution has prompted a reevaluation of the roles played by natural selection in the process of evolution.

Systemic mutation has also found its resurgence in a new theory called *punctuated equilibrium*. This theory is advocated by Stephen Jay Gould of Harvard University and Niles Eldredge of the American Museum of Natural History of New York (36). The essence of this theory is that during evolutionary periods individual species remain virtually unchanged. Speciation occurs only as "punctuations" caused by abrupt events at which a descendant species arises from the original stock. This view finds increasing acceptance among paleontologists who are dissatisfied with the imperfection of the fossil record, which lacks many transitional forms.

(4) *Concept of Species Selection.* Reacting to arguments of opponents of macroevolution, modern evolutionists have tried to reiterate their conviction that the process of natural selection is responsible for both microevolution and macroevolution. Yet the failure of natural selection (acting on individuals within a population) to account for the major features of macroevolution as represented by the fossil record has led to the formulation of the concept of *species selection* (37). It states that the random process of speciation favors species that speciate at high rates and survive for long periods; therefore, they tend to leave many daughter species. The concept was based on several extrapolations from the fossil record: (1) The time a new species appeared to its extinction or its pseudoextinction by gradually evolving into another species is between six to seven million years. (2) The duration time for mammalian species are shorter than those of some marine vertebrates with the major orders of mammals arising from their primitive ancestors within a span not ex-

ceeding 12 million years. (3) During an interval not greatly exceeding five million years, a new aquatic-animal family *Limnocardiidae* arose and developed over 30 new genera representing five subfamilies with members showing great morphological diversity. (4) The presence of "living fossils" such as the linguloid, brachipods, monoplacophoran mollusks, rhynchocephalian reptiles, mytilid and pinnid bivalve mollusks, sclerosponges, and the lungfishes indicate little or no evolutionary changes over a period of hundreds of millions of years after their origination. These phenomena are not adequately explained by the gradualistic accumulation of micromutations selected by geographic isolation (allopatric speciation), but instead they demand a rapid evolutionary mechanism to account for an initial fast apparent evolution rate followed by little if any change.

The concept of species selection bears a certain resemblance to the concept of sympatric speciation (*see* I.1.5) in that a sudden rapid mechanism is responsible for the formation of new species. It is analogous also to the process of natural selection in that species are selected on the basis of their ability to resist extinction and to form a new species. In contrast, natural selection occurs if individuals within a population exhibit genetic variabilities caused by mutation and recombination. These individuals are selected according to their abilities to survive and according to their rates of reproduction. While the concept of *species selection* may account for the apparent rapid evolution of certain lineages represented in the fossil record, it has no empirical documentation such as that of the mechanism of natural selection in microevolution. Once again the mechanism of natural selection fails to account for the major features of macroevolution in the concept of species selection.

All in all, the idea of Darwinian evolution is still venerated as the most comprehensive theory in biology. However, the concept of natural selection, by which the theory was given a scientific basis, is being gradually abandoned by the more radical biologists as the major mechanism that can account for the features of macroevolution. In addition, a recent conference on macroevolution has epitomized the growing contention that macroevolution occurs by a mechanism other than natural selection (36). The Darwinian evolutionists are no longer the dominating voice in the scientific debate on evolution. R. C. Lewontin has summed up his evaluation of natural selection as follows (38):

> During the last few years there has been a flowering of interest in evolution by purely random processes in which natural selection plays no role at all. If the empirical fact should be that most of the genetic change in species formation is indeed of this "non-Darwinian" sort, then where is the revolution that Darwin

made? The answer is that the essential nature of Darwinian revolution was neither the introduction of evolutionism as a worldview (since historically that is not the case) nor the emphasis on natural selection as the main force in evolution (since empirically that may not be the case), but rather the replacement of a metaphysical view of variation among organisms by a materialistic view.

In other words the only contribution that Darwin's natural selection theory made is in the form of an empirically testable mechanism that causes the diversification of genetic variability as exemplified by the process of microevolution. Macroevolution, then, is a very speculative theory that is becoming gradually divorced from the well-documented concept of natural selection (42).

b) *Chance as the Teleological Explanation of Evolution.* Aristotle has categorized four levels of explanation of an event: *material cause, efficient cause, formal cause,* and *final cause.* A sculpture can be used as an example. The material explanation of it is the stone or wood from which the sculpture is made, i.e., the sculpture is a piece of stone or wood. The efficient cause is the force, the act of carving, that forms the figure of the sculpture, i.e., the sculpture is a carved stone or wood. The formal cause is the pattern after which the sculpture is carved, i.e., a sculpture is a carved stone statue of man. The final cause is the purpose of the existence of the sculpture, i.e., the sculpture is a carved stone statue of Abraham Lincoln, commemorating his work as president of the United States.

According to *Webster's Third New International Dictionary,* the use of design, purpose, or utility as an explanation of any natural phenomenon is known as teleology. Thus, a teleological explanation of an event is equivalent to Aristotle's final cause. The English theologian William Paley argued eloquently in his *Natural Theology* that the intriguing features of nature evidence the design of the Creator. He cited the example of the human eye. Paley points to the fitting together efficiently and cooperatively of the lens, retina, and brain; enabling humans to have vision; as conclusive evidence of the design of an all-wise Creator. Thus the functional *design* of organisms and their features are taken as evidence of the existence of the designer.

Darwin rejected the notion of a designer and argued that the directive organization of living things is the result of a natural process—natural selection. In other words, he stressed only the material and efficient causes of the features of the organisms and tried to bring the origin and adaptation of organisms into the realm of empirical science. Evolutionists maintain the natural process can be accounted for by physiochemical

226

parameters; therefore, there is no need to resort to the design of a Creator or external agent. Nevertheless, they invoked natural selection as an agent capable of providing a purpose for the existence of certain features of organisms. Evolutionists have on the one hand regarded the teleological explanation of natural phenomena as untestable scientifically and thus untenable; but they have asserted, on the other hand, that chance, directed by natural selection, is the ultimate explanation of the necessity of evolution (39).

The results of natural selection as exemplified by the adaptive feature of the hand of humans, the wings of birds, and other biological structures or behaviors have been treated as the *reasons* why they exist at all. To put it more precisely, according to the evolutionists, the reason why there are streptomycin-resistant mutants in a population of *E. coli* bacteria is that they can propagate in the presence of the drug, whereas streptomycin sensitive bacteria cannot. Since streptomycin-resistant mutation arose spontaneously, the selection by the drug simply facilitates the differential multiplication of the mutant at the expense of the nonmutated bacteria. Therefore, according to the evolutionists, the "music of the biosphere" is composed of the unaided "noise of natural selection" feeding on "chance" alone (39).

Chance mutations can be subjected to the following fates: (1) selection by favorable natural environments thus providing the raw materials for further evolution, and (2) fixation by random drift or elimination by adverse conditions thus moving to oblivion. The assertion that the present biota is "entirely" the result of successful evolution of chance events by the process of natural selection is purely a posteriori, since natural selection is also known to cause extinction. The same assertion can be made to describe a hypothetical barren earth as the result of natural selection of unsuccessful chance events. Therefore evolutionists, while stressing the material and efficient causes of evolution in the mechanism of natural selection, have yet to come up with a valid counterargument to explain why chance alone can be in such marvelous harmony to produce the orderly array in the biosphere. Could not chance equally cause disruption of the whole structure? Both of these phenomena would be equally probable conditions implicit in the use of the term "chance."

c) *Empirical Unfalsifiability of the Theory of Organic Evolution.* After the triumphant Centennial Celebration of Darwinism in 1959, a mathematical and philosophical debate continued into the 1960s regarding the logical coherency of Darwin's concept of natural selection. The arguments focused on the circular reasoning of Darwin's premise of the *survival of the fittest.* Darwin did not provide any objective criteria to identify the fittest other than observing the survivor (40).

Evolutionists tried to get around the apparent tautology of their theory by redefining natural selection to mean differential reproduction that gives rise to changes in gene frequencies. In other words, a particular genetic variant confers higher *fitness* in a particular situation. Therefore it will leave more offspring in the course of time. The catch, however, is still present; i.e., the conclusion is essentially part of the premise, since the fitness is measured by the capacity to leave more offspring. Grene summarized this change as follows: "What have we? One more tautology: well, after all what survives survives. . . . When the theory [of natural selection] is summed up in a formula for measuring differential gene ratios, you have a theorem universally applicable because it is empty, totally comprehensive, because it expresses simple identity" (41).

The theory of evolutionary change as a consequence of natural selection promoting the adaptation of organisms to their environments is empirically demonstrable in the laboratory and in nature (*see* I.3.2). However, the difficulties involved in defining *adaptation* operationally and the subtle relationship between adaptation and fitness cast doubts on the integrity of the theory of natural selection as an all-inclusive theory to account for the origin of life. The *fact* is that the evolution of life from a single origin, an assertion adamantly maintained by most evolutionists, is more an a priori assumption than an empirically falsifiable theory.

The attempts to analyze the rate of molecular evolution by comparing amino acid sequences of proteins and determining the adaptive values of protein polymorphisms in order to illuminate the neutralist-selectionist controversy will yield nothing more than circumstantial evidence that will be subject to reinterpretation. No one can design any experiment or collect any amount of data from nature to falsify the claim that organic evolution *has occurred*. The legitimacy of extrapolating microevolutionary observations to macroevolution is increasingly being questioned (27, 28, 33, 38, 42).

The empirical unfalsifiability of the theory of organic evolution has removed it effectively from the realm of empirical science. It is apparent that theories of origins go beyond the limitations of verifiable empirical science and thus require philosophical assumptions and leaps of faith. We will now examine an alternative to the Darwinian theory based on a Christian theistic world view.

References 3.3

1. Oparin, A. I. Genesis and evolutionary development of life. New York: Academic Press; 1968: 29.

2. Popper, K. R. The logic of scientific discovery. London: Hutchinson; 1959.
3. England, D. A Christian view of origins. Grand Rapids, MI: Baker; 1972.
4. Kerr, R. A. Science. 210:42; 1980.
5. Hull, D. E. Nature. 186:693; 1960.
6. Lehninger, A. L. Biochemistry. 2nd. ed. New York: Worth; 1975: 1038.
7. Oparin, A. I. Genesis and evolutionary development (chapter 4).
8. Lehninger, A. L. Biochemistry. 1048.
9. Mora, P. T. The origins of prebiotic systems and of their molecular matrices. Fox, S. W., ed. New York and London: Academic Press; 1965: 39–52.
10. Mayr, E. Animal species and evolution. Cambridge, MA: Harvard Univ. Press; 1963: 488.
11. Grant, V. Plant speciation. New York: Columbia Univ. Press; 1971.
12. Simpson, G. G. The major features of evolution. New York: Columbia Univ. Press; 1953: 5.
13. Lewontin, R. C. The genetic basis of evolutionary change. New York and London: Columbia Univ. Press; 1974.
14. Nei, M. Molecular population genetics and evolution. Amsterdam: N. Holland; 1975: 231.
15. Ohta, T.; Kimura, M. J. Mol. Evol. 1:18; 1971.
16. Fitch, W. M.; Langley, C. H. Fed. Proc. 35:2092; 1976.
17. Simpson, G. G. The meaning of evolution. New Haven, CT: Yale Univ. Press; 1949: 108.
18. Dobzhansky, T.; Ayala, F. J.; Stebbins, G. L.; Valentine, J. L. Evolution. San Francisco: Freeman; 1977: 233.
19. Hubby, J. L.; Lewontin, R. C. J. Genet. 54:57; 1966.
20. Lewontin, R. C. Hubby, J. L. J. Genet. 54:59–61; 1966.
21. Harris, H. Proc. R. Soc. Lon. Ser. B. 164:298; 1966.
22. Marshall, D. R.; Allard, R. W. J. Genet. 66:393; 1970.
23. Marshall, D. R.; Allard, R. W. Heredity. 25:373; 1970.
24. Powell, J. R. In: Evolutionary biology. Dobzhansky, T.; Hecht, M. K.; Steere, W. eds. Vol. 8. New York and London: Plenum; 1975: 29–119.
25. Lewontin, R. C. The genetic basis of evolutionary change. 118.
26. Kimura, M.; Ohta, T. Proc. Nat. Acad. Sci. USA. 71:2848; 1974.
27. Nei, M. Molecular population genetics and evolution. Amsterdam: N. Holland; 1975.
28. King, J. L.; Jukes, T. H. Science. 164:788; 1969.

29. Stanier, R. Y.; Wachter, D.; Gasser, C.; Wilson, A. C. J. Bacteriol. 102:351; 1970.
30. King, M. C.; Wilson, A. C. Science. 188:107; 1975.
31. Hood, L. E.; Wilson, J. H.; Wood, W. B. Molecular biology of eucaryotic cells. Vol. 1. Menlo Park, CA: Benjamin; 1975.
32. Hacking, A. J.; Lin, E. C. C. J. Bacteriol. 180:832; 1977.
33. Goldschmidt, R. B. The material basis of evolution. New Haven, CT: Yale Univ. Press; 1940.
34. Goldschmidt, R. B. Am. Sci. 40:84; 1952.
35. Haldane, J. B. S. J. Genet. 55:511; 1917.
36. Lewin, R. Science. 210:883; 1980.
37. Stanley, S. M. Proc. Natl. Acad. Sci. USA. 72:646; 1975.
38. Lewontin, R. C. Genetic basis of evolutionary change. 4.
39. Monod, J. Chance and necessity. New York: Knopf; 1971: 118.
40. Eden, M. Mathematical challenges to the neo-Darwinian interpretation of evolution. Moorhead, P. S.; Kaplan, M. M. eds. Philadelphia: Wistar Inst. Press; 1967: 5.
41. Grene, M. Understanding of nature. Essays in the philosophy of biology. Boston: Reidel; 1974: 84.
42. Stebbins, G. L.; Ayala, F. J. Science. 213:967; 1981.

PART II

A CHRISTIAN VIEW
OF THE ORIGIN OF LIFE

CHAPTER 4

Christian World View and Its Contribution to the Scientific Enterprise

4.1 Christian Theism, Monism, and Dualism

We have seen that the naturalistic explanation of the origin of life has left much to be desired. It seems that the age-old question of man's origin cannot be satisfactorily answered by the scientific method that can only document observable and repeatable events. One has to approach this question from a historical perspective.

If there is a record of the history of people and the universe that has been demonstrated to be a reliable historical document, it is logical to examine that record to find the answer to the question of origins. The Bible is just such a record. It claims to be the inspired Word of God as written by humans under the influence of the Holy Spirit.

Although the historicity and the authenticity of the Bible have been attacked in the nineteenth century by the school of higher criticism (*see* III.8.7), the able defense by numerous biblical scholars such as Green (1), Harrison (2), and Bruce (3) has caused critics to modify their views. The historicity of the scriptural account has also been verified by other historical records such as recent archaeological findings (4). The Bible is thus taken by Christians as the only ultimate guide of faith and conduct and has become an influential force in shaping the outlook of the world and its destiny. The Bible also has an intimate relationship with the inception of the modern scientific era.

Ever since the dawn of human history, the advent of civilization has been shaped by people's perception of the world and the universe. Human civilization is actually a product of people's comprehension of reality and the application of this knowledge. People's awareness and appreciation of their existence helps them to develop a system of beliefs,

233

attitudes, and values that culminate as the "Weltanschauung" or world view—the philosophical outlook explaining history in general or the purpose of the world as a whole. Although the concept of a world view was developed only during the nineteenth century, it has found expression from the beginning of human civilization. The many diverse world views in human history can be summed up in three main philosophical systems: *Christian theism, monism,* and *dualism.* Figure 4.1 illustrates the differences of these three systems.

Christian theism is based on the assumption that the world and the universe were created by an eternal personality who sustains His creation by His providence. The world exists moment by moment only because of direct intervention of God the Creator. The task of the creatures in the world is to glorify the Creator in every way. The smaller circle in Figure 4.1 represents the Creation, and the arrow leading from God to creation represents the asymmetric dependence of Creation on its Creator. Both the Creation and the Creator are part of an external reality. This view is fundamental to biblical teaching.

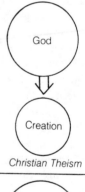

Christian Theism

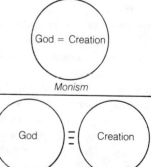

Monism

Dualism

Figure 4.1. Diagramatic representation of three leading world views.

Monism does not differentiate between God and creation. Everything in the world is treated as part of the eternal existence of reality. Therefore, to a monist, the only truth finds its expression in everything everywhere. Humans are reducible to but one of the many forms of the expression of this eternal truth. *Materialism*, as well as *naturalism* (*see* Part III), extrapolates the monist assumption that matter is eternal and therefore cannot be created. The idea of a personal Creator is easily eliminated. Monism also expresses itself in the various Eastern pantheistic religions (i.e., Transcendental Meditation, Divine Light Mission, Zen Buddhism, etc.).

Dualism assumes that there are two eternal realities—the material and the nonmaterial realms. They are coequal and they coexist throughout eternity as symbolized by the identical sign in Figure 4.1. Gnosticism is a classic example of dualism. To a Gnostic, the material world is evil, but the nonmaterial (spiritual) world is good. The human needs to be liberated from the evil material world and to attain the spiritual world by way of knowledge. However, the nature of this knowledge is poorly defined and has remained mysterious to many.

Each of these world views is pluralistic. Each has found its expression in different forms throughout human history, and all three play important roles in the unceasing quest for truth.

References 4.1

1. Green, W. H. The unity of the book of Genesis. New York: Charles Scribner's Sons; 1901.
2. Harrison, R. K. Introduction to the Old Testament. Grand Rapids, MI: Eerdmans; 1969.
3. Bruce, F. F. The New Testament documents: are they reliable? 4th ed. Downers Grove, IL: InterVarsity Press; 1953.
4. McDowell, J. Evidence that demands a verdict. Arrowhead Springs, CO: Campus Crusade for Christ International; 1972.

4.2 Quest for Truth

There are several approaches that humans have used in the pursuit of ultimate reality. They can be classified as *rationalism, empiricism,* and *rational empiricism* (1).

4.2.1 *Rationalism.* Rationalism is based on the Greek view of the existence of eternal *ideas.* These ideas pervade the universe, and the human being is an outward expression of them. Therefore, the human is rational and can perceive the mysteries of the universe by using reasoning power. Through rational preconceptions, the human can comprehend all observations in nature. Reason, then, becomes the final authority for truth. Any phenomena or theories that are unreasonable are thus untrue.

Rationalism seems to have a monistic overtone. It stresses the reasoning faculty at the expense of experience. The rationalist analyzes truth by *deduction*, sets up an a priori conception of reality from innate reasoning power, and proceeds to interpret specific events or observations. The medieval conflict between the church and its dissidents over the heliocentric issue (the sun is the center of universe) exemplified the fallacies of rationalism.

The medieval scholastic rationalist stipulated that the existence of God is connected with a long chain of natural events from the heavenly motions down to the most trivial terrestrial phenomena that appear to be governed by laws reasonable to humans. Anything that is not consistent with the dominant rationalistic view is thus heretic and false.

According to the popular naive interpretation of the Scriptures at the time, the earth was believed to be at the center of the universe. During the sixteenth century Copernicus enunciated his revolutionary heliocentric view of the solar system that clashed directly with the dominant rationalistic view. He and his followers were immediately labeled heretics and subjected to excommunication and chastisement by the church and state.

Many contemporary scientists have cited this incident as the classic example of the obscurant attitudes of the Christian church. In actuality, it is not the church that upheld obscurantism, but it was the rationalistic outlook the church had adopted at the time that hindered the scientific pursuit of truth.

4.2.2 *Empiricism.* Copernicus paved the way for the onset of empiricism. In the seventeenth century, Copernicus's followers Galileo and Kepler took up the task of promoting acceptance of the heliocentric "heresy." They were among the earliest empiricists who believed, together with the rationalists, that the universe is governed by a supreme "reason." However, they differed from the rationalists in their convictions that the supreme reason manifests itself also through observable events and phenomena in nature.

Galileo and Kepler stressed the importance of empirical observation as a valid avenue in the quest of truth. The results of their observations of the heavenly bodies led them to conclude that the sun instead of the earth was the center of the solar system.

In the eighteenth century David Hume and Immanuel Kant systematically developed the empiricist position by emphasizing the importance of experience in deciphering reality. To an empiricist, truth can come about only by interpreting what is observed or experienced through common senses. The empiricist arrives at a conclusion by *induction* through repeated observations of similar or identical events that either support or refute a presupposition.

The empiricists' emphasis on experience and induction gave birth to modern science. However, it also provided impetus for the followers of *skepticism*. The skeptics believe there is no absolute knowledge or true reality because knowledge and reality are only products of the senses. Therefore, total rejection of objective facts by the skeptics hindered the progress of modern science.

4.2.3 *Rational Empiricism.* Many Evangelicals believe that the Bible teaches a form of *rational empiricism*. The scriptural account provides for a rational Creator who created a rational universe. Humans are made in God's image (Gen. 1:27) and, through their God-given rational faculties, they can seek to understand the Creator through understanding the nature of God's creative order (Rom. 1:20). Therefore through the observations of nature (experience) coupled with deductive and inductive reasoning, humans can approach truth and reality systematically. This is essentially the major assumption of modern science. Scientists construct a hypothesis from what is known and then they seek to document, refute, or modify it by experimentation. Therefore, rational empiricism becomes the foundation of modern science.

Reference 4.2

1. Hooykaas, R. Religion and the rise of modern science. Grand Rapids, MI: Eerdmans; 1972.

4.3 The Relationships of Various World Views with the Development of Modern Science

4.3.1 *Platonic Dualism.* Plato believed the real world is formed by absolute immutable "ideas"; therefore the visible world is but a shadowy image of ideas. Humans can know about eternal ideas only vaguely by observing natural phenomena. In other words, one can at most formulate "opinion" concerning ideas of which the visible things are only distorted and partly unreal images.

The Gnostics extended Plato's ideas into the dualistic perception of the material and the spiritual realms during the time of Christ. Augustine (354–430 A.D.) also incorporated aspects of Platonic thinking into his theology. Even up through the twelfth century, some forms of Platonism dominated the thinking of the European intelligentsia. The stress on the inscrutability of ideas surpressed the human search for truth. Therefore this period of European history has been labeled the Dark Ages.

4.3.2 *Aristotelian Monism.* Aristotle deviated from Plato's conception by assuming that "nature coincides ideas." He believed that nature is the manifestation of ideas; therefore, it is eternally self-existing and self-rejuvenating. Nature is rational, and ideas are the essence of nature. Therefore humans should approach ideas by contemplating and interpret nature by contemplative insights.

Through the popularization of Thomas Aquinas, Aristotelian monism prevaded intellectual minds of Europe from the thirteenth to the sixteenth century. However, this rationalistic approach was not conducive to the development of modern science because it did not require the experimental method.

4.3.3 *Mechanistic World View.* The Greek philosopher Epicurus originated monistic materialistic thinking. He stipulated that everything in the universe can be reducible to "matter" that is eternal. His ideas fueled the later development of the mechanistic world view.

Descartes elaborated the mechanistic world view by treating the material world, including the human body, as a perfect machine reducible to exact mathematical and physical laws. He, however, maintained in his mind-body dualism that the mind is not under the control of these laws.

The naturalists extrapolated the materialistic and mechanistic perceptions to view the whole universe as a complicated machine definable in spatial-temporal terms. With the rise of empirical science, naturalists came to accept only statements that could be empirically verified as intelligible, and they precluded the existence of any non–spatio-temporal entities. To them, a person is but a part of the world machine, a product of chance, and people owe their ultimate accountability to none but themselves, for they can direct their own destiny. This naturalistic outlook of a mechanistic universe gave birth to the widespread acceptance of the evolutionary origin of life.

4.3.4 *Christian Theistic World View.* From the scriptural perspective, the universe is God's creation, and God established natural laws to govern nature. As contrasted with the mechanistic perception that God is not interested in His creation, God is constantly upholding the universe by "his powerful word" (Heb. 1:3 NIV).

The creation account gives humans two motivations for the pursuit of modern science. First, the Creation was good (Gen. 1), and "the heavens declare the glory of God; and the skies proclaim the work of his hands" (Ps. 19:1 NIV). Humans can know about the wonders of God by studying His creation. Therefore, the pursuit of scientific knowledge is not "thing-oriented" or "knowledge-oriented" but "God-oriented."

238

Second, God gave humans a mandate: "Be fruitful and increase in number; fill the earth and subdue it. Rule over the fish of the sea and the birds of the air and over every living creature that moves on the ground" (Gen. 1:28 NIV). Humans are to be stewards of God's creation, and the understanding of nature is a prerequisite of their effort to dominate and subdue it.

With these two strong motivating forces, Christians took the lead in the development of modern science. In fact, 90% of the membership of the Royal Society of Science in London during the early years of its existence were Christians who adhered to strict compliance with biblical doctrines. This was at a time when only 20% of England's population claimed to be Christians (1). Therefore it is well-recognized that Christianity was the mother of modern science (2). Although the naturalistic approach and the humanistic emphasis have since become the dominant world views among contemporary scientists, Christianity is a strong motivating force underlining the scientific endeavor, and it is the most consistent world view that can incorporate the scientific enterprise into the broad spectrum of the human search for truth (3).

References 4.3

1. Spradley, J. Faith and Learning Seminar. Wheaton College, Wheaton, IL: Summer, 1976. See also Merton, R. K. The Puritan Spur to Science. Sociology of Science. Chicago: Univ. of Chicago Press; 1973: 228–53.
2. Jaki, S. Science and Creation. New York: Science History Publication; 1974.
3. Sire, J. W. The universe next door. Downers Grove, IL: InterVarsity Press; 1976.

CHAPTER 5

Interpretation of the Genesis Account of Creation and the Flood

5.1 Some Exegetical Considerations

The systematic interpretation of the Old Testament can be traced all the way back to the earlier rabbinic rules of Hillel, one of the leading rabbis in the intertestamental period. He emphasized surrounding circumstances as a qualification for interpreting the Old Testament. He also stressed logical procedures in classifying the topical discussions of the Bible and setting up exegetical rules (1).

During the first century Greek influence was felt in Alexandrian Judaism in the form of *allegorism.* In this system a text is interpreted apart from its grammatical and historical meaning to reflect the thinking of the interpreter. Philo championed the allegorical method by ignoring the literal meaning of the Bible. He attempted by allegorical interpretation to reveal the presence of Greek philosophical ideas, such as Neoplatonism, that he saw in the Pentateuch.

The Alexandrian school of allegorism was matched by the Antiochian school of literal interpretation from the second to the fourth centuries. However, because of the theological controversies of the fourth and fifth centuries some members of the Antiochian school were accused of being heretics, and the school began to lose influence. It was further weakened by the later split of the church into the Eastern and Western segments. Therefore, allegorism became the dominant view of biblical hermeneutics for over a millennium.

Thomas Aquinas (1225–74) stressed the primary importance of the literal interpretation while maintaining at the same time the legitimacy of allegorization. He said, "The literal sense is that which the author intends, but God being the Author we may expect to find in Scripture a wealth of meaning" (2). Therefore, although he did take a step forward in the right direction, he did not rid the church of allegorism.

It was not until the Reformation, when the Bible came to be the supreme and sole authority, that the modern Protestant hermeneutical system came into being. In the Council of Trent held between 1545 and 1563, the Roman church issued a list of decrees setting forth the Catholic dogmas and canons anathematizing Protestants. Protestants replied categorically by drawing up creeds and theological systems in an effort to consolidate their biblical data. This led to great strides being made in the seventeenth and eighteenth centuries to determine the original text of the Bible. Grammars and lexicons of Hebrew, Aramaic, and Greek began to circulate. Historical backgrounds of biblical accounts came to the attention of biblical scholars. They started to study the Bible textually, linguistically, historically, and literarily, bringing in new dimensions of biblical hermeneutics.

Eighteenth-century rationalism gave impetus to the literal interpretation of the Scriptures. However, the extreme rationalistic emphasis led to preoccupation with historical higher criticism of the Bible and the elimination of the supernatural and miraculous elements from the Scriptures. The rationalists stripped the "historical" Jesus of all "irrational" elements, and He became no more than an ethical teacher. This required a naive dismissal of large sections of the Gospels.

In the twentieth century, a renewed interest among progressive theologians has been sparked in the quest for the historical Jesus. The traditional orthodox biblical interpreters who adhere to the Reformers' convictions of the inspiration and the authority of the Bible have emerged once again as major contending voices in biblical scholarship. This has been accompanied by a renewed interest in studying the Bible (3).

References 5.1

1. Blackman, A. C. Biblical interpretation. Philadelphia: Westminster; 1957.
2. Cited by Mickelsen, A. B. Interpreting the Bible. Grand Rapids, MI: Eerdmans; 1963: 37.
3. Mickelsen, A. B. Interpreting the Bible. 20–53.

5.2 Orthodox View

There are four presuppositions involved in the orthodox view of biblical interpretation (1):

1. *Scripture Interprets Scripture.* Viewed as a whole the Bible exhibits a marvelous harmony among the 66 books that were written by 40 different people over 1600 years. Each successive book in the time in which it was written presupposed the biblical books that went before. The earlier books in many passages were intended to point forward to Scriptures that were to come. Therefore, the Bible is internally consistent and interprets itself.

2. *Lexicography.* The meaning of words is established by studying their usage in a wide horizon by using available biblical and extrabiblical data. Then the words are composed into dictionaries (lexicography). The understanding of the usage of the words of human languages, by which the Holy Spirit conveys the Word of God to humans, sheds light on their meaning in the Scriptures.

3. *Context.* The context of Scripture must be taken into account. A study of the context of words and passages in the Bible includes not only the immediate context but the entire book in which the words or passages occur, as well as the historical background.

4. *Grammatico-historical interpretation.* The study of grammar includes lexicography, as well as the study of historical background, including immediate and remote contexts.

Reference 5.2

1. Buswell, J. O., II. A systematic theology of the Christian religion. Vol. 1. Grand Rapids, MI: Zondervan; 1963: 24–25.

5.3 Four Exegetical Principles

From the New Testament's usage of the Old Testament, Harrison (1) has cited four exegetical principles to apply when studying the Bible in general and for the Old Testament in particular. First is the *historical*. This principle regards the Old Testament as an authentic and reliable historical document. The second is the *propositional*. This principle views Old Testament statements as either fulfilled in the New Testament or employed as a basis for doctrine or conduct. The third point is the *homological* and expresses the identity or correspondence between Old Covenant and New Covenant situations. The last point is *illustrational* and employs historical material to reinforce truth and stress moral teachings.

The interpretation of the Genesis account is one of the focal points in the debate over the authenticity of the Pentateuch (1). The recovery of Mesopotamian creation and flood narratives led many scholars to believe that the Genesis account was a comparatively late composition stripped of

Babylonian paganism by postexilic priest and presented as the accredited Hebrew tradition. The Babylonian account of creation found in the *Enuma elish* and the account of a flood found in the eleventh tablet of the *Epic of Gilgamesh* were both dated back to the first Babylonian Dynasty around 1700 B.C.

The *Enuma elish* and Genesis accounts of creation are similar. Both commence with something analogous to a watery chaos and conclude with a creator at rest, and the intervening events follow the same general order. However, the differences in the two accounts are so striking that no real parallels can be found.

One similar flood account does emerge in the eleventh tablet of the Gilgamesh Epic. The survivor of the flood tells Gilgamesh, the legendary king of Uruk, how the powerful water-deity Ea warned him of the coming inundation and how he constructed a boat in the contemporary fashion. He preserved himself and his family together with his possessions and some local fauna. The flood lasted seven days, and the boat finally came to rest on Mount Nisir in northeastern Persia. These cuneiform accounts seem to be quite similar to the Genesis record of the Deluge. The *similarities* of the biblical and the Babylonian accounts of creation and the flood may be attributed to their reference to an actual event, or by the fact that a standard sequence of creation and a standard method of escaping from the devastating flash floods of Mesopotamia were being circulated in epical form.

The *differences* between the biblical material and the polytheistic compositions of ancient Mesopotamia cannot be overlooked. The Old Testament narratives were taken by the Hebrews as historical accounts whose traditions were taken seriously in the faith of Israel. While being explicit on the polytheistic environments they faced, the biblical writers never regarded nature as the life of God, whom they considered the independent Supreme Being. This stands in direct antithesis to the Mesopotamian traditions. The God of the Hebrews is distinct from the gods of Mesopotamian and Egyptian polytheism, for He demonstrated His personality and sense of purpose by significant continuous acts in history. Human beings are creatures of God, impregnated with a sense of destiny, and cautioned with diligence to formulate the pattern of their lives within the context of divine promise and fulfillment in history.

The Covenant concept pervades the Bible and relates metaphysical dynamism to specific events and periods within the temporal continuum of Israelite life. This stands in contradistinction to the Mesopotamian polytheistic patterns that made history in general dependent on rhythms of natural forces. In addition, after diligent comparison Alexander Heidel has pointed out succinctly nine striking differences between the Babylonian and Old Testament account of creation (2):

1. *Enuma elish* portrays Apsu and Tiamat as the masculine and feminine divine principles respectively who were the ancestors of the gods and living uncreated world-matter. Apsu was the primeval sweet-water ocean and Tiamat the primeval salt-water ocean. On the other hand, the Old Testament account of God depicts Him as the single divine principle existing apart from all cosmic matter.

2. The Babylonian account deems matter eternal. However, the Genesis account proclaims a creation from nothing *(ex nihilo)*.

3. *Enuma elish* and Genesis 1 both refer to a watery chaos. The former conceives of this chaos as *living* matter and being part of Apsu and Tiamat, in whom all elements of the future universe were blended together. The latter portrays the watery chaos as nothing but a mass of *inanimate* matter that was later separated into the waters above and below and then into dry land and ocean.

4. In both the Babylonian and Hebrew accounts of creation there seems to be an etymological equivalence in the terms by which the watery mass is designated, namely, *Tiamat* and *tehom*, respectively. However, the Babylonian Tiamat is a mythical feminine figure. *Tehom*, while it occurs in Genesis 1:2 and is translated "the deep," never has any personal connotation. It refers to the *entire* body of the vast expanse of water, whereas Tiamat can represent only *part* of it, the other part being represented by Apsu. Moreover, the masculine ending of the word *tehom* makes it inconceivable to be a loan word from Tiamat since the latter has a feminine ending.

5. Both *Enuma elish* and Genesis 1 refer to a primeval darkness. However, the idea of darkness in the Babylonian account can only be deduced from an additional Greek source. In the Genesis account, darkness is expressed in unequivocal terms (Gen. 1:2).

6. Both accounts refer to the existence of light and to the alternation of day and night before the creation of heavenly bodies. But light was spoken of as an *attribute* of the Babylonian gods, Mummu and Marduk, who defeated Tiamat and fabricated the world. In Genesis, light is only a *creation* of God.

7. While the Genesis account concentrates on the creation of the universe, only two of the seven tablets of *Enuma elish* speak of creation. The other tablets record the conflict between Marduk and Tiamat.

8. The conflict between Marduk and Tiamat has been compared to the conflict of the Lord and Rahab (Isa. 51:9) and Leviathan (Ps. 74:12–17). However, the Marduk-Tiamat conflict occurred *before* creation, and the

conflict of God with Rahab and Leviathan took place *after* creation.

9. In *Enuma elish*, the world and humans were not created in the biblical sense of the term. They were merely *fashioned* from the elementary world-matter as by a craftsperson, and they are made with the blood of a deity that might be called a devil among the gods who had the assigned task of serving the gods. However, in the Genesis account, the Lord, who is *one* God throughout creation and eternity, does not first develop Himself into a series of separate deities. God creates matter out of nothing, and by His sovereign *word* the world was created. Humans were created in the image of a holy and righteous God, to be the lords of the earth, air, and sea.

Heidel concluded his treatise with the following succinct comments: "We have a number of differences between *Enuma elish* and Genesis 1:1–2:3 that make all similarities shrink into utter insignificance. These exalted conceptions in the biblical account give it a depth and dignity unparalleled in any cosmogony known to us from Babylonia or Assyria" (3). Therefore, the authenticity of Genesis is not easily dispensed with by its comparison with Near Eastern mythological writings.

References 5.3

1. Harrison; R. K. Introduction to the Old Testament. Grand Rapids, MI: Eerdmans; 1969: 447.
2. Heidel, A. The Babylonian Genesis. The story of the creation. Chicago: Univ. of Chicago Press; 1942.
3. Heidel, A. The Babylonian Genesis. 118.

CHAPTER 6

Interpretation of the Genesis Account by Evangelical Scholarship

Evangelical Christians accept the Bible as the inspired Word of God, the only unerring guide of faith and conduct. However, there are numerous theories put forth by evangelicals to try to interpret the Genesis account in light of modern scientific findings. Donald England summarizes the major Christian interpretations of Genesis 1, as well as the atheistic evolutionist position, and suggests a few objections to each view in his recent book *A Christian View of Origins*. This is shown in Table 6.1

6.1 Three Tenets

The three most widely discussed tenets in the contemporary dialogues on the issue of creation and/or evolution are *fiat creationism, theistic evolutionism,* and *progressive creationism* (1). The three beliefs are reviewed briefly.

6.1.1 *Fiat Creationism.* Fiat creationism includes all the *literal* views. It demands a young earth and cataclysmic flood geology as well as the total repudiation of any forms of evolutionary development of life.

To the fiat creationists, evolution and creation are diametrically antithetical to each other with no room for reconciliation. They believe evolution is the culmination of the atheistic offensive to undermine the trustworthiness of the Bible. Therefore, to them, to give in by the least amount in the evolution issue would open Pandora's box for the ultimate destruction of the biblical foundation of the Christian faith (2).

6.1.2 *Theistic Evolutionism.* Theistic evolutionism accepts the historicity of the Bible but allegorizes the Genesis account to treat the whole creation story as a "poetic" representation of the spiritual truths of the human's dependence on God their Creator and their fall from God's grace by the symbolic act of disobedience. They accept the processes of organic evolution as the ways God used to create humans; however, they believe God endowed humans with His spiritual capacity by supernatural means.

The theistic evolutionists sees no conflict whatsoever in harmonizing organic evolution with the creation account despite the necessity to dispense with the historicity of the human Fall. They feel the fundamental Christian doctrines of original sin and the human need for redemption are unshaken by the incorporation of organic evolution into the Christian interpretation of life and origins (3, 4, 5, 6). Richard Bube summarized these two positions: "If the evolutionist usually puts too much emphasis on these [scientific] data, the antievolutionist usually puts too little" (5).

6.1.3 *Progressive Creationist.* Progressive creationists (1) are more liberal than the fiat creationists in that they are more open-minded to reinterpreting the creation account when necessitated by the findings of science. However, they are more conservative than the theistic evolutionists in their acceptance of the theory of organic evolution. They hold to the geologically demonstrated antiquity of the earth and limited microevolutionary processes occurring subsequent to God's original creation of the prototypes of present-day varieties. They also adhere strictly to the exegetical principles of the Bible and find ample room for the "day-age" (or similar) interpretation of the Genesis account.

While the hypertraditional fiat creationists and the enlightened theistic evolutionist have been outspoken for some time in Christian circles on the creation and evolution controversy, an increasing number of scholars are revealing that their views are in line with those of the progressive creationists (1, 7, 8, 9, 10, 11). It is the author's contention that progressive creationism is the best available model that maintains the scriptural integrity of the Genesis account and at the same time does no injustice to known scientific facts. This position and its rationale, as contrasted with the views of the fiat creationist and the theistic evolutionists, is reviewed in the following section.

References 6.1

1. Ramm, B. The Christian view of science and Scripture. Grand Rapids, MI: Eerdmans; 1954.
2. Morris, H. Evolution and the modern Christian. Philadelphia: Presbyterian and Reformed; 1967.
3. Bube, R. J. Am. Sci. Affil. 23:140; 1971.
4. Bube, R. J. Am. Sci. Affil. 27:171; 1975.
5. Bube, R. The human quest. Waco, TX: Word; 1971: 207.

Table 6.1. A summary of popular Genesis 1 concepts and objections to them.*

CONCEPT	PRINCIPLE
The so-called Literal View	Six 24-hour consecutive days of creation, 4000 B.C. Assumes Bible chronology is complete.
Apparent Age	Same as Literal View but earth has a "built in" age.
Flood Catastrophe	Same as Literal View. Noachian Flood caused all present geological phenomena.
Successive Catastrophe	Same as Literal View. Several catastrophes, including the Great Flood, caused present geological phenomena.
Gap or Restitution	Genesis 1:2; was = became. Creation—destruction—restitution. Modern "fossil men" belonged to a pre-Adamic race.
Multiple Gap	Sometimes confused with Day—Age. Six 24-hour creation days separated by indefinite periods. Fiat creation of animal and plant families.
Day-Age	Daysof Genesis 1 = geologic ages. Yom is used metaphorically. Divine creation activity gradual over long periods.
Revelatory Day	Indefinite time allowed. God revealed the story of creation to Moses in six days.
Theistic Evolution	God created matter and natural law. Life evolved according to current evolutionary thought.
Atheistic Evolution	Everything is a "great coincidence"—matter, life—ALL.

*NOTE: Reprinted, with permission, from England, D. A Christian view of origins. Grand Rapids: Baker Book House; 1972. © 1972 by Baker Book House.

TIME INVOLVED	OBJECTION
6000 yrs.	Earth appears older than 6000 yrs. Overworks biblical chronology.
6–10 000 yrs. but earth looks much older.	This view implies that God has misled or deceived man. Why fossils? Ancient earth.
6–10 000 yrs.	Ancient earth; radioactive dating. This view attributes too much to the Great Flood of Genesis 6.
6–10 000 yrs.	Ancient earth; radioactive dating. Overworks catastrophism.
Any time for first creation. Re-creation about 6000 yrs. ago	Overworks limited parts of Scripture, by putting too much emphasis on one word. However, a favorite view of many fundamentalists.
Any time	No Scriptural basis for assuming indefinite periods between 24-hour days.
Any time	Day in Genesis 1 seems to be a 24-hour day. Genesis 1 "reads like" a historical account.
Any time	Genesis 1 reads like history. No Scriptural basis for the principle.
Any time	Requires spontaneous generation of life. Evolution is deficient. Genesis 1 must be understood figuratively.
Any time	Rejects the idea of God. Offers no first cause. Evolution is deficient.

6. Berry, R. J. Adam and ape, a Christian approach to the theory of evolution. London: Falcon; 1975.
7. Mixter, R. Creation and evolution. 2nd ed. Monograph. Am. Sci. Affil.; 1967.
8. Buswell, J. L., III. In: Evolution and Christian thought today. Mixter, R. L. ed. Grand Rapids, MI: Eerdmans; 1959.
9. Pun, P. P., J. Am. Sci. Affil. 29:84; 1977.
10. Newman, R. C.; Eckelmann, H. J. Genesis one and the origin of the earth. Downers Grove, IL: InterVarsity; 1977.
11. Young, D. Creation and the flood. Grand Rapids, MI: Baker; 1977.

CHAPTER 7

Justification
of a Personal Point
# of View

In the age-old debate of the conflicts between science and Scripture, the most conscientious Christian position seems to be the one that accepts the validity of God's revelation through nature (the realm of scientific investigation), as well as God's special revelation through the Bible (the realm of theological interpretation). Both of these avenues of God's revelation should lead one into a "consistent" though incomplete understanding of the Creation and the Creator. The scientific enterprise, despite its theory-laden nature, has the methodological element that enables one to perceive God's general revelation regardless of the scientist's presuppositions.

Apparent conflicts that have arisen between science and the Bible can be attributed to a misinterpretation of either scientific data or biblical data. The Bible is not a textbook of science. The cultural backgrounds of biblical writers have to be considered in the interpretation of descriptive accounts such as Genesis.

The writers of the Bible conveyed to their contemporaries the message of God, and their only way was to use the languages and customs of their time. Therefore, it is unreasonable to expect Moses to describe creation in twentieth-century scientific language. Nonetheless, the Genesis account is historical, depicting what actually transpired in history. This is clearly evident in the eleven tablets, each ending with "These are the names [generations, decendants] of . . ." found in the first 36 chapters of Genesis. The contents are linked together to form a roughly chronological account of primeval and partriarchal life (i.e., Gen. 1:1–2:4; 2:5–5:2; 5:3–6:9a; 6:9b–10:1; 10:2–11:10a; 11:10b–27a; 11:27b–25:12; 25:13–19a; 25:19b–36:1; 36:2–36:9; and 36:10–37:2) (1, 2). The New Testament also regards certain events mentioned in Genesis 1 as actually having taken place (e.g., *see* Mark 10:6; 1 Cor. 11:8–9).

7.1 The Hurdles

In the attempts to harmonize the Genesis account and scientific evidence supporting the theory of evolution without debasing one category at the expense of the other, there are quite a few hurdles to overcome because of the incompleteness of scientific as well as theological data. The hurdles that progressive creationists encounter seem to be far fewer and less insurmountable than those faced by fiat creationists and theistic evolutionists. If the fiat creationists have exalted a particular interpretation of the Bible at the expense of the objectivity of science, the theistic evolutionists have conceded important theological grounds to the liberals and atheists in allegorizing the Creation and the Fall of humans.

7.1.1 *Fiat Creationists and the Earth's Age.* The major hurdle facing the fiat creationists is the antiquity of the earth. Since the dominant neo-Darwinian view of evolution requires a vast amount of time, fiat creationists maintain that the acceptance of the ancient-earth concept opens the door to atheistic evolution. They adopt essentially the chronology worked out by Archbishop Ussher (1581–1656) and Dr. John Lightfoot who fixed the date of creation at 4000 B.C. (3) based on the naive assumption that the biblical genealogies were intended to be used for chronology. This is the young-earth theory. Therefore, fiat creationists ignore much of the dating information on the antiquity of the earth that is discussed in an earlier section (I.2.1).

Fiat creationists reject the principle of uniformitarianism and all of the dating methods pertaining to the antiquity of the earth in favor of the universal cataclysm (4). However, they have yet to come up with enough data to support their theory in light of the lack of visible evidence of the universal Deluge and the intriguing patterns of biogeography (*see* I.2.4). They also overlook the vast amount of data supporting the observable microevolutionary processes in nature and the laboratory. The refusal to be open-minded to scientific inquiry because of the espousal of a particular interpretation of the Bible seems to be more conducive to the continuation of the medieval mentality with its obscurant attitude than to the defense of absolute biblical truth (5).

7.1.2. *Theistic Evolutionists and Creation.* If man is a product of the chance events of natural selection, theistic evolutionists have the problem of convincing the secular world of the biblical basis of humans as created in the image of God and of the first sin. The figurative interpretation of the Genesis account of creation seems to weaken these two fundamental doctrines of the Christian faith. By denying the historicity of the first Adam, this position also invites skepticism for the meaning of the cross of Christ, the second Adam (Rom. 5:12-21), as a historical event and thus endangers the whole structure of the Christian message (6, 7).

The materials in Genesis 1:1 to 2:4 are formal and arranged in balanced structure with recurring formal phrases. This led some theistic evolutionists to treat the formal structures as "poetic." However, this interpretation is untenable for two reasons. First, the creation account in Genesis 1:1 to 2:4 bears no resemblance to any known form of poetic arrangement. Second, the account has nothing of the emotional tone of poetry. The abundance of Hebrew poetry in biblical and extrabiblical Semitic literature provides no comparison with the Genesis account and thus does not lend itself to the support of the poetical interpretation of this passage (7). The commandment to honor the Sabbath day is rooted in the sequential events of the creation week (Exod. 20:8-11). A figurative interpretation would provide no factual basis for this commandment, and thus, it would be untenable (8).

The creation of Eve (Gen. 2:21-22) also constitutes an enigma for the theistic evolutionists who accept the naturalistic explanation of humanity as being genetically derived from a nonhuman ancestor. Furthermore, in Genesis 2:7 it is stated that "the Lord God formed man from the dust of the ground and breathed into his nostrils the breath of life, and man became a living being" (NIV). Although the process of formation is not specified, it seems to convey the thought of "special creation" from inorganic material rather than "derived creation" through some previously living form.

The Hebrew word for "living being" in Genesis 2:7 (NIV), *nephesh*, is the same as the words translated "living creatures" or "living and moving thing" in Genesis 1:20-21, 24. The same word *nephesh* is used in the translation of "living being" (Gen. 2:7). The difference between humans and beasts is that humans were created in God's image whereas the beasts were not. Therefore, Genesis 2:7 seems to imply that humans became living beings just as other beasts. The interpretation that humans are derived from a preexisting living being is entirely inappropriate in light of this consideration. Of course, to go so far as to imply that God, who is a Spirit, has a mouth or nose that can breathe the breath of life is to ignore the common Scriptural metaphor symbolizing spiritual activities by the act of breathing (Ps. 33:6; John 20:22; 3:8). The breath of God in Genesis 2:7 can be easily taken to symbolize the special spiritual creative activities whereby a human was made a living being without overworking the metaphoric use of the word (7).

Theistic evolutionists also give too much credence to the as yet poorly formulated theory of organic evolution. In their efforts to reconcile the naturalistic and theistic approaches to the origin of life, they have inadvertantly got themselves into the inconsistent position of denying the miracles of creation while maintaining the supernatural nature of the Christian message. The overworking of the multilevel structure of reality according to Bube's dictim (i.e., there are many levels at which a given situation can be described. An exhaustive description on one level does not preclude meaningful descriptions on other levels [9]) seems to run the danger of compartmentalizing reality into spiritual and physical realms that are independent of each other. This dualistic connotation seems to be implicit in the theistic evolutionist position of the human being, with a body that is a product of naturalistic evolution and a spiritual capacity that is given by God in a supernatural act.

7.1.3 *Progressive Creationists' View of the Earth's Age and Creation.* Progressive creationists seem to be able to keep an open mind scientifically and yet maintain the integrity of the Genesis account. The definition of progressive creationism is given clearly by Ramm as follows (10):

> In Gen. 1 the [fundamental] pattern [of creation] is a "development" from vacancy (Gen. 1:2) to the finished creation at the end of the sixth day. In "manufacturing," the pattern is from raw materials to finished product. In "art" the pattern is from unformed materials to artistic creation. In "life" the pattern is from the undifferentiated ovum to the adult. In "character" the pattern is from random and uncritical behavior to disciplined and moral behavior.

Let us analyze the progressive creationists' perspective in the treatments of the antiquity of the earth and the creation account in light of the findings of modern science.

The progressive creationists' view fits nicely with the well-documented estimate of the age of the earth and the universe as being more than four billion years. They maintain the infallibility of the Bible but find ample room for the reinterpretation of the length of the creation days of Genesis 1 and the genealogies of the Bible. Some say the progressive creationists fall into the trap of letting science pass judgment on the Scriptures (11). However, it can be seen from the following discussion that, aside from external evidence of present-day scientific determination of age, there is adequate exegetical data to demonstrate that the days of Genesis 1 can be considered long indefinite periods of time, and the genealogies of the Bible were not intended and cannot be used for the construction of an accurate chronology.

a) *How long were the creation days in Genesis 1?* The purpose of the

254

six-day account of creation seems to be to show how God changed the uninhabitable and unformed earth into a well-ordered world (12). The late Dr. James O. Buswell, II, theologian and third president of Wheaton College, has written a concise article on "The Length of the Creative Days," which is reprinted in the appendix, pp. 299–311. He argues that Moses used the word *yom* (day) in many ways in addition to its normal usage of a solar day. Day can be taken to mean a period of time of undesignated length (Gen. 2:4; Ps. 90:1–4) and periods of light as contrasted with darkness (Gen. 1:5). The sun's visible function of defining days and years did not begin until the fourth day, when the sun was revealed. Therefore, the first four days were definitely not 24-hour solar days as we have.

The citation of the fourth commandment, "Remember the Sabbath day by keeping it holy" (Exod. 20:8–11), to argue against the day-age interpretation is not necessarily valid because the argument is based on analogy but not identity (13). The substance of the keeping of the Sabbath is that people must work six days and rest one day, for God also worked in six creative periods and rested on the seventh.

The establishment of a Sabbath year (Exod. 23:10–11; Lev. 25:3–7) and a Jubilee Sabbath (Lev. 25:8–17) also suggests that the emphasis on the Sabbath is rest instead of the strict interpretation of "day." The phrase "and there was evening, and there was morning" that is found at the end of every creation narrative in Genesis 1 has been used to argue for the literal 24-hour interpretation of "day." However, since the word "day" can be interpreted as a period longer than 24 hours, the components of the day, "evening" and "morning," can also be interpreted figuratively (12) (*see* Ps. 90:5–6). Moreover, the evening and the morning make a night, not a day, if one wants to press the literal interpretation of these two items.

R. J. Snow has also made several observations on the length of the sixth day (14). As illuminated from the account in Genesis 2, several events transpired on day six: (1) God "formed" man from the dust of the ground (Gen. 2:7 NIV). (2) God "planted" a garden (Gen. 2:8a NIV). (3) God "put" man in the garden (Gen. 2:8b). (4) God said "I will make" a helper fit for him (Gen. 2:18b). (5) God brought all the beasts of the field and the birds in the air to the man for naming (Gen. 2:19–20). (6) The Lord God caused a deep sleep to fall upon the man (Gen. 2:21). (7) God took the rib from the man and "made" (or "built") a woman (Gen. 2:22 NIV). All these events involved a considerable amount of time.

Although God used supernatural processes to complete all the remarkable acts mentioned above, the words "formed," "planted," "put," "I will make," and "made" seem to suggest a certain amount of elapsed time. The naming of all the beasts and birds would take Adam a good deal of time even considering that the land animals were less numerous than the varieties observed today. In addition, Adam's deep sleep during God's "operation" suggests a prolonged period of time.

The most important time consideration seems to be the term *happa'am* translated in Genesis 2:23 as "at last" (RSV) or "now" (NIV, NASB) in Adam's exclamation as he showed appreciation of the woman whom God had made. The word *happa'am* seems to imply that Adam had waited for a long time for a mate, and finally his desire was satisfied. This interpretation is borne out by several passages in Genesis and other places in the Old Testament (Gen. 29:34–35; 30:20; 46:30; Exod. 9:27; Judg. 15:3; 16:18) where *happa'am* has been translated "now," "this time," or "this once" ("once more" NIV) in the Revised Standard and King James versions. These examples were used in the contexts of periods of elapsed time. Although the length of time that elapsed between God's bringing the animals before Adam to be named until Adam awoke from his deep sleep to see Eve was not specified, it seems more reasonable that Adam had developed loneliness after tending the Garden of Eden for a period of time until he found comfort in Eve. Thus it seems exegetically unwarranted to restrict the interpretation of the sixth day as a literal 24-hour solar day.

b) *Genealogies of the Bible.* Dr. W. H. Green, late professor of Old Testament at Princeton Theological Seminary and a contributor to the famous *Fundamentals* papers, has succinctly analyzed the genealogies of the Bible. He concluded that they were not intended and cannot be legitimately used to construct a chronology (15). His conclusions have been collaborated by other biblical scholars (16, 17). The arguments against the chronological treatment of the biblical genealogies can be summarized in the following three points:

1. *Abridgment and omission of unimportant names is the pattern in the genealogies of the Bible.* There are numerous examples of this observation. One prime example is the omissions in the genealogies of the Lord Jesus. In Matthew 1:8 Ahaziah (2 Kings 8:25), Joash (2 Kings 7:1), and Amaziah (2 Kings 23:34; 1 Chron. 3:16) are dropped between Joram and Ozias (or Uzziah). In Matthew 1:1 the entire genealogy of Jesus is summed up in two steps, "Jesus Christ the son of David, the son of Abraham." A comparison of 1 Chronicles 6:3–14 and Ezra 7:1–5 also reveals that six consecutive names in the genealogy of Ezra were omitted in the book that bears his name. The genealogy in Exodus 6:16–25 makes Moses the great-grandson of Levi though 430 years intervened (Exod. 12:40). It is,

therefore, evident that many names have been omitted from Moses' genealogy.

Another convincing proof is found in Numbers 3:19, 27–28. Four sons of Kohath, or grandsons of Levi, appear respectively to give rise to the families of the Amramites, Izharites, Hebronites, and Uzzielites. The number of males in these families one month and upward was 8600 only one year after the Exodus. It is inconceivable to assume that the father of Moses had given birth to 8600 descendants of the male sex alone, and 2750 of them were between the ages of 30 and 50 (Num. 4:36).

2. *Genealogies include significant names.* Biblical writers did not have chronology in mind when they wrote the genealogies. The genealogy of our Lord Jesus in Matthew 1 covered three lists of 14 generations. Each list covered different lengths of time, according to archaeological findings: Abraham to David nearly 1000 years, David to the Exile about 400 years, and the Exile to Christ more than 500 years. In verse 6 David is counted as the last of 14 generations extending from Abraham through David. David is also counted again as the first of 14 generations extending from David to the Exile. Therefore, David is counted twice in the genealogical record.

At the same time, the four women listed in the genealogy of Jesus— Tamar (v. 3), Rahab (v. 5), Ruth (v. 5), and the wife of Uriah (v. 6)—were not counted in Matthew's final tabulation of generations. The listing of these women in the genealogy was contrary to the Jewish custom. Yet each of these women was remarkable in some way. Three were once guilty of gross sin (Tamar, Rahab, and the wife of Uriah), and Ruth was of Gentile origin. This circumstance seems to indicate that Matthew did not simply copy the genealogical history of Joseph. He seemed to have a specific purpose in mind, and he omitted what did not suit the purpose or added what did.

The genealogies in Genesis 5 and 11 pertain to the generations elapsed from Adam to the Flood and from the Flood to Abraham, respectively. There is no passage in the Bible specifying the total length of time that actually transpired from Adam to the Flood and from the Flood to Abraham. However, some dates after the Flood-to-Abraham period are given—the period from Joseph to Moses was recorded as 430 years (Exod. 12:40), and the time elapsed from the Exodus to the building of the temple was 480 years (1 Kings 6:1). The absence of recorded elapsed time from Adam to Abraham suggests that this was an indefinite period of time on which Moses was not given exact information by God.

The structures of the genealogies in Genesis 5 and 11 seems to be symmetrical. Each genealogy includes 10 names; Noah is 10 persons from

Adam, and Terah is 10 persons from Noah. Each ends with a father having three sons, and the Cainite genealogy (Gen. 4:17–22) ends this way also. The Cainite and Sethite genealogies (Gen. 5) both culminate in their seventh member in terms of Lemech's polygamy, bloody revenge, and boastful arrogance, and Enoch's godliness and direct ascent to God, respectively.

The absence of accurately recorded time from Adam to Abraham and the symmetrical structures of the genealogies in Genesis 5 and 11 are highly suggestive of intentional arrangement in a form similar to that of Matthew. If one assumes that a long period of time elapsed between Adam and Abraham, the meager biblical record of events that transpired during this period is not surprising, for it is not uncommon for Scripture to pass over very long periods of time with little or no remark. For example, the greater part of the 430 years of the sojourn of the Israelites in Egypt is left blank in the sacred history.

3. *"Father," "son," and "begot" were used in a broad sense.* Several Biblical passages contain ancestral titles used in a broad sense. We know from earlier discussion that several names have been omitted in Matthew 1:8 after Joram. Therefore, Joram was actually the great-great-grandfather of Urriah. It is obvious that the "father" used in verse 8 between Joram and Uzziah means "ancestor" instead of its conventional meaning. In 1 Chronicles 1:36 the Hebrew text includes seven names after "the sons of Eliphaz," making it appear that all the seven named are sons. Actually one of the names, Timna, was that of a concubine, not a son. Only the New International Version translates clearly that Timna was Eliphaz's concubine as recorded also in Genesis 36:11–12 and that the other six are sons.

The genealogy of Samuel in 1 Chronicles 6:22–24, 37–38 suggests that an individual is a son of the preceeding descendant: "The descendants Kohath: Amminadab his son, Korah his son, Assir his son, Elkanah his son, Ebiasaph his son, Assir his son" (vv. 22–23 NIV). However, the first Assir, Eklanah, and Ebiasaph were all sons of Korah and thus brothers. Korah's father, Amminadab is also called Izhar in verse 38. This practice of listing dual names is common throughout the Bible.

Matthew 1:1 reads, "Jesus Christ the son of David, the son of Abraham." "Son" here obviously means descendant. Therefore, the biblical writers and translators seem to use the words "father" and "son" freely to mean "ancestor" or "descendant," and sometimes the persons are not closely related.

The regular formula in the genealogies in Genesis 5 and 10 is "A lived _____ years and begat B, and A lived after he begat B _____ years and

begat sons and daughters. And B lived _____ years and begat C . . ."
(KJV). The Hebrew word "begat" is sometimes used for succeeding generations. Zilpah is said to have "born to" Jacob her great-grandchildren (Gen.
46:18 NIV) and Bilhah her grandchildren (Gen. 46:25). Canaan is recorded
to have begotten whole nations (Gen. 10:15–18). Furthermore, if the
dates are true, Adam was contemporary with every generation until the
Flood, except Noah. Methuselah died in the year of the Flood. Shem
survived Abraham for 35 years; Salah, 3 years; and Eber, 64 years. For 58
years Noah was the contemporary of Abraham, and Shem actually survived Abraham for 35 years. Such conclusions are contrary to the spirit of
the record that presupposed a much longer gap between Adam and Noah
and between Noah and Abraham.

A comparison of the Hebrew text with the Septuagint (Greek) and the
Samaritan Pentateuch also reveals discrepancies in the years assigned to
the antidiluvial patriarchs. Different versions seek to bring the ages of the
patriarchs into closer conformity. The Samaritan and the Septuagint versions vary systematically from the Hebrew text, suggesting that these
translations were trying to accommodate the Mosaic narratives to the
demands of the accepted Egyptian antiquity at the time. However, the
Hebrew text (A.D. 980), although it came much later than the Septuagint
(250–150 B.C.) (18) and the Samaritan Pentateuch (143–37 B.C.) (19), was
well established as the most accurate original transcript of the Old Testament.

Moses, who lived for some time in Egypt, must have known as much
about the age of Egypt as the Septuagint translators or any other translators. If some translators felt that the original genealogy from which they
drew their information was inadmissible to fit the antiquity of Egypt and
that they had to introduce up to 900 years into the lives of the patriarch, it
is highly suggestive that Moses did not intend for the genealogies to be
interpreted chronologically. This suggestion was born out by the inclusion
of Cainan (Luke 3:36) in the genealogy of Jesus. This name was not found
in the Hebrew text, but it occurs in Genesis 11:13 in the Septuagint Old
Testament (20).

W. H. Green concluded his paper with the following statement: "On
these various grounds we conclude that the Scriptures furnish no data for
a chronological computation prior to the life of Abraham, and that the
Mosaic records do not fix and were not intended to fix the precise date
either of the Flood or of the creation of the world" (15).

Thus the purpose of the genealogies in Genesis 5 and 11 seems to be
more to show the effect of sin on human vitality and longevity rather than
to establish chronology. In the formula discussed above, B could be the

literal son of a distant descendant, and the age of A may be his age at the birth of the child from whom B was descended. This may allow centuries, millenniums, or hundreds of thousands of years to intervene between A and B.

The proponents of a recent creation have revised their date of creation back to 10 000 B.C. or so because of these arguments. However, they will not make any further concession, for this would introduce too large a gap into the genealogies (21, 22). However, it is entirely personal preference and not based on any exegetical data.

Bible passages referring to "the last days [times]" (Matt. 28:20; Acts 2:17; Heb. 1:2; 9:26; 1 Peter 1:20; 1 John 2:18) and the promise of Jesus' imminent return (Rev. 1:3; 22:10, 12, 20) fit in nicely with the assumption that humans have existed for hundreds of thousands of years prior to Christ's first coming. The use of "last days" implies that the major part of the world's history has been finished. The passages indicate that Christ's coming is to be expected within a short period, yet over 2000 years have passed since the promises. When contrasted with the thousands of years people have existed on earth, it *is* a short time. However, the passages are far-fetched if it is assumed that created life has existed for only 4000–10 000 years, because one would be forced to interpret the "last days" to mean the last one-half to one-fifth of the created order. This assumption seems to misread the intent of the "last days" passages (13).

7.1.4 *Creation Account in Light of the Findings of Modern Science*

a) *Day-age Interpretation of Creation.* The traditional day-age interpretations of the creation account assign days to various geological periods (23, 24). However, this seems to ignore the inconsistency of the creation of land plants, including herbs that yield seeds and trees that yield fruit, in the third day that is usually treated as corresponding to the Silurian Age. In the geological record the first fossil of fruit-bearing Angiosperms was found in the Cretaceous period that is more than 220 million years *later* than the Silurian Age (*see* Table 2.8).

Some try to explain away this problem by assuming that God in His revelation of creation to Moses revealed only the organisms existing at Moses' time. Thus the extinct organisms found in the Paleozoic and Mesozoic eras were ignored in the creation account. The third day was interpreted as corresponding to the Tertiary period where the land plants were abundant, and the fifth and sixth days are credited to the Quaternary and recent periods, respectively (25). (The fourth day did not involve the creation of any living organisms and is thus not included in the alignment of the geological timetable.) This view encounters the difficulties of implying that God misled or deceived humans and also of the fact that quite a few species of "living fossils" that persist in much of the geological column are extant today.

b) *Overlapping Day-age and Modified Intermittent-day Models.* The two views this author finds most consistent with the findings of modern science and the exegesis of the Genesis account are, namely, the *overlapping day-age model* (26, 13) and the *modified intermittent-day model* (13). They are represented in Tables 7.1 and 7.2. Several remarks can be made concerning these two models.

1. Both views maintain the orthodox position of creation *ex nihilo* (from no previously existing material). This is based on Genesis 1:1 as an independent sentence. Liberals have charged that this verse should be a dependent clause. They suggest that instead of the original statement of "In the beginning God created the heavens and the earth," it should read, "In the beginning of the creating of God. . . ." If this new translation is used together with verse 2, "The earth was formless and empty . . ." (NIV), it would imply that when God created, He used chaotic material that was presumably already there. This interpretation then reduces the unique Judeo-Christian God to a god similar to that of Plato's *Timaeus* who can only shape the world according to the design of eternal ideas.

The controversy revolves around the translation of the Hebrew word for "beginning." The word is eloquently defended in E. J. Young's work *Studies in Genesis One.* Young said that according to Hebrew lexicography and the usage of the word in other parts of the Bible, the most exegetically sound interpretation of this word in verse 1 is "In the beginning God created the heavens and the earth." This stands as a simple declaration of the fact of absolute creation.

2. Both views assume that the Genesis account is a description of what God revealed to an earthbound observer as if he had been present during God's creative activities. Therefore, Moses tended to use the language of his day to describe what he actually observed. Moses' observations are interpreted through his particular mental processes and recorded in the simplest terms understandable to his contemporaries. His early language naturally had a limitation in that it had no scientific terms of a technical nature. This means that when Moses said that "God made two great lights—the greater light to govern the day and the lesser light to govern the night. He also made the stars" (Gen. 1:16 NIV), he was really describing the first appearance of the sun, moon, and stars. This point will be elaborated in the following remarks.

3. The current popular *Star Formation Model* of the origin of the earth and the solar system has been nicely harmonized with the Genesis account (13). The model incorporates some of the elements of the well-

Table 7.1. The overlapping day-age model.

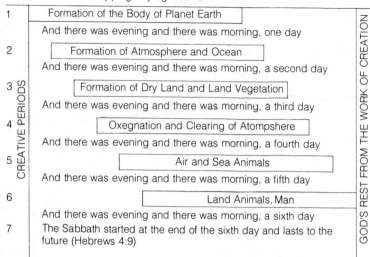

Table 7.2. Synopsis of creative activity according to proposed modified intermittent-day-view.*

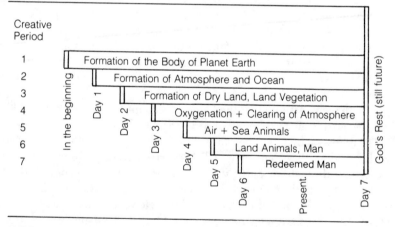

*NOTE: Reprinted, with permission, from Newman, R. C.; Eckelman, H. J., Jr. Genesis one and the origin of the earth. Downers Grove, IL: InterVarsity Press; 1977. © 1977 InterVarsity Press.

accepted *Big Bang* theory of the galaxies. This theory pictures the universe as expanding from a super dense state that exploded 13 billion years ago. The earth and the planets are natural products of a cloud of interstellar gas and dust as it cooled down during the process of expansion.

Genesis 1:2 states that "the earth was formless and empty, darkness was over the surface of the deep . . ." (NIV). This would imply that the earth at this point of the narrative is not yet a solid body but is shapeless, empty, and hardly visible. Genesis 1:2 then states that "the Spirit of God was hovering over the waters" (NIV). "Waters" can be interpreted as a large fluid mass of ice or water vapor. Thus the earth was covered with a watery mass, and this is in agreement with the scientific model of a dark nebula containing water vapor.

Genesis 1:6–8 seems to indicate the formation of the earth's atmosphere by the creation of the expanse or firmament, separating the waters above and below. The creation of plants in the latter part of the third day (Gen. 1:12) is also consistent with the scientific view that plants that can undergo photosynthesis and give off oxygen are presumably responsible for the introduction of oxygen into the reducing atmosphere (see I.3.3.1.b). It is believed that microscopic photosynthetic organisms may have been created prior to land plants to aid in the oxygenation process as indicated in the geological column. These organisms, which would probably have escaped the unaided naked eyes of an earthbound observer, were not recorded. With the oxygenation of the atmosphere, the surface of the earth that had been covered with watery masses and clouds began to clear up. Therefore, from the viewpoint of the earthbound observer, there is recorded the creation of the sun, moon, and stars as they were first visible in the fourth day.

4. Both the overlapping day-age model and the modified intermittent-day model allow for processes of change to take place after the creation of each prototype of living creatures. We have seen in previous discussions that the human was created from nonliving materials, and the stipulations "according to their kinds (its kind)" in Gen. 1:12, 21, 24 seem to imply there is only a limited amount of change among each "kind." However, the Genesis account never specifies what the biological boundaries of "kind" are, and one should be cautious in suggesting what these really might have been. The term "produce" in Genesis 1:12, 24 also suggests that processes may be involved.

The late Arnold Guyot, Blair Professor of Geology and Physical Geology of the College of New Jersey (later Princeton University), has observed that the Hebrew word *bārā*, translated "created," occurs on only three occasions in Genesis 1: verse 1, at the creation of the heavens and the earth; verse 21, at the creation of animal life; and verse 27, at the creation of humans (27). Therefore, he believed that the Bible teaches the creations of matter, animal life, and humans are distinct events, demanding direct divine intervention. Guyot's interpretation implies that the evolution from matter to life and from animal life to humans is impossible. Although the overworking of this interpretation is unwarranted, it is possible that the processes of microevolution are not at all excluded.

It is reasonable to interpret that "kind" of the Genesis account may mean the original ancestral form of a certain group of organism such as the fruit fly *Drosophila*, which later on developed into the present-day species through microevolution (*see* I.3.2.2.b). It is unlikely that the term "good" pronounced by God in Gen. 1:10, 12, 18, 25, 31 means completion and that each creation is a finality incapable of further changes and development, for God did not pronounce "it was good" after the creative activities of the second day. Moreover, 1 Timothy 4:4–5 states that "everything God created is good, and nothing is to be rejected if it is received with thanksgiving, because it is consecrated by the word of God and prayer" (NIV). This passage seems to suggest that "good" is used in contrast with "evil," so that we can receive everything God created with thanksgiving because it is not evil.

5. The succession of the creation of the living forms given in Genesis 1 seems to be as follows: (1) plants (third day); (2) invertebrates and some vertebrates (fifth day); (3) mammals, or the higher vertebrates (first half of the sixth day); (4) humans, the highest form of mammals (second half of the sixth day). Both the overlapping day-age and modified intermittent-day models provide for the paleontological record because the difficulty of the fruit plants appearing earlier than the invertebrates and some vertebrates is resolved. The models assume that the third creative period extends to a time contemporary with or later than the creation of the invertebrates and some vertebrates.

The problem of the propagation of land plants, which are immotile, in the third day without the aid of pollinating insects can also be resolved by assuming the overlapping or contemporaneousness of the creation of the land plants and some of the land animals. However, all microscopic organisms found in earlier geological times would have escaped the unaided eye of Moses and therefore are not recorded in the creation account. Both models suggest that God created all living organisms with a similar blueprint. This accounts for the similarities of the comparative structures and functions among organisms and their similarities in physiology and biochemical genetics.

6. The overlapping day-age model differs from the modified intermittent-day model in two respects. First, the former takes the phrase "there was evening, and there was morning" to symbolize the beginning and the end of a creative period. The latter assumes that "evening . . . morning" actually represents a 24-hour day that precedes each creative

period that extends into the present and will be ended only in the future. The overlapping day-age model and the traditional view assumes creation was ended at the conclusion of the sixth day (Gen. 1:31). However, the modified intermittent-day model suggests that each time "evening . . . morning" is mentioned, a new creative era is introduced by a 24-hour day, and this is followed by a long indefinite period of time in which all the creative activities of that era take place. Second, the overlapping day-age model accepts the literal meaning of Genesis 2:2 that God has rested from His creative activities in the Sabbath that extends through the present into the future. Therefore, God's activities today (John 5:17) are those of redemption (2 Cor. 6:2) and providence (Heb. 1:1–3).

The modified intermittent-day model, on the other hand, suggests that we are still observing God's creative activities in the earth through the changes and developments of the inorganic as well as the organic world. This model proposes that we are living in the creative period that intervenes between the sixth and seventh days in which God's principal activity is the creation of redeemed humans. For this latter position, Hebrews 4:1–11 is taken to mean an absolute rest in which God ceases all activities in the seventh day and will commence again only at the inception of the new heavens and the new earth (Rev. 21:1–8). At the second point of diversion between the two models, the overlapping day-age model seems to be at a slight advantage since it does not strain the interpretation of Genesis 2:1 that states "thus the heavens and the earth were completed in all their vast array" (NIV).

The creation or a redeemed people (2 Cor. 5:17) seems to be qualitatively different from the creation of the earth. The former is concerned with the spiritual rebirth of humans whereas the latter is primarily concerned with the bringing into existence of the world and humans. The overlapping day-age position views the microevolutionary processes observed today in nature and the laboratory as development and differentiation of preexisting life instead of creation of new life, and this is borne out by scientific findings.   •

The conjunction "and" that follows all of the concluding "and there was evening, and there was morning—the _____ day" (Gen. 1:3, 8, 13, 19, 23) and precedes a new creative narrative seems to suggest overlapping between the subsequent events and the previous ones. However, "and" is replaced by "thus" in Genesis 2:1 immediately following "and there was evening, and there was morning—the sixth day" of Gen. 1:31. It seems to end too abruptly for the modified intermittent-day view that takes Genesis 1:31 as the beginning of the sixth creative era.

It can be criticized that both the overlapping day-age model and the modified intermittent-day model read too much into the Genesis account and an ordinary person would never obtain such ideas from the account without external reference. However, if both of these models are exegetically sound, which is the contention of this author, and circumvent much of the apparent conflict between science and the traditional interpretation of the Bible, an open-minded person should seriously consider them viable options. C. Hodge, a leading evangelical theologian, stated:

> It is of course admitted that, taking this [Mosaic] account by itself it would be most natural to understand the word ["day"] in its ordinary sense; but if that sense brings the Mosaic account into conflicts then it is obligatory on us to adopt that other [overlapping day-age theory] (28).

7.1.5 *Difficult Problems in the Attempts to Harmonize the Bible and Science.* Any scientific model may find phenomena that cannot be accounted for reasonably, and thus, it may need constant modification or revision. Our models are subjected to this same criticism and revamping. Although this author maintains that the progressive creationist position faces fewer problems than the fiat creationist and theistic evolutionist positions, there are nonetheless problems to be resolved. However, these problems are not insurmountable, and the progressive creationist has a conscientious attitude in the search for answers. It will suffice to mention only two of the most perplexing questions that are constantly being tackled in the attempt to relate the Bible to scientific data.

a) *Antiquity of Humans.* How does the antiquity of humans fit in with the seemingly advanced civilization of Genesis 4 although the human fossils that have been found lack cultural artifacts?

If the cranial characteristics and the capacity of toolmaking are the criteria for identifying humans, then people have been around in the form of *Australopithecus* for as long as five million years (*see* Figure 2.16). On the other hand, if the use of fire is a distinctively human characteristic, *Homo erectus* who roamed the earth close to one million years ago is a good candidate for early humans. However, if the practice of burial rite is considered the characteristic human trait, then human status can be assigned to only *Homo neanderthalensis*, who lived as early as 150 000 years ago. The *Homo sapiens* fossils dated arround 40 000 years old with modern cranial features and characteristic human civilization are unquestionably human and bear close resemblance to modern humans. It is safe to conclude that physical anthropology suggests that humans have been on earth for perhaps millions of years.

Both current scientific theories and the scriptural account agree on the basic unity of the human race, i.e., the present human varieties all stem from a common stock. However, since the advent of human civilization was only a relatively recent event (*see* Figure 2.14), the Neolithic culture that involves the domestication of plants and animals did not come on the scene until approximately 9000 B.C. (29). However, the account of Genesis 4 seems to suggest a fairly complete culture for humans immediately after the Fall.

The large gap that exists between the first human as evidenced from the fossil record and the advent of human civilization is a major problem. It deserves diligent efforts by scholars intimately involved in anthropological studies. There are several suggestions in the attempt to resolve this apparent enigma.

We have seen the fiat creationist position that ignores the early human fossils and the theistic evolutionist position that ignores the Genesis account. Both of these theories create more problems than they solve.

Still another idea is suggested in the *gap theory* as mentioned in Table 6.1 and the appendix. The gap theory attributes early human fossils to pre-Adamites in a first creation "implied" by Genesis 1:1. The theory states that pre-Adamites were subsequently wiped out before the onset of the events recorded in Genesis 1:2 and the rest of the Bible.

Another theory suggests there were *two Adams*. This idea states that Adam of Genesis 1 is not the same as the Adam in Genesis 2, the former being the Old Stone Age Adam and the latter being the New Stone Age Adam. This theory suggests that the rest of the Bible is about the Fall and salvation of the New Stone Age Adam (30). The last two theories are not exegetically sound and seem to impinge on the fundamental concept of the unity of the human race.

A theory by Buswell III (29) suggests that the description of Cain and Abel in Genesis is comparatively meager and that they may not really be "domesticators" of plants and animals. He says that they may appear to be such due to the translation of Moses' language. Their respective concern with vegetable and animal provision might have been vastly more primitive. This would date them to an early time.

Buswell II (20) believes Cain could have lost his cultural attainment because of the prevalence of sin based on Genesis 4:12. Thus a considerable part of the economic culture as God gave it to humans before the Fall might have been lost at an early date and then rediscovered gradually (*see* Gen. 3:17–19). The advanced culture suggested by Cain's descendants can then be attributed to the arrival of civilization after many generations had elapsed and the human population had grown. This interpretation is borne out by Genesis 4:17 that suggests the presence of dynasties or tribes instead of individuals, and this necessitated the building of a city.

The lost civilizations implicated by the archaeological remains found in South and Central America lend credence to the possibility of an advanced culture that was wiped out suddenly. The question is raised as to whether there is a connection between this culture and the cities of Genesis 4:17. However, without solid prehistoric findings of cultural artifacts these theories remain speculative and need to be reevaluated when more data becomes available.

b) *What Is the Extent of the Noachian Deluge?*

(1) *Universal Flood.* There are two theories propounded in the attempt to answer this question. The universal-flood theory is based on the literal interpretation of Genesis 7:1 to 8:22 and the fact that some type of flood story is found in every culture of the world, except Japan and a few places in Africa. Readers are referred to the recent extensive treatments of this theory by Whitcomb and Morris (4), Patten (31), and Filby (32). The difficulty in this theory is mainly the lack of clear geological evidence to indicate that a cataclysmic event did cover the broad area required by a universal flood (33).

Another perplexing phenomenon that cannot be accounted for successfully by the theory of a universal flood is the biogeographical distribution of fauna (*see* I.2.4). The distinct biotic regions separated from each other by land masses or ocean barriers are very difficult to reconcile with a universal flood that devastated the fauna of the earth. This would mean that the present fauna all originated from the animals saved by Noah's ark. However, the physical barriers separating the biotic regions are too harsh for land animals to cross (*see* Figure 2.24).

If the theory of continental drift correctly describes the configuration of the land masses of the ancient earth, the continents existed in close proximity with each other more than 60 million years ago. If the migration of animals is to be used to account for the present biotic distribution, one has to postulate that the Flood must be dated back to the time when the continents were together so that when the animals were released from the ark after the inundation, they could migrate to repopulate the earth. Since humans came on the scene only a few million years ago by the most liberal estimate, this date for the Flood is totally unacceptable.

(2) *Local Flood.* The local-flood theory (33) is the second theory dealing with the Noachin Deluge. It tries to get around the difficulty of accounting for biogeography. There are two forms of this theory, and both hold to the view that the waters inundated only the Mesopotamian Valley and its vicinity. The two views are (1) the Flood was universal in the sense that it wiped out all humans, who had not spread very far from the Mesopotamian Valley when the Flood occurred, and (2) the Flood wiped

out only the inhabitants of the Mesopotamian Valley.

The major argument of the local-flood theory is that there is a sort of metonymy commonly employed by the ancient Near Eastern Culture to speak of a considerable part as a whole. This seems to be evident in numerous biblical passages (Gen. 41:57; Deut. 2:25; 1 Kings 18:10; Ps. 22:17; Matt. 3:5; John 4:39; Acts 2:5). These are cases when "all" means "all" and "every" means "every," but the context tells us where this is intended. Therefore, the universality of the flood may simply mean the universality of the experience of the one who reported it. There was no knowledge concerning the scope of the earth, not to mention the New Continents, at Moses' time. It is difficult to conceive how Moses would visualize the universal flood without knowing the entire scope of the earth. The universal legendary flood stories can be attributed to the people with the common origin of being from the area that experienced the Deluge. This theory is held by most anthropologists.

The local-flood theory also avoids the necessity to propose a mechanism by which the whole globe could be covered by water. It is estimated that to cover the highest mountains would require eight times more water than what the earth has now. Therefore, the local-flood theory seems to be facing fewer obstacles than the universal-flood theory.

For more details readers are referred to Hugh Miller's classic treatment (18) of the local-flood theory and a more updated version by Bernard Ramm (10). Davis Young also criticizes the views held by the flood geologists who advocate a universal flood (33).

In summary, we can state that the Christian world view has made a substantial contribution to the development of modern science. Since nature is God's handiwork, Christians are obligated to search for truth about God through biblical as well as natural revelation. Some Christians believe in a God-directed evolutionary origin of life. Others reject any mechanistic explanation of the origin of life as anti-Christian. There are also Christians who believe God created basic life forms that subsequently diversified into many varieties and species through the natural forces God has put into place. To this author the last group avoids the constraints of humanistic extrapolations of science that are made at the expense of the integrity of the Scriptures. This view also is not constrained by adherence to theological traditions that suppress the objectivity of science.

References 7.1

1. Harrison, R. K. Introduction to the Old Testament. Grand Rapids, MI: Eerdmans; 1969: 548–51.
2. Buswell, J. O., II. Systematic theology of the Christian religion. Vol.

1. Grand Rapids, MI: Zondervan; 1963: 156.
3. Newman, R. C.; Eckelmann, H. J. Genesis one and the origin of the earth. Downers Grove, IL: InterVarsity; 1977: 57.
4. Whitcomb, J. C.; Morris, H. M. The Genesis flood. Nutley, NJ: Presbyterian and Reformed; 1961.
5. Ramm, B. The Christian view of science and Scripture. Grand Rapids, MI: Eerdmans; 1954: 22.
6. Orr, J. God's image in man. London: Hodder and Stoughton; 1906: 157.
7. Buswell, J. O., II. Systematic theology. 140, 159–61.
8. Young, E. J. Studies in Genesis one. Nutley, NJ: Presbyterian and Reformed; 1964: 78.
9. Bube, R. The human quest. Waco, TX: Word; 1971: 207.
10. Ramm, B. Christian view of science and Scripture.
11. McCain, A. J. Christian theology. Revised by Smith, C. R.; Whitcomb, J. C. Winona Lake, IN: Grace Theol. Sem.; n.d.: 29.
12. Young, E. J. Studies in Genesis one. 104–5.
13. Newman, R. C.; Eckelmann, H. J. Genesis one and the origin of the earth.
14. Snow, R. J. In: Genesis one and the origin of the universe. Newman, R. C.; Eckelmann, H. J., Jr. Downers Grove, IL: InterVarsity Press; 1977: 125.
15. Reprinted from: Green, W. H. Bibl. Sacra. (April):285–303; 1890. Newman, R. C. Genesis one. 105–23.
16. Raven, J. H. Old Testament introduction. New York: Revell; 1910.
17. Robinson, A. T. A harmony of the Gospels. New York: Harper & Row; 1950.
18. Archer, G. L., Jr. A survey of Old Testament introduction. Chicago: Moody; 1964: 37–38.
19. Purvis, J. D. The Samaritan Pentateuch and the origin of the Samaritan sect. Cambridge, MA: Harvard Univ. Press; 1968: 16–17.
20. Buswell, J. O., II. Systematic theology of the Christian religion. 24–25.
21. Morris, H. M. Biblical cosmology and modern science. Grand Rapids, MI: Baker; 1970: 60–71, 79–81.
22. Whitcomb, J. C., Jr. The early earth. Grand Rapids, MI: Baker; 1972: 107–11.
23. Miller, H. Testimony of the rocks. New York: Hurst; 1856.
24. Magoun, H. W. Bibl. Sacra. (Oct.):347–57; 1931.
25. Warring, C. B. Bibl. Sacra. (Jan.):50–67; 1896.
26. Dana, J. D. Bibl. Sacra. (April):201–24; 1885.

27. Guyot, A. Creation. New York: Charles Scribner's Sons; 1884.
28. Hodge, C. Systematic theology. Vol. 1. Grand Rapids, MI: Eerdmans; 1960: 570–71.
29. Buswell, J. O., III. Faith and thought. J. Victoria Inst. 96(1):1–23; 1967.
30. Pearce, E. K. V. Who was Adam? Exiters: Paternoster; 1969.
31. Patten, D. W. The biblical flood and the ice epoch. Seattle, WA: Pacific Meridian; 1966.
32. Filby, F. A. The flood reconsidered. Grand Rapids, MI: Zondervan; 1970.
33. Young, D. Creation and the flood. Grand Rapids, MI: Baker; 1977.

PART III

A BRIEF SURVEY
OF THE INTERRELATIONSHIP
OF NATURALISM AND DARWINISM

CHAPTER 8

Evolution as a Paradigm to Explain Human Experience

Naturalism is a philosophy that maintains several propositions. It states that all processes and all things are explained in terms of space-time conditions so that no non–space-time existence is possible. Naturalism holds that the only intelligible statements are those referring to empirical inquiry and those amenable to empirical verification. The philosophy contends that the cosmos exists as a uniformity of cause and effect in a closed system. In dealing with humans, naturalism states that humans are only a complex machine and that death is extinction of personality and individuality. Naturalism considers history a linear stream of events linked by cause and effect but without an overarching purpose. Finally, naturalism states that humans are the central reference point of ethical values (1).

In the intellectual history of western civilization, many thinkers have contributed to the development of naturalism. However, some contributors were not themselves naturalists. The roots of naturalism can be traced to the ancient Greek atomists who postulated an infinite number of indivisible and unalterable atoms of an infinite variety of sizes and shapes that move in an infinite empty space, and these atoms are eternal, unchangeable, and self-sufficient. All things happen according to this *law of necessity* inherent in the properties of atoms (2).

Naturalism was first formulated as a systematic school of thought in the eighteenth century. René Descartes (1596–1650) set the stage for naturalism by his conception of the material world as a perfect machine that is rigidly deterministic and reducible to exact laws.

Many traditional thinkers regard God as the maker of the universe, but they contend He is not personally interested in it. On the other hand, naturalists have elevated human reason as the sole criterion for truth.

Georg Wilhem Friedrich Hegel (1770–1831) summed up the naturalists' view of history. He stated that history is a rational process that provides an ideal reality of dialectical reason that underlies all natural phenomena. He suggested that the world known to our senses is only the external manifestation of the *essence*, or the *absolute*, more simply defined as logic. Progress is made by the dialectic process. For example, in a conversation a first statement is made (thesis), then it is answered (antithesis), and then a new statement is made (synthesis). This new statement may then be answered, and so the process goes on. The dialectic works in all things that proceed toward fuller freedom and eventually toward the complete self-realization of essence. Hegel was opposed to the static formulations of *Enlightenment* thought (belief in the power of human reason). He had everything in motion, to be grouped only when its growth and development are understood. Hegel's views contributed directly to the nineteenth century's evolutionary outlook (3).

Hegel's naturalistic philosophy undoubtedly influenced the thinking of Charles Darwin (1809–82) when Darwin formulated his theory of evolution based on natural selection. Although reared in the Church of England, Darwin did not encounter strong pressure for religious orthodoxy from either side of his family. His father did not attend church, and his mother was a liberally oriented Unitarian (4). His gradual change from the acceptance of the traditional view of Christianity to agnosticism seemed, to a large extent, to be influenced by the naturalistic philosophy that was in vogue.

Darwin wrote in one of his most controversial treatises: "A belief in all-pervading spiritual agencies seems to be universal; and apparently follows from a considerable advance in man's reason, and from a still greater advance in his faculties of imagination, curiosity and wonder. . . . The idea of a universal and beneficent Creator does not seem to arise in the mind of man, until he has been elevated by long-continued culture" (5).

Over the years since the publication of Darwin's *Origin of Species*, advocates of Darwin's ideas have to a large extent succeeded in the universalization of the theory of evolution and have thus established it as a new paradigm to explain most areas of human experience. Evolution and naturalism have become interwoven although evolutionary thought is not

276

always naturalistic. Both naturalism and Darwin's ideas have influenced past as well as present thinking in philosophy, psychology, education, political theories, economics, sociology, and religion.

References 8

1. Sire, J. The universe next door. Downers Grove, IL: InterVarsity Press; 1976: 61.
2. Hooykaas, R. Religion and the rise of modern science. Grand Rapids, MI: Eerdmans; 1972: 2.
3. Stromberg, R. N. An intellectual history of modern Europe. New York: Appleton-Century-Crofts; 1966: 245.
4. West, G. Charles Darwin, the fragmentary man. London: G. Routledge and Sons; 1937.
5. Darwin, C. The descent of man. New York: Rand McNally; 1974: 607.

8.1 Evolutionary Thinking in Philosophy

Darwin's evolutionary concept broke down the principle of fixity. This idea had pervaded the field of philosophy ever since the view that each form of living organism is immutable was introduced by Aristotle and elaborated by Thomas Aquinas. In addition, new philosophical postulates in ontology, epistemology, and ethics incorporated Darwin's ideas (1).

The most influential philosophy that has Darwinian roots is pragmatism. Pragmatic theory emphasizes the evolution and changing character of reality, as well as the relevance of knowledge to practical situations. The emphasis is also on the need to test truth by its ability to "work" and on the instrumental nature of ideas (2).

Well-known pragmatists like Charles S. Peirce (1839–1914), William James (1842–1910), and John Dewey (1859–1952) have exerted a great influence on twentieth century thinking. John Dewey has been especially vocal in applying the Darwinian concepts in philosophy. He wrote, "A universe describable in evolutionary terms is a universe which shows, not indeed design, but tendency and purpose; which exhibits achievement, not indeed of a single end, but of a multiplicity of natural goods at whose apex is consciousness" (3). Naturalism as a philosophy does contain an element that treats the universe like an organism. This view, which was first expounded by Hegel, was based on the organic approach: nothing can be understood except by reference to the whole of which it is a part. Our minds and the universe are parts of a single whole; hence, they obey the same law.

With the monistic overtone, pragmatism also makes truth a subjective

277

affair. "Truth, in general or in the abstract," Dewey maintained, "is just a name for an experienced relation among the things of experience: that sort of relation in which intents are retrospectively viewed from the standpoint of the fulfillment which they secure through their own natural operation or incitement" (4).

Dewey attempted to explain away the ethical theory that there exists a final goal of absolute reality, absolute truth, and absolute goodness, and a separate moral force that moves toward that goal. He maintained that the progress of biology has accustomed our minds to the notion that moral force is not an outside power that presides supremely but statically over the desires and efforts of humans. Instead, he contended that moral force is a method of adjustment of the capacities and conditions within specific situations. Thus he advocated the abolition of final goals and single motive power, as well as the separate and infallible faculty in morals. Dewey thought that the business of morals is not to speculate on the final goal of human beings and what is ultimately right, but to utilize physiology, anthropology, and psychology to discover all that can be discovered in humans, namely, their organic powers and propensities. He felt that morals are to help humans resolve problem situations that arise in the course of social evolution.

This expedient definition of the morally good has become one of the major presuppositions of situation ethicists. They maintain that *love* only is always good and that there are no universals of any kind. On this basis, when a small neighborhood merchant tells a lie to divert a "protection" racketeer from a victim because of his compassion for the latter, the merchant is doing the most loving thing in the situation and thus the right and good thing (5).

Pragmatism has penetrated various facets of modern human thinking. The pragmatists' ideas are being put into practice in many ways.

References 8.1

1. Henry, C. F. H. Remaking the modern man. Grand Rapids, MI: Eerdmans; 1946: 116–78.
2. Bixler, J. S. Pragmatism. An encyclopedia of religion. New York: Philosophical Library; 1945: 601.
3. Dewey, J. Influence of Darwin in philosophy. New York: Henry Holt; 1910: 34.
4. Dewey, J. Influence of Darwin in philosophy. 190.
5. Fletcher, J. Situation ethics, the new morality. Philadelphia: Westminster; 1966: 40, 64.

8.2 Evolutionary Thinking in Educational Theories

Evolutionary thinking can lead to the following conclusions: (1) Since species arise and disappear by natural selection, reality is not a static, closed system but is a dynamic process of change and development. (2) Humans and their cultural achievements are only the products of a natural process of development. The latter conclusion undermines the theory that human beings are a special creation of God, a theory that is grounded in a Judeo-Christian monotheistic presupposition.

Evolution can be applied to both body and mind. The body is the culminated product of biological evolution, and the mind is an adjustive behavior in response to social evolution (1). Based on these presuppositions, the role of experience in the educational process was reevaluated in Dewey's theory of *Reconstruction*.

Traditional philosophies assert that since experience never rises above the level of the particular, contingent, and probable, only a power transcending the origin and content can impart to experiences a universal, necessary, and certain authority and direction. In contrast, Dewey elevated experience by declaring it a guide in science and moral life. He adopted a biological perspective and defined the essence of life as *behaviors* and *activities*. He visualized that an organism acts in accordance with its own structures. Thus, changes produced in the environment react on the organism and its activities. As a result, the living creature suffers or undergoes the consequences of its own behavior, and this becomes the organism's experience. In this sense, the interaction of the organism with its environment is the primary factor for the attainment of knowledge. This knowledge is derived from and is involved in the process by which life is sustained.

Sensational experiences that may be relative are emotional and practical, not cognitive and intellectual. However, the experiences are to provoke and incite challenge to decide what is to terminate as knowledge. The true "stuff" of experience is recognized to be the adaptive courses of action, liabilities, active functions, connections of doing and undergoing, as well as sensory and motor coordinations. Experience carries within itself the principle of connection and organization that renders unnecessary a supernatural and superempirical synthesis (2).

The outcome of Reconstruction was *progressive education*. The progressive educationist's motives were to discover how a newborn is influenced by organic needs, drives, and potentialities and how that child acquires the determinate interests, patterns, and values that interact with the social human environment. The progressive educationist stresses the present interaction of humans and their environment against a cultural heritage. It identifies the end as the result of the process in which change of experience brings about added power of subsequent directive or control (3). The resulting objective of education is not to eliminate bias or preferential acts but to learn to justify the bias (1). Progressive education has put the traditional essentialist educators on the defensive. In contrast, the traditional essentialists educators stress the so-called subject-centered curriculum and demand that essential skills and basic knowledge be taught to all (4).

References 8.2

1. Childs, J. L. American pragmatism and education. New York: Henry Holt; 1956.
2. Dewey, J. Reconstructionism in philosophy. Boston: Beacon; 1959.
3. Dewey, J. Democracy and education. New York: Macmillan; 1916.
4. Johnson, J. A.; Collins, H. W.; Dupuis, V. L.; Johansen, J. M., editors. Foundations of American education readings. Boston: Allyn and Bacon; 1969: 336.

8.3 Social Evolutionism

Although Auguste Comte (1798–1857) pioneered an evolutionary approach to explain the development of social institutions (*see* III. 8.7), Herbert Spencer (1820–1903) was the first key thinker who applied the principles from *Struggle for Existence* and *Survival of the Fittest* to society. He believed *nature* would reveal that the best competitors in a competitive situation would win. This process would lead to a continuing improvement, and the outcome is the natural law of competitive struggle.

Spencer was heavily influenced by concepts in thermodynamics as well as natural selection in formulating his social theories. The natural process starts from the persistence of force. It proceeds to redistribute matter and motion by evolution and dissolution until a final state of equilibrium is achieved. Thus Spencer believed that evolution ends only in the establishment of the greatest perfection and the most complete happiness.

Spencer maintained that conscious control of societal evolution is an absolute impossibility. He felt that all attempts to reform social processes are efforts to remedy the irremediable, would interfere with nature, and would lead only to degeneration. In the interest of survival itself, cooperation in industrial society must be voluntary, not compulsory. State regulation and distribution, according to Spencer, is more akin to the organization of a militant society. He believed this would be fatal to the survival of the industrial community. Spencer condones natural right instead of utilitarianism. He tried to reconcile evolution and idealism by forming a bridge between militarism and peace, egoism and altruism.

William Graham Sumner (1840–1910) incorporated Spencer's emphasis on natural selection with his own interpretation of Protestant ethics. He equated the Protestant ideal with the strongest or the fittest. Sumner argued against natural right and equality on the basis that powers will be developed according to their measure and degree. He believed that better qualified people will be favored if nature provides the environment where all can exert themselves. Sumner concurred with Spencer in opposing legislative meddling with the natural events of society (1).

Some radical *Social Darwinists* exploited natural selection to justify indifference to the suffering of the poor. Their thinking can be traced to Thomas Malthus's *Essay on Population* that expounded the tendency of the population to increase faster than the food supply. Malthus's stress on the inevitability of human disaster and perpetual poverty led Darwin to formulate his concept of the struggle for survival in which less durable human organisms would die and fail to reproduce themselves (2).

Critics of Social Darwinism stress the capacity of the human mind to mold the narrow genetic process of natural selection. Lester Ward (1841–1913) maintained that although the human mind lies within the domain of cosmic law, it has deliberately and capably adapted to the social environment of humans and thus directs the process of human evolution (3). William James (1842–1910) believed that the human mind is not just a quiet, cognitive organ. He felt it is intelligent mental reactions that promote survival by arranging internal relations to suit the environment. James believed that humans can change history and society because of their adaptability to the social situation. However, Spencer attributed social changes only to geography, environment, and external circumstances that a human cannot control (2).

With the beginning of the twentieth century and the havoc of the two world wars, the optimism of Social Darwinism was shattered. Old notions of inevitable progress had to be discarded, and evolutionism metamorphosed and reappeared in the functionalistic approach of sociology. Talcot Parsons put social development in an evolutionary context by suggesting a continuity of human ways with those of subhumans. However, support for this hypothesis must include evidence of continuity of cultural patterns as evidenced by cultural artifacts between human and subhuman populations. Cultural evolution among early humans probably represents adaptations to a changing environment (4).

References 8.3

1. Hofstadter, R. Social Darwinism in American thought. Rev. ed. New York: G. Braziller; 1965.
2. Stromberg, R. N. An intellectual history of modern Europe. New York: Appleton-Century-Crofts; 1966: 275.
3. Becker, H.; Barnes, H. E. Social thought from love to science. 2nd ed. Washington: Harren; 1952: 972.
4. Parsons, T. Evolutionary universals in society. Am. Soc. Rev. 29:339; 1964.

8.4 Evolutionary Thinking in Economics

Traditional economic thought has been dominated by an equilibrium approach in which an economic system is viewed as being in equilibrium. The French *physiocrats* advocated working out the *law of nature* in its economic bearing toward the highest welfare of the human race. The law of nature, in their view, is immutable and irrefragable. It is a propensity working to an end, the accomplishment of a purpose (1).

The physiocrats' British counterpart, Adam Smith, put the traditional economic view in a theistic context. He envisaged the Creator as being very restrained in the matter of interference with the natural course of things. The guidance of His invisible hands takes place not by way of interposition but through a comprehensive scheme of contrivances established from the beginning of creation. Humans are considered to be consistently self-seeking. This economic person is part of the mechanism of nature, and the self-seeking endeavor is but a means by which general welfare is worked out (2).

The classic economic model was accommodated by Social Darwinists. They maintained that natural selection is the law of nature that favors the strongest and fittest in self-seeking traffic. Therefore, this eventually leads to the inevitable progress of society (3).

The major contending school of thought was developed around the turn of the century by Thorstein Veblen (1857–1929). He systematically applied the evolutionary concept of change in formulating his economic theories. According to Veblen, society is a process and not a static system. It develops an existence of its own that is independent of individuals and groups functioning within the society or culture.

Veblen believed the factor that causes society to be emergent is technological change. The cultural process is not teleological, for it does not move toward any predetermined end. Veblen held that human beings can contribute little to provide guidance for social evolution, for it seems to be a matter of drift.

Social institutions are the key element of human culture. They are the end products of individuals who seek to satisfy their instinctive drives by using reason and following customary and habitual ways of behaving. Institutions develop over time as aids for people to organize and control individual and social behavior in order to satisfy their wants.

Veblen categorized institutions into two types: serviceable and disserviceable. Serviceable institutions involve human workmanship and parental instincts for race survival. Disserviceable institutions are the products of human predatory and acquisitive drives that elevate the individual over the community. Therefore, the economic system develops from the dichotomy of the serviceable and disserviceable human drives in culture and in institutions and classes (4). Veblen's evolutionary thinking has inspired the inception of an influential school of economic thought, *neoinstitutionalism*. This view finds favor among such prominent contemporary economists as Clarence E. Ayes, John Kenneth Galbraith, Gunnes Myrdal, and Gerhard Colm, to name but a few.

Neoinstitutionalists differ from convential economists in their treatment of the social system. They contend it is an evolving open system rather than a static closed system. Neoinstitutionalists favor comprehensive governmental involvements and national control in economic development. However, the conventional economists fight against complicated fiscal and monetary control to preserve free market competition.

References 8.4

1. Stromberg, R. N. Intellectual history of modern Europe. New York: Appleton-Century-Crofts; 1966: 156.
2. Ibid., 157.
3. Hofstadter, R. Social Darwinism in American thought. Rev. ed. New York: G. Braziller; 1965.
4. Gruncy, A. G. Contemporary economic thought. New York: Auguste M. Kelley; 1974: 20.

8.5 Evolutionary Thinking in Political Theories

Karl Marx (1818–83) helped set the stage for *communism* by stressing the materialistic nature of history and the unpaid labor of the working class that accumulates as surplus value. He elaborated the Hegelian System (a proposition is opposed by equal idea and reconciled by third proposition). Marx used this system by representing the history of humankind as the evolution of humanity in the discovery of the dialectic law (elevation of matter over mind, material existence). Thus, he attempted to free history from metaphysics (spiritual existence).

To Marx, nature works dialectically through a nonrecurring historical evolution. He credited Darwin as the one who had brought about the transition from the metaphysical to the dialectic conception of nature by *proving* that all organic beings, including humans, are the products of an evolutionary process that has been going on for millions of years. The methods of dialectics with their constant regard to the innumerable actions and reactions of life and death and of progressive or retrogressive changes provided Marx with the driving force for his system of historical evolution. The struggle for individual existence that culminates in the evolution of humans from animal ancestors disappeared when humans became really human. At that point humans could dominate the conditions of life and make their own history by controlling the extraneous factors that govern history. Humans try to regulate commodity production and appropriation, for they are the major factors by which society evolves.

Thus political systems evolve from the medieval balance of individualistic production and appropriation to the capitalistic conflict of social production versus individualistic appropriation. Marx believed the system would evolve finally to the triumph of classless society where production and appropriation are equally controlled by all people. He taught that proletarian revolution is the means by which the exploited working class can seize power and transform the socialized means of production, which is owned by the capitalists, into public property. Marx believed the development of public production would eventually abolish the different classes of society, and the culmination of human historical evolution would be achieved (1).

Engels (1820–95) built on Marx's theory. In spite of Engels' disregard for individual competition (2), he justified class struggle by Darwin's concept of the struggle for existence. He also exploited Hugo de Vries's mutation theory (*see* I.1.3–1.4) to explain the necessity of sudden and drastic reconstruction of the economic basis of societies (3).

Another political theory was put forth by Militaristic National Socialism (*Nazism*). They adopted a crude Darwinistic outlook and held that life is a ruthless struggle in which the weak, wounded, and allegedly biologically inferior must perish. They believed the Germans belong to the purest Aryan race who alone created civilization. Nazism held that decadent members of society are the intellectualist, internationalist, uprooted, and atomist and that they have to be purged to maintain national tradition, close group integration, and people's intuition and customs. This system was an irrational and inherently destructive force with no doctrinal center. It was committed to eternal dynamism for the sake of dynamism.

Other political systems developed that extended Nazism. Nihilistic thinkers Nietzsche and von Bernhardi glorified wars and contributed directly to the inception of *militarism*. In addition, the political system of *Fascism* was influenced by the same thinkers. It shared with Nazism the conceptions of the survival of the fittest, the superiority of institution over intellect, and the organic nature of society.

References 8.5

1. Engels, F. Socialism: utopian and scientific. Chicago: C. H. Kerr; 1900. Aveling, E., translator.
2. Selsam, H.; Martel, H., editors. Readers in Marxist philosophy. New York: International; 1963: 188.
3. Ghent, W. J. Socialism and success. New York: John Lane; 1910: 47–49.

8.6 Evolutionary Thinking in Psychology

Darwin was a dualist and he applied his theory of evolution to both the mind and body (1). His influence in the later development of psychology was particularly felt in psychoanalysis, functionalism, and behaviorism. He made a direct contribution to psychology in his theory of emotion developed in his book *Expression of Emotion in Man and Animals*. Darwin, also, prepared the foundation for ethology and comparative psychology.

Sigmund Freud (1856–1939), the physician founder of psychoanalysis, was influenced by the deterministic implication of Darwin's natural selection in formulating his theories on the development of the human's normal and neurotic personalities. Freud also based his conception of the irrational nature of the human's instincts on the evolutionary kinship between animals and humans.

Freud divided a person's mental apparatus into three categories: the *id*, the *ego*, and the *superego*. The id is the primary unconscious pleasure principle that includes the instincts. It acts like a spoiled child who wants immediate gratification of all desires. The ego is the secondary process evolved out of the control of the id in facing reality in which the superego has to be placed in balance with the id. The ego is partly conscious and partly unconscious. The superego is the product of moral principles learned from society and is totally conscious. It consists of the *conscience*, which tells what is wrong, and the *ego-ideal*, which tells what is right (2).

Freud developed his theories on instincts according to a more or less biological outlook. He distinguished two classes of instincts. The first instincts are the life instincts that find their source in the physiological needs of the organism for survival. The second instincts are the death instincts that are based on the decay process in biological degradation of tissues (3).

The *functionalists* took from Darwin the theme that behavior is adaptable and in order to survive psychologically, humans have to be able to adjust to their environment both physically and mentally. They stressed the survival values of the solution of a mental problem. To them, psychology is concerned with mental functions rather than contents, and these functions are adjustments and adaptations to the environment. They emphasized the utilitarian aspect of psychology that asks the question of applicability of mental functions. They also saw a close relationship between mental and physical responses, the biological and psychological understanding of humans in terms of interaction between mind and body (4). The evolutionary philosophy of pragmatism also contributed much to the functionalist's thinking through William James (1842–1910) and John Dewey (1859–1952). In addition, the functionalists influenced later theories of perception, e.g., James J. Gibson's writings (5).

The application of Darwinian evolutionary ideas to both mind and body led to a controversy on whether an animal has consciousness and, if so, to what extent, and at what point on the scale to simpler forms consciousness ceases. The *behaviorists* solved this problem by confining psychology to the studies of observable behavior and leaving open the question of whether mind exists.

In one of the animal- and man-consciousness studies Ivan Petrovich Pavlov (1849–1936) experimented with the salivation of dogs in response to food and pioneered the techniques of *conditioning* (6). Early behaviorist James Broadus Watson (1878–1958) stressed the continuity between humans and animals. He elevated the experimental aspect of psychology at the expense of introspection and consciousness as the only tool in the behaviorist method (7). Contemporary outspoken behaviorist B. F. Skinner elaborated the art of conditioning and stressed the manipulatability of human behavior. To him, the autonomous agent to which behavior has traditionally been attributed is replaced. The new agent is the environment where the species evolves and that same environment shapes and maintains the species behavior (8). In the fifties behaviorism emerged as the dominant view of psychological thinking.

References 8.6

1. Darwin, C. The expression of education in man and animals. London: Murray; 1973.
2. Freud, S. An outline of psychoanalysis. New York: Norton, 1949.

3. Freud, S. Beyond the pleasure principle. London: Hogarth; 1955.
4. Lundin, R. W. Theories and systems of psychology. Lexington, MA: Heath; 1972 (chapter 9).
5. Gibson, J. J. The senses considered as perceptual systems. Boston: Houghton Mifflin; 1966.
6. Pavlov, I. P. Conditioned reflex. London: Oxford Univ. Press; 1927.
7. Watson, J. B. Psychology as the behaviorist views it. Psychological Review. 20:158; 1913.
8. Skinner, B. F. Beyond freedom and dignity. New York: Banton; 1971.

8.7 Evolutionary Thinking in Religion

With the advent of Darwinism, religion has been treated by the naturalists as man's evolving concept of a felt practical relationship with what is believed to be a supernatural being or beings. This supernatural concept emerged because of man's eternal quest for the meaning of life and death (1). Humans in some way seem to be in conflict with their own reason. Naturalists believe the universal instinctive religious impulse serves the important social function of providing a supernatural nonrational sanction that impels people to act in a socially responsible way. Such an impulse has survival value for it is indispensable for social progress (2).

Auguste Comte (1798–1857), a contemporary of Darwin, had devised an evolutionary scheme to explain the development of social and religious institutions even before the publication of *Origin of Species*. According to him, the craving of man's religious impulse for simplication and unification of ideas leads religion through three stages of metamorphosis: *fetishism* (separate will animating material objects), *polytheism* (many gods acting through things without the things being themselves alive), and *monotheism* (everything being brought under a single, abstract will) (3).

Comte believed that evolutionary ideas also took the form of *progressive revelation* in the exegesis of the Bible. However, the liberals' view of biblical revelation is in contradistinction with the view held by evangelicals. Every idea in the Bible is viewed by liberals as having undergone an evolution from a primitive and childlike origin to the culminated scope and height in Christ's gospel. On the other hand, evangelicals believe God unfolds more and more concerning Himself and His will for humans in the course of biblical history. Liberals believe that the revelation of God has progressed from the crude Old Testament idea of God as a fearful and merciless tyrant who does not care for individuals except as they are temporary members of the social group. They believe this idea of God was modified throughout the shattering experience of the Israelites being exiled. The Psalms are treated as an anticipation of a personal God who finds expression in the person of Jesus Christ (4).

The rise of *higher criticism* also strengthened the perspective of liberalism on the Bible. It is alleged that a substantial portion of the earlier books of the Bible (e.g., the Pentateuch) were not written until hundreds of years later than the events they describe. In addition, the great similarities between the biblical version and the Babylonian version of the Flood (*see* II, 5.3) cast doubts on the originality and authenticity of the biblical record (5). The Bible has since been treated by liberal scholars as containing human errors and outgrown teaching, despite its essential message of vital personal realization.

In a bold step of the total incorporation of the evolutionary concepts into the biblical framework, Pierre Teilhard De Chardin (1881–1955) attempted to modify the entire Christian message. In his analysis, original sin is not treated as the result of a particular historical event but rather the negative forces of counterevolution—evil. This evil is a mechanism of the creation of an incompletely organized universe, according to Teilhard De Chardin. He believed God has been creating since the beginning of time through a continuous creative transformation from within the universe and individuals. He taught that the cross of Christ does not symbolize as much the atonement of sins as the ascent of the creation and the progress of the world through revitalization that is symbolized by the blood of Christ. According to Teilhard De Chardin, Christ is no longer the Redeemer of the world from the damnation of sin, but He is rather the apex of evolution and gives meaning and direction to the world.

Christianity, then, is preeminently a faith in the progressive unification of the world in God. It is more universalistic, organic, and monistic than individualistic, revelational, and monotheistic (6). Under the liberal tradition, the mission of the church is to alleviate human suffering in direct harmony with the inevitable progress fostered by evolution. The concern with the life to come is largely repudiated.

Although some of the evolutionary concepts may have provided useful working tools in certain areas of human experience, e.g., economics and education, the outcome of the naturalistic emphasis is a relativistic humanism. Despite the optimistic outlook of some naturalists such as Bertrand Russell or John Dewey, recent naturalists, particularly in Europe, have been quite *nihilistic*.

Nihilists do not have a basis to justify the significance of their actions. Since humans are a product of chance in the evolutionary scheme that has somehow adopted a purpose and duplicated the chance-produced pattern, their actions are absurd. Chance is irrational, causeless, purposeless, and directionless. It does not justify the teleological process of evolution and disallows humans to be free from the closed system of the universe to have self-determination. Therefore, nihilists cannot make a positive statement about whether what they seem to know is illusion or truth.

The naturalist perceives man as a complex machine with a brain that has arisen from the functioning of matter. Since it is not logical to assume that matter has an inclination to lead a conscious being to true perception of itself, humans do not have any solid reason for confidence in their own reasoning capacity. Darwin questioned the trustworthiness of the convictions of the human mind because of its lowly origin (7). His own theory of a human's origin must therefore be accepted by an act of faith (8).

Naturalistic influence in theology with its overextended attitude of analytical criticism of the Bible has smothered the reverent appreciation that has been afforded to it throughout Christendom. The Bible is no longer treated as a unique revelation of God but rather as a great book of religion to be studied just like any other great book of humankind. Using the naturalistic approach, the naturalist considers most of the traditions and philosophies of the Israelites to be outgrown with time, and the only essential message of the Bible is considered to be the practical experience transmitted by the Hebrews to represent the deepest needs, direst struggles, noblest aspirations, and the finest hopes of the human soul. However, the search for this unformulated experience for a human's inward salvation and love without exercising mental discipline in perceiving the historicity of the biblical account has degenerated into sentimentality (9).

The direct social consequence of naturalism is the introduction of ethical *relativism*. James Sire summarizes it this way:

> Naturalism places man in an ethically relative box. For man to know what values within that box are true values, he needs a measure imposed on it from outside the box; he needs a moral plumbline by which he can evaluate the conflicting moral values he observes in himself and others. But there is nothing outside the box; there is no moral plumbline, no ultimate, non-changing standard of value (10).

This form of relativism has expressed itself in the development of situation ethics that shifted from a hierarchy of values to a fluid spectrum of values in the relativization of the absolute by "agapeic love" (11).

Evolutionistic naturalism suffered a staunch defeat with the turning of the century. The havoc of two devastating world wars shattered the evolutionists' dream of inevitable progress. The rise of National Socialism in Germany and its incredible travesty on human dignity has deepened man's inward frustration and cultural discontent.

New theories have developed in the quest to understand humankind. *Existentialism*, which stresses existence rather than essence, with the human's subjectivity being the meaning of existence, has flourished in atheistic and theistic forms to try to quench man's yearning for meaning in life. In recent years, Eastern pantheistic monism has lured disillusioned young minds who are fed up with the contradictions they have perceived in naturalism. They have observed its antirationalism, syncretism, quietism, and its simplistic lifestyle. Naturalism, Eastern mysticism, and animism find their expressions in the popular *New Consciousness* movement, which points humans to their salvation through a mystical experience transcending time, space, and morality. Supposedly this is brought about by evolutionary transformation of the inner being to be united with world spirits who inhabit the natural universe (12).

A revitalizing trend has also been initiated in American religious life in the reemergence of evangelical Christianity in the public scene as a life-transforming power with its balanced development both in biblical scholarship and in spiritual maturity (13). Dissatisfied with the naturalistic interpretation of life, humans are awakening to the reevaluation of their own nature in increasingly diversified directions and in a more holistic context.

References 8.7

1. Lewis, J. The religions of the world made simple. New York: Doubleday; 1958.
2. Hofstadter, R. Social Darwinism in American thought. Rev. ed. New York: Braziller; 1965.
3. James, E. O. The beginning of religion. London: Hutchinson's University Library; 1952: 11.
4. Fosdick, H. E. The modern use of the Bible. New York: Macmillan; 1930: 11.
5. Stromberg, R. N. Intellectual history of modern Europe. New York: Appleton-Century-Crofts; 1966: 349.
6. Teilhard De Chardin, Pierre. Christianity and evolution. New York: Harcourt Brace Jovanovich; 1971.
7. Darwin, C. The autobiography of Charles Darwin and selected letters. Letters to W. Graham (July 3, 1881). New York: Dover; 1958.
8. Sire, J. The universe next door. Downers Grove, IL: InterVarsity; 1976: 78–91.
9. Fosdick, H. E. Modern use of the Bible. 169–207.
10. Sire, J. The universe next door. 90.

11. Fletcher, J. Situation ethics, the new morality. Philadelphia: Westminster; 1966: 44–45.
12. Sire, J. The universe next door (chapters 6–9).
13. Henry, C. Evangelical summertime? Christianity Today. 21 (13): 38; 1977.

PART IV

A CHRISTIAN ATTITUDE
TO EVOLUTION

CHAPTER 9

Criteria
for Forming Opinions
on Evolution

This book has attempted to show how evolutionary theory has been elevated to a paradigm that finds its expression in many areas of human experience (Part III). It elaborates also on the strengths and weaknesses of evolutionary theory (Part I) as well as the important and difficult task of harmonizing scientific findings with the Bible without doing injustice to either (Part II). It is the hope and prayer of this author that the reader will develop the following attitudes after having reviewed this book.

9.1 To Be Well Informed Concerning the Scientific Bases of Evolutionary Theory

Since evolutionary theory is encountered in almost every avenue of learning, it is paramount for a conscientious, intellectual Christian to be aware of the scientific bases of this theory. Since the publication of Darwin's *Origin of Species*, evolution by natural selection has undergone much revision. Evolution (microevolution) taken in its *narrowest* meaning in terms of changes and diversification of living organisms within a certain boundary as a result of natural selection has been well substantiated. However, the mechanism by which transpecific evolution (general, macroevolution) in the higher categories can occur is still mysterious and awaits unraveling by scientific methodology or other means. It is entirely possible that the general theory of organic evolution will never be proven or disproven by the scientific method because of its all-inclusive nature and its lack of well-defined parameters.

Informed intellectuals are able to decide if a new paradigm that is based on evolutionary theory (the so-called Darwinian revolution) is well established when it is compared to the historical paradigms introduced by Newton's laws of motion and Einstein's theory of relativity. By being exposed to the scientific bases of evolutionary theory, Christians are able to decide conscientiously on the degree of conformity they can make with a current evolutionary paradigm. After all, since the dawn of the scientific era, the paradigm shifts have been sparked by a minority of scientists who did not conform to dominant views (1).

Reference 9.1

1. Kuhn, T. S. The structure of scientific revolution. Chicago: Univ. of Chicago Press; 1962.

9.2 To Understand the Intellectual Mind of the Post-Christian Era

A Christian must strive to understand the intellectual mind of the post-Christian era that allows the wide acceptance of the general theory of evolution. Bernard Ramm suggests several salient observations that brought about this post-Christian era (1):

1. Since medieval times a continuing revolt away from the religion and authoritarianism of the Roman Catholic church has taken the form of deep-moving secularism—life without God, philosophy without the Bible. Thus a community without the church surfaced in the Renaissance and in the modern scientific era and became hostile to both Catholic and Protestant orthodoxy.

Evolutionary theory, though accepted by some Christians as God's way of creation, in its popular form is largely atheistic. However, the intellectual mind of the post-Christian era welcomes this explanation of life, for it fits very nicely into the secularistic outlook.

2. Since the inception of the scientific era, the rapid advance of science has come to dominate the lifestyle of modern people. The scientific method was proposed by the humanist to be the only reliable way to truth. Anything religious, theological, or metaphysical was debased as unintelligible. This form of scepticism, or *scientism*, finds many practical apologists who are employed in such areas as the aerospace industry, industrial chemistry, and biomedicine.

3. Division in Christendom stands in sharp contrast to the unity of science. The major cleavages of Eastern Orthodoxy, Roman Catholicism, Protestanism, and Protestant denominationalism disillusion the secular world. Science, on the contrary, has developed a sense of unanimity. Newton formulated the law of universal gravitation, and it was checked and accepted by fellow scientists. Pasteur disproved the theory of spontaneous

generation, and the scientific world accepted his conclusion. The anti-Christian philosophies preempt the apparent unity of science and impress the populace that orthodoxy and science are divorced.

4. Most recent scientific achievements have been made by non-Christians. Christians have moved away from science since theologians lost the battle to the scientists in the classic debates over evolution. In the last few decades the proportion of American scholars with an evangelical background in institutions of higher education and in major research-oriented universities is much smaller than their proportion in the general population (2). This has many ramifications. The prestige of science goes to the scientists and to their philosophical and religious beliefs. Presently science develops on non-Christian premises. This forms a vicious cycle. Most science faculties of higher institutions of learning are made up of non-Christians with atheistic ideas, and they recruit new people with their perspectives. When Christian students join the scientific community, these faculties often shatter their beliefs.

References 9.2

1. Ramm, B. The Christian view of science and Scripture. Grand Rapids, MI: Eerdmans; 1954: 15–21.
2. Press Digest. Current contents, life sciences. Philadelphia: Institute for Scientific Information; 1975. Also see Ladd, E. G., Jr. Chronicle of Higher Education. 11(2):2; 9–22–1975.

9.3 To Be Exposed to the Various Interpretations of the Genesis Account

A Christian must study the various interpretations of the Genesis account, as well as be current on new data on the subject and keep an open mind as to the validity of each idea. One charge leveled by the scientific community against the church is its apparent obscurant attitude toward scientific truth. This was prompted by some medieval church leaders who adhered dogmatically to a certain interpretation of the Bible. Galileo was denounced as a heretic for believing the Coperican theory that proposed the sun was the center of the solar system because leading theologians of the day believed the Bible taught otherwise. Psalm 19 and the account of Joshua's long day (Josh. 10:12–15) were quoted as sure scriptural proof that the earth was the center of the universe (1). One wonders if some people who adhere now to a given interpretation of Genesis would not have agreed with those theologians had they lived then, and they, too, would have had to suffer the embarrassment of revising their hermeneutics in light of scientific fact.

Galileo rightly stated (1), "Scripture deals with natural matters in such a cursory and allusive way that it looks as though it wanted to remind us that its business is not about them but about the soul and that, as concerns nature, it is willing to adjust its language to the simple minds of the people."

It is apparent that failure to consider various interpretations of the Bible and the unwillingness to forsake a traditional interpretation to adopt an alternative view that fits well-established facts of nature can do great harm to the cause of Christ.

Reference 9.3

1. Snow, R. J. In: Genesis one and the origin of the universe. Newman, R. C.; Eckelman, H. J.; Jr. Downers Grove, IL: InterVarsity; 1977: 125.

9.4 To Be Aware of the Basic Problem

A Christian must be aware that the basic problem is not scientific so much as a world view and philosophical. The world view is summed up in the January/February 1977 issue of *The Humanist* published for the American Humanist Association and the American Ethical Union. A statement signed by 179 scientists, educators, and religious leaders asserted that evolution has been "well established" scientifically and therefore has been "accepted into humanity's general body of knowledge by scientists and other reasonable persons who have familiarized themselves with the evidence."

The philosophical view of leading scientists has certainly not been Christian. Darwin, Huxley, Spencer, and other early evolutionists were shown to have strong bias against God, the Bible, and Christianity, and they tended to interpret physical evidence as favoring a materialistic explanation of things (1). The Nobel laureate molecular biologist Francis Crick, commenting on the teaching of evolution in British schools, said, "Personally, I myself would go further, and think it is also regrettable that there is so much religious teaching." He disapproved the "tremendous institutional support given to religion by such a body as Cambridge University. . . ." (2).

The late Jacques Monod, another Nobel laureate molecular biologist, expressed his conviction of the correctness of scientism in his controversial book attributing humans to the fate of evolution this way:

For their moral bases the "liberal" societies of the West still teach—or pay lip service to—a disgusting farrago of Judeo-Christian religiousity, scientistic progressism, belief in the "natural" rights of man, and utilitarian pragmatism. . . . However this may be, all these systems rooted in "animism" exist at odds with objective knowledge, face away from truth, and are strangers and fundamentally "hostile" to science, which they are pleased to make use of but for which they do not otherwise care (3).

The harbinger of modern evolutionism Theodosius Dobzhansky disposed of the absolute values of ethics when he said, "The process of evolution has produced a human species capable of entertaining ethical beliefs; the biological function of ethics is to promote human evolution; ethics may consequently be judged by how well they fulfill this function" (4). The outspoken advocate and crusader for evolutionism George G. Simpsons echoed Dobzhansky's humanistic conviction by saying:

> The propensity for developing moral precepts and the dispositions to learn them as well as the precepts themselves are adaptations acquired in the course of our biological and social evolution. When viewed in this way, rather than as mere edicts from a stern and incomprehensible source, those precepts achieve a higher sanction and become the more impelling (5).

These quotations emphasize the point that many outspoken evolutionists are under the strong influence of the naturalistic and humanistic world view. Evolution to them is more than a scientific theory applicable only to the description of the living world. It is a philosophy of life. Therefore, the issue of evolution is not scientific so much as a philosophical world view. Christian theism is in direct confrontation with the naturalistic monism of most evolutionists. Marjorie Grene, a philosopher long involved in the philosophies of science, has succintly summarized the philosophical basis of evolutionism, and I will conclude by quoting from her (6).

> Yet, if all this is so, why is neo-Darwinian theory so confidently affirmed? Because neo-Darwinism is not only a scientific theory, and a comprehensive, seemingly self-confirming theory, but a theory deeply embedded in a metaphysical faith in the faith that science can and must explain all the phenomena of nature in terms of one hypothesis, and that hypothesis of maximum simplicity, of maximum impersonality and objectivity. Relatively speaking, neo-Darwinism is logically simple. There are just two things happening, chance variations, and the elimination of the worst ones among them, and both these happenings are just plain facts, things that "do" or "don't" happen "yes" or "no". Nature is like a vast computing machine set up in binary digits, no mystery there. And—what man has not yet achieved—the machine is self-programmed, it began by chance, it continues automatically, it master plans itself creeping upon itself, so to speak, by means of its own automation. Again, no mystery here; man seems at home in a simply rational world.

References 9.4

1. Clark, R. J.; Bales, J. D. Why scientists accept evolution. Grand Rapids, MI: Baker; 1966.
2. Crick, F. Of molecules and man. Seattle: Univ. of Washington Press; 1966: 89–91.
3. Monod, J. Chance and necessity. New York: Knopf; 1971: 171.
4. Dobzhansky, T. Mankind evolving. New Haven, CT: Yale Univ. Press; 1962: 344.
5. Simpson, G. G. This view of life, the world of an evolutionist. New York: Harcourt, Brace and World; 1964: 233.
6. Grene, M. The knower and the known. New York: Basic Books; 1966: 199–200.

Appendix

The Length of the Creative Days

Dr. J. Oliver Buswell, Jr.

	Eternal Past	
First Day	*Darkness*	
	Light	
	Day and Night	
Second Day	*The Expanse or*	
	"Firmament"	
Third Day	*Land*	
	Vegetation	
Fourth Day	*Sun, Moon and Stars*	
	for Times and for	
	Seasons and for	
	Days and Years	
Fifth Day	*Certain forms of*	
	Animal Life	
Sixth Day	*Man*	
Seventh Day	*Innocence*	
	Conscience	
	Human Government	
	Promise	
	Israel	
†	*Church*	
	Kingdom	
	New Heavens and New Earth	
	Eternal Future	

THE QUESTION STATED

The question before us is not what God can do or could have done in the creation of this world. God could have created a universe in an instant of time as easily as in any length of time.

The question is not how Scripture can be harmonized with geology or with any theory of cosmogony. Of course, we are thankful for any light from natural or historical facts upon the interpretation of the Scriptures. This, however, is a secondary question. The question before us does not lie within the field of those who specialize in the physical sciences.

The question is, what do the Scriptures teach in regard to the length of the creative days described in Genesis 1:1 to 2:4. This is primarily a question of hermeneutics and exegesis.

We shall proceed first of all to a general statement of interpretation. We shall then discuss objections to our interpretation, after which we shall take up a certain theory held by many Christian people and present our objections to it.

The chart at the beginning of this article sets forth what we believe to be the best interpretation of the days of the creative week.

We hold that the word "day" is used here as elsewhere, figuratively and represents a period of time of undesignated length. This does not mean that the several days correspond to periods into which geologists have divided the physical history of the earth. Moses, as inspired by the Spirit, did not describe the periods marked off by the modern geologist, though the facts which Moses does give and the order of these facts are not in conflict with any established facts of geology. If the word day is used figuratively, then the words referring to the parts of days are figurative. We commonly refer in English to "the dawn of a new day" when we mean literally the beginning of a new era. According to Hebrew usage the literal day began with the evening, and concluded with the daylight. Thus "the evening and the morning" taken figuratively, represent the opening and the closing of great eras of time included in the creative work of God. There is no line of division between the "days", but one period follows another in unbroken sequence as morning follows evening. Examples of the figurative use of "day" are very numerous in Hebrew and in English. In fact, the usage is identical in the two languages. "The day of Jehovah", "That Day", are expressions which actually include at least one thousand years. Similarly in English we refer to Wycliffe as "the morning star of the reformation" and we say "in Luther's day" meaning in Luther's period of time.

WHAT WAS MOSES' USAGE?

It is important for us to inquire first what was Moses' own use of the word "day". I shall proceed from those references which are most clear to those which are not quite so readily understood.

Genesis 2:4—"These are the generations of the heavens and of the earth when they were created, in the day that the Lord God made the earth and the heavens."

In this reference, the entire period of six days is referred to as one day. There can, therefore, be no possible doubt that Moses was in the habit of using the word "day" sometimes at least, to refer to a period of time of undesignated length. This is the only possible explanation of the fact that a period of six days is referred to as one day by the words "in the day that the Lord God made the earth and heavens."

Psalm 90:1–4—"Lord, thou hast been our dwelling place in all generations. Before the mountains were brought forth, or ever thou hadst formed the earth and the world, even from everlasting to everlasting, thou art God. Thou turnest man to destruction; and sayest, Return, ye children of men. For a thousand years in thy sight are but as yesterday when it is past, and as a watch in the night."

Conservative scholars tell us that the headings of the Psalms are quite accurate and that we have no reason to doubt that, as stated in the heading, Moses is the author of the ninetieth Psalm. That being the case, we have in his own language a very clear reference to the attitude of God toward our earthly measures of time. Here we see that a thousand years in God's sight are as only a day, "yesterday", or as only three or four hours, "a watch in the night".

Genesis 1:5—"And God called the light Day, and the darkness he called Night. And the evening and the morning were the first day."

It appears from this verse that within the first creative "day" or period of time, the series of earthly days and nights, periods of light and darkness, was instituted. The inference is that the first day began with a long period of darkness on the earth, then with the coming of light, periods of darkness and light followed each other, and days and nights in our literal earthly sense of the word, began to occur. This was all within the "first day" of the creative work of God.

The references in the Scofield Reference Edition of the Bible argue here against the twenty-four hour day theory.

"1. The word 'day' is used in Scripture in three ways: (1) that part of the solar day of twenty-four hours which is light (Genesis 1:5, 14; John 9:4; 11:9); (2) such a day, set apart for some distinctive purpose, as 'day of atonement' (Leviticus 23:27); 'day of judgment' (Matthew 10:15); (3) a period of time, long or short during which certain revealed purposes of God are to be accomplished, as 'day of the Lord.'

"2. The use of 'evening' and 'morning' may be held to limit 'day' to the solar day; but the frequent parabolic use of natural phenomena may warrant the conclusion that each creative 'day' was a period of time marked off by a beginning and ending."

Genesis 1:14–19—"And God said, Let there be lights in the firmament of the heaven to divide the day from the night; and let them be for signs, and for seasons, and for days, and years: And let them be for lights in the firmament of the heaven to give light upon the earth: and it was so. And God made two great lights; the greater light to rule the day, and the lesser light to rule the night: he made the stars also. And God set them in the firmament of the heaven to give light upon the earth, And to rule over the day and over the night, and to divide the light from the darkness: and God saw that it was good. And the evening and the morning were the fourth day."

It is obvious here that the visible function of the sun "for days and years" did not begin until the fourth day of the creative period. This fact was noted by St. Augustine long ago. (See "City of God" Book 11, Chapters 6 and 7.) The clear inference of Moses' teaching here is that the whole visible periodic function of the sun and the other heavenly bodies began to operate within the fourth day. It is hard to see how this fourth day could have been a twenty-four hour day. Obviously, Moses did not intend it to be so understood.

James Orr, "The Christian View of God and the World", page 421 says, "Even in regard to the duration of time involved,—those *dies ineffabiles* of which Augustine speaks,—it is at least as difficult to suppose that only ordinary days of twenty-four hours are intended, in view of the writer's express statement that such days did not commence till the fourth stage in creation, as to believe that they are symbols." Orr here quotes Augustine as follows: "Of what fashion those days were it is either exceeding hard or altogether impossible to think, much more to speak. As for ordinary days, we see they have neither morning nor evening, but as the sun rises and sets. But the first three days of all had no sun, for that was made on the fourth day, etc.—De Civitate Dei, xi 6, 7. Cf. De. Genesi, ii 14."

Exodus 20:8–11—"Remember the sabbath day, to keep it holy. Six days shalt thou labour, and do all thy work: But the seventh day is the sabbath of the Lord thy God: in it thou shalt not do any work, thou, nor thy son, nor thy daughter, thy manservant, nor thy maidservant, nor thy cattle, nor thy stranger that is within thy gates: For in six days the Lord made heaven and earth, the sea, and all that in them is, and rested the seventh day: wherefore the Lord blessed the Sabbath day, and hallowed it."

The other examples of Moses' usage given above seem to me quite clear in indicating that Moses was in the habit of using "day" to denote long periods of time. The fourth commandment, in the twentieth chapter of Exodus, is frequently referred to as evidence on the other side.

If we had no other examples of Moses' usage, this example would not necessarily imply that the length of days in the creative week is the same as the length of days in man's ordinary week of time on this earth. We suggest, on the contrary, that those to whom Moses delivered these commandments of God were quite familiar with Moses' own language. They had heard him discussing the substance of the first chapter of Genesis; they knew that he referred to the period of six days as one day (Genesis 2:4). They had heard him use language similar to that found in the ninetieth Psalm. They knew that he regarded God's attitude towards earthly time as quite different from man's attitude. It is not difficult to see, therefore, that those who were familiar with the ninetieth Psalm and Moses' general attitude toward God's time, would draw no such inference from the fourth commandment as is drawn by those who hold to the twenty-four hour day theory. What Moses says is in fact thoroughly in accord with the idea that the days in God's creative program are long periods. The substance of the fourth commandment is that man must work six days and rest one day, for God in creation worked six of God's days and then rested on the seventh day from His creative work. There is no more reason to conclude that God's creative days are as short as man's days of the week, than there is to conclude from the same Scripture that God Himself is no greater than man. The argument is one of analogy between the infinite greatness of God and the little activity of man. Man must work six days and rest one because God in His greatness has chosen to observe a similar practice.

Hebrews 4:1–11—Outside of the writings of Moses we have a very interesting reference to one of the days of the creative period in the fourth chapter of Hebrews, verses 1–11. The author of the Epistle to the Hebrews in this passage teaches that the "rest" of God is originally described in Genesis 2:1–3, "For He spake in a certain place of the seventh day on this wise, and God did rest the seventh day" (Hebrews 4:4). The author argues then that "rest" was available for God's people in Moses' time, in Joshua's time, in the time of the writing of the ninety-fifth Psalm, and in his own time "There remaineth therefore a rest unto the people of God" (Hebrews 4:9). Thus, it is clear that in the inspired judgment of the writer of the Epistle to the Hebrews the seventh day of the creative period was still going on when this epistle was written.

This probable continuance of the seventh day in which God has ceased from His work of creation is indicated above in the chart. Immediately

305

after the creation of man, God stopped His work of creation. He is now carrying on His work of providence, and His work of redemption, but God will not again undertake any work of creation until the end of the millennium. After that He will create new heavens and a new earth. This new creation will end the seventh day referred to in Genesis 2:1–3.

Genesis 1:1–2:4—In addition to the above argument, the reader's attention must be called to the fact that we have here in the very first part of our Bible a beautiful orderly, systematic account of creation. We have first of all an introductory statement covering the entire creative activity of God, "In the beginning God created the heavens and the earth." Then follow detailed statements in regard to the process of the creation of the earth, including a statement that on the seventh "day" God ceased from His creative activity after having seen that it was "all very good". Then follows a general conclusion summing up the entire creation record "these are the generations of the heavens and the earth when they were created in the day that the Lord God made the earth and the heavens." The reader must note that the entire record is called "creation", not "renovation". It is summed up at the beginning and at the end as the divinely inspired account of creation.

A SUGGESTED INTERPRETATION

We began by saying that this is a question of Scripture interpretation, not of geology. Having examined the Scripture on this question, it is not out of place to inquire whether Biblical statements have any reference to geology. Let the reader follow through the account in the first chapter of Genesis day by day and note the marvelous orderliness of the description. The following explanation is given independently of any particular geological theory except that the earth was at one time in a state of intense heat, and has been through a cooling process. This, I believe, is the view of most geologists. If so it coincides with the fact of darkness on the first "day", followed by light and vegetation before the sun was visible. If this assumption should ever prove to be untrue we should then have to seek some other explanation for light and vegetation before the visibility of the sun. The twenty-four hour day theory would not be established by the abandonment of this one geological assumption. The following interpretation is not based on geology, and can be harmonized with any reasonable geological theory.

The first statement in the creation record has to do with the entire physical universe, "In the beginning God created the heavens and the earth". This includes the sun, moon, and stars as well as the earth on which we live. Next we find specific reference to the earth itself and from this point forward we are dealing with the earth as the future habitation of man. The point of view, as others have pointed out, is the surface of the earth and not the universe in general. "And the earth was without form and void and darkness was upon the face of the deep." The words (thohu wa-bhohu) "without form and void" simply mean "empty and waste". The earth or any given country on the earth may be described by these words after a desolation, but may also be described by these words when it is simply in a virgin condition, empty and waste, not having been desolated, but not having been completely prepared for the habitation of man.

THE FIRST DAY

It seems quite apparent from the study of the nature of this earth that it has at one time been much hotter than it is now. Nobody knows how many fluctuations between colder periods and periods of greater heat may have taken place. Just now glaciers are receding in many parts of the earth. In the large the history of the earth, with much fluctuation, is a history of a cooling process of an enormous ball. We are not here concerned with the way in which this ball may have come to be in its present shape. The planetesimal theory or the nebular theory or whatever theory we may have of cosmogony does not enter into this question. The earth, since it has been the earth, has been much hotter than now, and has been through a long process of cooling off. Now doubtless when the earth was much hotter than at present, all the water in the earth and a large part of the other liquids, would have existed in the form of vapor. Thus, the earth would have been surrounded by dense banks of clouds and the surface of the earth would have been for a long period in dense darkness. The heavens had been created, the earth had been created, or rather was in the process of creation as the habitation of man. Gradually by the cooling process the dense banks of cloudy vapors surrounding the earth began to become slightly transparent, and the first great event of significance in the preparation of the surface of this earth for the habitation of man was the penetrating through of light from the sun. A dim, diffused light at first, yet such that at some points on the earth's surface, day and night could soon be distinguished, though the heavenly bodies were not yet visible. This is the process of the first day as Moses describes it.

THE SECOND DAY

In the second day the cooling process continues. The heavy banks of clouds begin somewhat to condense, the earth is still in a diffused light coming through this cloudy atmosphere, the heavenly bodies are not yet visible, but there is a clearing up of the atmosphere on the surface of the earth, an "expanse", (the word incorrectly translated "firmamentum" (firmament)) developed between the cloudy waters about the expanse or firmament and the waters which covered the surface of the earth. This is the process of the second day.

THE THIRD DAY

The third day continues the cooling process. The dry land appears, the heavenly bodies are still invisible through the dense banks of clouds, but the earth continues to cool and the great masses of the continents buckle and heave above the surface of the waters. Volcanic action probably was violent in this part of the process. God brings forth from the dry land vegetation. The presumption is that the first part of the earth's surface cooled sufficiently for vegetation would be the polar regions. The tropical regions were still too hot for the vegetation but the great masses of vegetation which now form the coal beds in the Arctic and Antarctic regions, developed. Vegetation then spread over all the earth. All this was pursuant to the divine command "Let the earth bring forth grass, herb yielding seed and fruit tree yielding fruit after his kind whose seed is in itself, upon the earth". Nobody knows how many times various parts of the earth may have been elevated above the sea and then submerged again. Let the fossils be found where they may. The Scripture simply says the dry land appeared and the vegetation was brought forth.

In all of this interpretation the key thought is that the physical point of view after the first verse of the chapter is the surface of the earth, being prepared for the habitation of man. (See "The Creative Days" by Prof. L. Franklin Gruber. Bibliotheca Sacra Oct. 1919.)

THE FOURTH DAY

On the fourth day the atmosphere clears sufficiently so that God places in the firmament of heaven the sun, moon, and stars. Note that the word "create" is not here used. God created the heavens and the earth before this fourth day. The sun, moon, and stars are now made to function "for times and for seasons and for days and years."

THE FIFTH DAY

The fifth day shows the orderliness of God's creation of animal life.

THE SIXTH DAY

The sixth day continues the creation of animal life. Finally as a distinct creation, the great climax, God "created man in his own image, in the image of God created he him, male and female created he them." The rhetoric of Genesis 1:26 seems to suggest a pause, perhaps a lapse of some time, between the creation of "the beasts of the earth" and the creation of man. This ends the creative process.

THE SEVENTH DAY

After the creation of man God ceased from His creative activity and "rested the seventh day from all his work which he had made."

The above interpretation is not the only possible one. It is only tentatively suggested, but it seems to us the most reasonable. It assumes as has been said, a long cooling process in accordance with the second law of thermodynamics and in accordance with the evidence from the igneous rocks. It has nothing to say one way or another about cataclysms or glacial periods within any of the creative "days". We do hold with J. Frederick Wright that the last glacial period was connected with the cause of the flood (See "The Deluge of Noah" I.S.B.E. Vol. II) but that is another question.

OBJECTIONS

Let us now give attention to certain objections in matters of detail.

Objection 1—It is objected that the creation record cannot be true since vegetation appears before the sun. Vegetation is made on the third day, the sun does not appear until the fourth day.

Answer—The creation record does not state that the sun was created on the fourth day, but that it was then made to appear in the firmament. Probably the light which appeared on the first day was diffused light from the sun, coming through dense banks of clouds.

Objection 2—Vegetation is said to have been created before the insects were created, whereas many forms of vegetation depend upon insects for pollinization.

Answer—The creation of insects simply is not mentioned in the creation record. The record does not claim to be exhaustive in detail. The "creeping things" referred to in Genesis 1:24, 25 are not insects, but four-footed animals walking on the earth. If insects are actually necessary to the existence of vegetable life from the beginning, then probably God created them along with vegetation. Whether this is true, or whether God provided some other method of pollinization we do not know. The insects simply are not mentioned.

Objection 3—If the days are long periods of time, then half of the days must have been dark and half light. Vegetation could not exist during long periods of darkness including thousands of years.

Answer—In claiming that the days are long periods of time, we claim

ENDIX

t the word day is used in a familiar figurative manner. Thus these long periods included the regular progress of solar days and nights as described in Genesis 1:5 and Genesis 1:14–19. All of this will be made clear by examination of the chart.

Objection 4—All God's creative acts are instantaneous "He spake and it was done, He commanded and it stood forth." Some go so far as to say that to recognize any process in time is to recognize evolution.

Answer—It is true that "He spake and it was done, He commanded and it stood forth", but it is not correct to insert, either consciously or unconsciously, the word "instantaneously" before the verbs in this sentence. It simply is not a fact that all of God's creative activity is instantaneous. The verb "bring forth" in the sentence "Let the earth bring forth grass" implies a process of time if it has any meaning at all. This is not a question of what God can do. He can create anything in an instant of time, but the Scripture plainly teaches that He chose to use at least some time during the creative process. God often works cataclysmically but He also works sometimes in temporal processes.

Objection 5—The theory that the days of creation represent long periods of time is said to contradict the statement of the age of Adam in the fifth chapter of Genesis.

Answer—This objection is based upon the false idea that after the sixth day of creation the seventh day intervened before anything went forward in the world. It is clear from the first chapter of Genesis that man was created at the very end of the creative process. The interpretation which we advance does not interpose a seventh day between the creation and the beginning of world history, but regards God as now resting from His work of creation until such time as He shall choose to create the new heavens and the new earth. The years of Adam's life began as soon as he was created at the end of the sixth creative day.

Objection 6—"Wherever the word 'yom' (day) is preceded by a numerical article, we are forced to accept it as a literal day."

Answer—In the first place, the very form of this objection reveals the fact that the author had never had a course in Hebrew before he made this statement. There are such things as "numerals" and there are such things as "articles" in the various grammars of the various languages. The words "numerical article" however do not refer to any known grammatical phenomena.

It may be true that this is the only case in which the word day is used figuratively when preceded by any numeral, but the reason is that this is the only case in Scripture in which any indefinitely long periods of time are enumerated. The words "aion" in Greek and "olam" in Hebrew are literal words for "age", but we do not happen to have any case in which God has said "first age", "second age", "third age", etc. The attempt to make a grammatical rule to the effect that the numeral preceding the word day makes it literal, breaks down on the simple fact that this is the only case in all the Scriptures, and in all Hebrew language, I think, in which ages are enumerated one after the other. There is no such rule in anybody's Hebrew grammar anywhere. The author of this objection, or the one from whom he has attempted to quote, has simply put forth with a sound of authority a grammatical rule which does not exist.

Objection 7—"The word 'day' (Hebrew 'yom') when used figuratively to denote a period of time longer than a literal solar day, is never used to denote time outside of the scope of history."

Answer—Genesis 2:4 "in the *day* that the Lord God made the earth and the heavens," refers to the whole creative work of God "the heavens and the earth when they were created." Let the writer of this objection search through the entire range of Scripture to find one example of any word but "day" denoting successive periods of prehistoric time.

Objection 8—"It is never permissible in serious thought to have a double meaning [both literal and figurative] of the same word in the same context, unless it is accompanied by an explanation."

Answer—Let the writer of this objection look up the difference between a simile and a metaphor. Were the disciples to "catch men" with a physical net? or is the "water of life" a physical substance?

Objection 9—The existence of plant life for long periods of time before the creation of time before the creation of man would be "prodigious waste."

Answer—Are all uninhabited times and places wasted? Rather the Scriptures (Psalms 8 and 90) seem to emphasize the littleness of man in the physical universe.

Objection 10—"Not even an evolutionist would claim that fowls came into existence at the same time marine animals first appeared." (With reference to Genesis 1:20–22.)

Answer—No! It is Moses who states that. And it is remarkable that the Hebrew words here used include the reptiles and seem to imply that birds were created soon after reptile forms of life. This the facts of biology and geology confirm.

A THEORY WHICH WE REJECT

Let us now turn to a theory which has been popular among Christian people for quite a number of years. It is held by some that after the creation of the heavens and the earth and before the situation described in the second verse of the first chapter of Genesis, a great cataclysm and a long period of time took place, in which the earth was desolated. Our objections to this theory are (1) that it rests upon not one single grain of evidence, and (2) that it was invented in order to harmonize geology with the Scripture and not simply in order to interpret the Scripture as it stands. Christian geologists have felt the problem of light and vegetation before the visibility of the sun, to be a difficulty in the Genesis account. They have therefore invented the theory of a long period of time inserted between the first two verses in chapter one.

In the notes in the Scofield reference edition of the Bible we read the following comment on Genesis 1:2:—"Jeremiah 4:23–26; Isaiah 24:1 and Isaiah 45:18 clearly indicate that the earth had undergone a cataclysmic change as the result of a divine judgment." We reply that this is a definitely untruthful and misleading statement which anyone can examine for himself if he will but look up the references cited. No one can intelligently read Jeremiah 4:23–26 in its context without seeing that this is a reference to events still future to Jeremiah. It refers to the desolation of men and cities, as Jeremiah specifically states. Similarly Isaiah 24:1 taken in its context is positively predictive and does not refer to any past event unless language has lost all meaning. Isaiah 45:18 reads as follows: "For thus saith the Lord that created the heavens; God Himself that formed the earth and made it; He hath established it, He created it not in vain, He formed it to be inhabited: I am the Lord; and there is none else." Surely we can understand that God did not create the earth "in vain" ("thohu"), that He formed it to be inhabited; but to distort this statement to mean that there was no stage in the process of creation at which the earth could be described as empty and waste before it was yet formed to be inhabited, is to do violence to language.

It is argued that during this supposed period of time between the situations described in the first two verses of the creation record, the fall of Satan and the fallen angels took place.

Our reply is that we do not have the slightest hint in the Scriptures as to the time and place of the fall of Satan and his evil angels, except that Satan was a fallen creature when man was created. There is all eternity past and all space in which the fall of Satan and his evil angels may have taken place. We do not need violently to disrupt an orderly passage of Scripture and insert a cataclysmic period of time, to make room for the fall of devils. It is argued that "ha yethah" the word translated "was" in the second verse of the first chapter of Genesis should correctly be translated "became". Our answer is that this verb is a very simple grammatical form, the third person feminine singular perfect of the verb to be. Its primary meaning is simply "was". It is true that the verb "to be" in Hebrew is sometimes used to mean "became" if the context demands it, but the verb as it stands is "was" as anyone who has studied Hebrew will testify. There is not the slightest hint in the context that the unusual meaning "became" should be read. In fact, we should either find the preposition "to" ("l—") before the descriptive adjective or noun if the word is to read "became" (See Genesis 2:7), or else we should find from the context that "was" has some such meaning as "was potentially". Neither of these is the case.

It is argued that the word "replenish" in Genesis 1:28 means "fill over again", therefore the earth must once have been full, then devastated, before man was to replenish it.

The answer is that the word in Hebrew ("mala'") means simply "to fill" and does not convey the idea of anything beyond this simple meaning. The correct translation would be "Fill ye the earth". This is an example of argument from the etymology of an English word, the etymology of the English word having no substantiation whatever in the Hebrew original.

(The above notes are tentatively set forth in an attempt to assist those who are bewildered by fanciful interpretations. The author will welcome criticisms. The same argument in briefer form was published in an article by the author in "Christian Faith and Life", April 1935.)

J. OLIVER BUSWELL, JR.

From: "Chronology," *Davis Bible Dictionary*, 1935.

Glossary

alleles: Specific locations on DNA carrying information for contrasting forms of the same trait (e.g., blue eyes and brown eyes) (I.1.4.2).

allopatric: Living in different areas (I.1.5.1).

anaerobic cell: A cell that grows only in the absence of oxygen, i.e., it derives its energy by fermenting nutrients in the absence of oxygen (I.3.3.1.b).

archosaurian reptiles: Ruling reptiles that are specialized toward bipedal life; the dinosaur is the famous example. They were the dominant land reptiles in the Mesozoic era. Today they survive only in the form of aberrant crocodiles and alligators (I.2.2.2).

cataclysmic flood: The flood recorded in Genesis 6–9. It was a universal, sudden, and violent deluge that covered the whole earth and wiped out all the land animals (II.6.1.1).

Cavendish balance: A device invented by Rev. John Mitchell but first used by Sir Henry Cavendish in 1798 to measure the force of gravitational attraction between two bodies. It consists of a light, rigid T-shaped member supported by a fine vertical fiber. Two spheres with known mass are mounted at the ends of the horizontal portion of the T, and a small mirror fastened to the vertical portion reflects a beam of light onto a scale. To use the balance, two large spheres with gravitational attraction to the small spheres mounted on the balance are brought to juxtaposition with the latter. The forces of gravitational attractions between the large and small spheres result in the twisting of the system through a small angle, thereby moving the reflected light beam along the scale (I.3.1).

clone: A group of cells with identical genetic make-up (I.1.3).

colinearity: The exact correspondence between the nucleotide sequence on the DNA with the amino acid sequence on the polypeptide encoded by the DNA; e.g., a mutation on the DNA code will change the amino acid to be inserted into a corresponding site on the polypeptide (I.3.3.1.d).

colony: An area of bacterial growth on an agar plate containing millions of bacterial cells of the same genetic make-up (I.1.3).

cornified: Hardened (I.2.5.2.c).

dimorphism: Distinctness in structure and appearance usually associated with the different sex role of male and female; e.g., differences between man and woman, both being in the same species (I.1.2).

echinoderm: A member of the phylum Echinodermata (spiny-skinned animals such as sea stars, sea urchins, and sea cucumbers) (I.2.5.3) *endemic:* Regularly found in a particular locality (I.2.4).

fidelity: Accuracy, exactness (I.2.6.1).

formal: Having to do with form (I.2.3.3).

genetic polymorphism: The existence of two or more forms of individuals in the same species. These forms have detectable differences that are controlled genetically; e.g., the human blood groups (I.1.2).

geological column: A geological timetable that divides the earth's history into the Precambrian, Paleozoic, Mesozoic, and Cenozoic eras characterized by various fossilized plants and animals. The age of the rocks found in each era was estimated by both radiometric and non-radiometric methods (I.2.1.2).

geological time scale: Each geological stratum in the earth's crust (geological column) has been correlated with quantitative measurements of radiometric data, resulting in the construction of a geologic time scale (I.1.5; 2.1.2.b.4).

haploid: Having a single set of chromosomes per individual or cell, as in gametes (I.1.2).

heliocentric: Referring to the view that the sun is the center of the solar system. This view challenged the medieval belief that the earth was the center of the universe. It was first promulgated by Copernicus and later elaborated by Galileo and Kepler (II.4.2.1).

homology: A similarity of specific organs of living members of an animal group, albeit with slight or marked modification, to corresponding organs in their presumed common ancestor (I.2.3.1).

lymphocytes: White blood cells of a certain type produced in the bone marrow that are involved in the immune system of the body (I.2.5.2.d).

lymphoid tissue: Tissue that is rich in lymphocytes. Some of the lymphoid tissues in the body are the thymus, the lymph nodes, the spleen, and the bone marrow (I.2.5.2.d).

macrogenesis (saltation): A sudden change in the genetic make-up of an organism leading to a new species (I.1.5.1).

manus: The proximal part of the hand below the radius and ulna bones (I.2.2.2).

marsupial: Pertaining to mammals whose young are born quite early in development and complete their development attached to a nipple in the mother's marsupium, or pouch (I.2.4).

mechanistic: Referring to the theory that everything in the universe is produced by matter in motion; materialism (I.4.3.3).

meiosis: A process involved in sexual reproduction in which the number of chromosomes is reduced by half (I.1.4.2).

musculature: The muscular system (I.2.3.3).

mutator locus: A region of DNA in certain bacteria and bacteriophage (virus) that has been known to produce DNA polymerase, the enzyme responsible for the replication process of DNA. Mutations in this region of the DNA alter the behavior of this enzyme, leading to an increase in the spontaneous mutation rate for all detectable genetic loci due to base mispairing (I.2.6.3.[3]).

neonatal thymectomy: The surgical removal of the thymus from newborn (I.2.5.2.d).

neontologist: A developmental biologist (I.2.2.2).

occipital: Pertaining to the back part of the head or skull (I.2.3.3).

organic infusions: Liquid extracts (of meat, vegetable, or any other kind of organic matter) that contain an abundance of nutrients for growth of microorganisms (I.3.3.1.a).

outcrossing: Outbreeding, mating with genetically unrelated individuals (I.2.6.5).

phagocytic cells: Cells that are capable of phagocytosis (I.3.2.1.c). (*See* definition of phagocytosis, I.2.6.)

phagocytosis: The process by which certain cells such as the leukocytes (white blood cells) engulf large particles into a sac or membrane-bound vacuole in the cell (I.2.6.1).

phenotypic: Pertaining to the structural and functional appearance of an organism that results from the interaction of genes with one another and with the environment (I.3.2.2.c).

phylogenetic: Pertaining to the presumed evolutionary relationship (I.2.2.1.b).

placental: Pertaining to mammals that carry their young in the mother's uterus where they receive food and oxygen via the placenta until a fairly advanced stage of development (I.2.4).

point-mutations: Changes in the DNA molecules that are confined to a single base (i.e., adenine, guanine, cytosine, or thymine) (I.1.5).

polyploidy: Possession of more than two complete sets of chromosomes (I.1.5.1).

sagittal: Vertical and lengthwise from snout to tail in the body as in sagittal section (I.2.3.3).

saltation (macrogenesis): Sudden change in the genetic make-up of an organism leading to a new species (I.1.4.1; 1.5.1).

spatial: Pertaining to space (I.2.3.3).

sympatric: Living in the same area (I.1.5.1).

synapse: The pairing up of homologous chromosomes during meiosis (*see* I.2.6, Figure 2.62) (I.3.3.1.c).

taxon (pl. taxa): One of the hierarchical categories in which organisms are classified, i.e., species, order, class, etc. (I.2.2.1.b).

temporal: Pertaining to time (I.2.3.3).

thymus: A lymphocyte-rich organ located in the chest behind the top of the breast bone; important in the production and maintenance of immune cells (I.2.5.3).

tundra: A treeless terrestrial community north of the artic circle (I.2.4, Figure 2.25).

universal cataclysm: A world-wide, sudden, and violent flood (Genesis 6–9) that covered the whole earth and wiped out all land animals (II.7.1.1).

venous blood: Blood that flows from the peripheries of the body toward the heart via the veins; it is usually deoxygenated (I.2.5.2.c).

young earth: The view that the universe was created in six solar days so that the earth is only 10 000 to 20 000 years old (II.6.1.1).

Abbreviations

Am. Geophy. Un.	American Geophysical Union
Am. J. Phys. Anthropol.	American Journal of Physical Anthropology
Am. Min.	American Mineralogist
Am. Sci.	American Scientist
b.	born
Bacteriol. Rev.	Bacteriological Reviews
Bibl. Sacra	Bibliotheca Sacra
Biograph. Rev.	Biograph and Review
Biol. Bull.	Biological Bulletin
Bull. Geol. Soc. Am.	Bulletin of the Geological Society of America
C	centigrade
Canad. Min.	Canadian Mineralogist
cc	cubic centimeters
Cold Spring Harbor Symp. Quant. Biol.	Cold Spring Harbor Symposia on Quantitative Biology
dpm	disintegrations per minute
Earth Planet. Sci. Letters	Earth Planetary Science Letters
ed.	edition, editor
Fed. Proc.	Federation Proceedings
Geochim. Cosmachim. Acta	Geochimica et Cosmochimica Acta
J. Am. Sci. Affil.	Journal of the American Scientific Affiliation
J. Appl. Phys.	Journal of Applied Physiology
J. Bacteriol.	Journal of Bacteriology
J. Exp. Med.	Journal of Experimental Medicine
J. Genet.	Journal of Genetics
J. Geophys. Res.	Journal of Geophysical Research
J. Hyg. Camb.	Journal of Hygiene (Cambridge)
J. Infect. Dis.	Journal of Infectious Diseases
J. Mol. Biol.	Journal of Molecular Biology
J. Mol. Evol.	Journal of Molecular Evolution
km.	kilometers

mm	millimeters
Mutat. Res.	Mutation Research
n.d.	no date
Physiol. Rev.	Physiological Reviews
Proc. Natl. Acad. Sci. USA	Proceedings of the National Academy of Sciences of the United States of America
Proc. R. Soc. Lon. Ser. B	Proceedings of the Royal Society of London, Series B
Q. Rev. Biol.	Quarterly Review of Biology
Rec.	recorded
Sc. Am.	Scientific American
sp.	species
suppl.	supplement
Syst. Zool.	Systematic Zoology
trans.	transactions
univ.	university
vol.	volume

Index

Note: When the word or phrase of an entry appears on a figure or table, the page number is printed in boldface type.